Supervisor's Training Guide

The How-To Book for New and Experienced Supervisors

By Joyce Karnes

Produced by Positive Options, Inc.

Published by
Cincinnati Book Publishers
Division of PSA Consulting Inc.

President: Anthony W. Brunsman

www.cincybooks.com

Printed in Cincinnati USA by The John S. Swift Co., Inc.

First Edition 2008

ISBN 13   978-0-9817269-0-8

ISBN 10   0-9817269-0-9

Contents

Introduction

Most of my career, I have been training supervisors in companies in the Midwest. As I sit here at the keyboard, I can remember so many of them talking about their struggles, questions, stories, successes, and failures. Some of them were new supervisors, intimidated by the challenges, searching for some technique that would work for them. Some of them were experienced supervisors who got some cooperation but were exhausted with the daily struggle of coping with so many people problems. Some supervisors thought that they were doing a great job, but their bosses disagreed and expected much more. All of them needed a new way to look at their jobs, some education in people skills, and lots of time and attention to help them work through their unique problems, discouragements, and mindsets. Along the way, there was a lot of frustration, distrust, resistance, and anger to overcome, but the goal was to make the job easier and more effective.

I remember the managers who depended on the supervisors and had to solve the problems that poor supervisors created. They were frustrated because they got little improvement with problems discussed with their supervisors. They needed some breakthroughs and didn't know how to get them.

I remember the classes. In the beginning, the supervisors were suspicious as to what this lady could possibly tell them about their jobs. But slowly, as we talked about their problems and goals (and they began to listen to each other), the group realized that all of them were all pretty much alike—same problems, frustrations, and needs.

As we got into the case studies and roleplays, the humor started to come out. We all laughed at the common situations, the futile efforts, the personalities, and stories from their own lives. As we got into the personality types, they sat in rapt attention as I described their personalities to them. They recognized traits in themselves, each other, their workers, their bosses, their parents, spouses, and children. They took the handouts home and their families confirmed their traits.

Soon the group began to see themselves in a clear light and understand the need to change some of their behaviors, but also to assert others. As some of them changed, others were impressed and attempted some new behaviors themselves. As a part of our program, we do on-site, one-on-one coaching sessions called *walkarounds*. These generated much positive anticipation, many confidential conversations, and new strategies to try. In the final classes, the roleplays got more difficult and the solutions got better and better. As supervisors experimented with better ways to talk to their workers, they started to see success one step at a time. I am so proud of their efforts and appreciate every effort and success that they shared with me.

I always miss the program when the classes are over. It seems that it goes by so fast, but runs so deep that it is like leaving all of your school friends behind. Fortunately, the managers often request a similar program for themselves. Their experience in the program forges a new communication and respect for their supervisors. And I get to see a newfound trust and teamwork between supervisors and managers develop.

When I started Positive Options Inc., I could not have predicted such a satisfying outcome, and I am humbled and grateful for how well it has turned out. I hope to share this experience with you, the reader, as well as with many more companies who want programs. Thanks for reading this book and I would welcome your feedback.

"It is never too late to be who you might have been."
George Elliot

Class One

Welcome

Welcome to this seminar entitled *Supervisors Training Guide*. I will be writing to you as if I were there speaking so that we can simply and easily explore our topic. Imagine yourself in a class of 20 or so other supervisors, all of you seeking to better understand yourselves and learn how to be better supervisors. I will include comments typical of those made in the classes, so participants will be speaking to you as well. I promise to make this experience enjoyable, but more importantly interesting and useful.

Each class will be devoted to topics that are of vital interest to you. There will be explanations and thought-provoking questions and exercises. Finally, each class will offer a role-play or case study for you to test your skills and to compare your words and thoughts with others. References will be made to both male and female supervisors, so you can visualize how anyone can use these skills. But more important than what you read is what you do. Take these skills and try them out every day on your job. The more you experiment with new ways of thinking and talking, the more you will benefit from this seminar. Participate, experiment, and improve.

Goals for this seminar

1. Learn about supervisory skills
   - Communication
   - Motivation

- Discipline
- Teamwork
- Decision-making

2. Discover why people do what they do

3. Learn about our own strengths and weaknesses

4. Discuss actual problems on the floor and come up with solutions

5. Assist with quality and productivity improvements

6. Have fun learning and communicating

7. Recognize your service to the company

Supervisory performance consists of a comprehensive battery of skills, including communicating, motivating, disciplining, teamwork, planning, problem solving, decision-making, teaching, and organizing. That is a lot of competence to have. Possibly, you possess some of these abilities, but others might seem remote and challenging. All of these skills are required for a supervisor who does an effective job of motivating, so I will presume that you have some of them.

Our first goal will be to understand the importance of people skills. In my experience, understanding people skills is the most important, because lacking good people skills can get you in the most trouble, and mastering good skills can lead to the greatest success. In addition, people skills are the most difficult to learn and the most difficult to teach. That is why we will focus most of this course on people skills. After all, you are not supervising things—you are supervising people.

That leads us to our second goal—to discover why people do what they do. To most of us, human behavior is something of a mystery, as we wonder why people do the things that they do. We secretly wonder why friends, family, and co-workers don't behave like us. But understanding people and predicting what they are likely to think is so far beyond us. We never even attempt to explore the issue, at least not until we are standing in front of a person we are supervising and they are giving us fits. *How in the world am I going to get this person to respond the way I need them to,* you are thinking. This problem is the topic of our seminar, so sit up and pay attention.

The first place that we will start in our study of people is the person you know the best and can change the most easily—you. We will identify your individual strengths and weaknesses, which is possibly the most useful part of this whole class. I find that people, (including you and me) keep making the same mistakes over and over again in their careers and personal lives. But they never see that their own behavior is causing them most of their troubles. Bosses, co-workers, and spouses can see these errors clearly and secretly wish that the behaviors would change, but they are at a loss to explain what to do differently. Even if they explain it—and their words fall on open ears—an individual must correctly analyze what changes to make and carry them out over a long period of time. Rather than tackle this task, most of us just go on with life and hope for the best.

You may be thinking that everything and everybody in your work life is causing your problems. But consider that most of your problems are caused by your own behavior. The personality type system that I teach will give you a new tool for understanding yourself and others and an easy way to direct the appropriate changes. The good news is that you can change your own behavior and vastly reduce your problems. Don't overlook the fact that these behaviors also affect your life outside work. If you've noticed that you've had repeated failed relationships, problems on the job, longstanding disagreements, and unhappiness in your life, exploring these weaknesses will offer you relief.

Since I have learned the personality-type system, I have seen the same problems acted out in different settings and played by different people. These include foundries, machine shops, sales organizations, charities, publishing firms, medical firms, and service companies. I have included stories and case studies from all of these settings. In these stories, you will find similarities to your situation that you can use. As a result of your attention and participation, you will be able to apply what you have learned in your job—and in your life— and see a huge difference for the better.

I will share other participant's comments, stories, and thoughts in boxes so you can read what other participants are thinking. If you go to our website and complete the feedback form found at the end of the book, I may include some of your comments in future editions. Here is a sample:

> When you are promoted to supervisor, you wear a white hardhat. It's funny how the color of your hardhat changes people's perceptions of you—especially when they are older than you. They are thinking, *Who do you think you are?* You have to dig down deep inside and find out for yourself why you deserve to wear the white hat of a supervisor.

Good Supervisory Skills are Important

In today's competitive environment, the difference between success and bankruptcy is often only a few percentage points or the loss of one customer. Your performance as a supervisor is critically important to the quality and productivity of your organization. Every day you fight to keep customers, prevent mistakes, and save costs. You are the frontline representative of management's goals and strategies for success. Because you represent the company to its employees, in their minds you are the company. If you communicate a well-organized, helpful, successful, fair picture, the employees believe that the company is just that. The reverse is also true. If you communicate that all is not well, then the employees think the company is a bad place to work and they will not be successful there.

Other supervisors and managers depend on the performance of your department in order to do their jobs well. Improving performance can cause other departments to improve or to weaken, which causes the whole company's performance to shift. You are very important to the success of your company. You make a difference and doing better makes a big difference.

Learning new skills and trying new things should be fun, so I will suggest interesting and fun activities. I do not expect you to be perfect, so don't think that you have to get everything right. I do not allow criticism in the class, nor do I allow self-criticism, so, feel free to review your own successes and failures in the spirit of self-acceptance and humor. I invite all participants to write in their own voice. There is no need to be fancy. Some people are comfortable speaking out and writing volumes, while others are quiet, but think deeply about what is being discussed. Each style is acceptable and is necessary for success. Mark up this book with questions, thoughts, and stories. Scribble in the margins and underline to your heart's content. This book is your record of your learning.

Finally, I would like to **thank you** for your work every day as a supervisor. You most likely are not appreciated nearly as much as you should be for the determination, responsibility, and plain old hard work that you pour into your job day after day. And then, after working a long day, the fact that you take the time to pick up this book and explore ways to do your job even better is a tribute to your dedication. In fact, the better supervisor you are, the more management and employees bring problems and complaints to your door. They don't intend to communicate negatives, but I'm sure that they don't often enough say: *Job well done.* Thanks *for being here today. We appreciate you.*

How you learned to be a supervisor

We all started to work one fine day, possibly when we were quite young, and met our first supervisor. That supervisor either made our work experience a good one or a bad one. We all have clear memories of our first supervisor, sometimes the very words that they said. When we changed jobs, we learned from many other supervisors and made comparisons in our minds. It is from these events, as well as from our experiences with our parents and teachers, that we started to form ideas about what makes a good or bad supervisor. Take some time to answer the following questions:

What makes a bad supervisor?

Select someone who represents the worst supervisor that you recall. What did that person do wrong?

1. How did you react in these situations?

2. What problems did this create for you and for others?

Characteristics of the worst supervisors

Here are some examples of what other supervisors have shared with me:

- Bad supervisors ridicule people and destroy their self-respect. This leads to high turnover because people leave and try to find a better supervisor as soon as possible.

- Bad supervisors can be out of control themselves, have drinking problems, or other personal issues that seriously interfere with their work and hurt their employees.

- Poor communication leaves their people in the dark. Workers are left to decide what to do and are often criticized for doing it wrong.

- Taking credit for others' work causes people to look for ways to sabotage their supervisor.

- A poor supervisor does not admit when he or she makes a mistake and may blame it on others. (It actually improves credibility to admit to and correct them, just as an employee has to do.)

- Confusion seems to follow bad supervisors. They may assume that someone knows something and not follow up or train the employee thoroughly. This sets the worker up for failure.

- Second guessing a person detracts from trust. (Checking work and pointing out strengths and weaknesses increases trust.)

- Being inflexible and unrealistic makes people anxious. Workers know that no situation is black or white. When a supervisor does not listen to what team members are saying, it tells workers that their point of view has no value. This is *the do it my way or else* approach.

- Being a liar is a bad trait. People need to hear the truth delivered in a personable way so they can improve.

- Being unavailable to your people leads to confusion and a feeling of lack of support. The most frequent cause of being unavailable is a supervisor who has not trained a worker well and is essentially doing their job for them. This makes both the worker and the supervisor ineffective.

- Not being organized communicates a lack of support –employees have to redo work or wait around while things are organized.

- Using employees to satisfy ego needs to feel important is a poor way to lead.

- A lack of consistent and fair policies leads to jealousy and resentment that is difficult to resolve.

One Supervisor's Story

I'll never forget my first supervisor, Donald. He made it his personal business to humiliate me when I made a mistake. He would tell me in front of my co-workers that I was stupid and would never be a success. They too would have made fun of me, except they knew that it could be one of them being reamed the next time. I suspected that Donald wanted to see me fail. He assigned me the worst duties to punish me for a mistake and demanded even more than before. To this day, I am still angry with him. I would do anything to get back at him. I vowed that I would never be like him when I was a supervisor.

Discussion Notes: Donald probably thought that being hard on people would push them to excel, but he was really building resistance and revenge within his team. Memories of personal humiliation motivate people to react negatively. This is the first time I have used the word *motivation*. Go ahead; underline it. Donald is an example of how negative approaches create negative outcomes. I speculate that Donald had little cooperation from his team and possibly even sabotage. People would want to avoid working for him and look for an opportunity to quit or to transfer. Donald was making his job harder and his employees miserable. Add this to your list of don'ts.

Supervisory Story

My worst experience was with my father. He and I would do home projects together, but I could never please him. No matter how carefully he described what he wanted, and how I tried to do it, he would find something wrong. I don't ever remember him praising me or saying *job well done*. I was soon discouraged and stopped trying to please him. He had a lot to teach me. He was a good handyman but eventually, we no longer worked together. I guess he was a perfectionist. He never lost his temper with me, but he also never smiled or appreciated my efforts. One of the greatest sorrows of my life is that we could never overcome this problem. It took me a long time to gain my self-confidence and to be able to work for other people.

Discussion Notes: Do you hear the tone of hopelessness because of the breakdown of the working relationship? All of this was over a bad habit of always pointing out what is wrong and never seeing the positive. Maybe this man's father thought that telling his son he had done a good job when there was something wrong was a lie. He was just being honest. The truth is that when much of a job is right and little is wrong, it should be acknowledged with positive feedback. The motivational impact of being positive far outweighs the discouragement caused by being negative as you can see in this story. What is the point of honesty if no one can work with you?

Second Discussion Point

1. Who was your best supervisor? What did this person do right?

2. How did you react to what this person did?

3. How did this benefit you and others?

Here are some examples of what other supervisors have shared with me about the best supervisors in their lives:

Characteristics of the best supervisors

- Good supervisors always look for ways to help their people and to make them a success. Their training and discipline comes across as helpful.

- Successful managers organize detail so that the job goes smoothly.

- They follow up on tasks assigned to others and their own responsibilities. Getting things done well is a priority.

- Good supervisors are knowledgeable of the equipment, the product, customers, and policies. They can answer questions credibly. Most of this knowledge comes from actual experience of having done the job themselves.

- Effective supervisors have a positive attitude toward problem solving and avoid finger pointing. Even if an employee makes a mistake, a good supervisor looks at it as a retraining opportunity. They rarely lose their temper when mistakes are made.

- Good supervisors have charisma—a good leadership skill. They seem to magnetize people to work hard to achieve goals. As a result, their employees feel loyal and satisfied.

- All good supervisors lead by example and observe all policies. They can demonstrate the job processes themselves and model good attitudes.

- The best leaders are positive and open to all and do not hold grudges or exclude people. Communication is consistent, open, and friendly to everyone without exception.

- Personable managers are approachable. Bad news delivered in a personable way is easier to bear.

- Professional supervisors delegate tasks so that they don't do work that their people should be doing. To do so would show a lack of confidence in the employee. These supervisors have time to attend to many duties and to address employee issues when they arise.

- Good leaders are good communicators—they listen well and give clear instructions.

- Some supervisors are hard driving, meaning they push their people to work hard. They keep busy all day, while providing both positive and negative feedback to their workers. They are mindful of each person's abilities, but everyone is challenged to improve.

- Good supervisors are organized. They avoid wasting time and creating rework. They effectively schedule the day and provide necessary materials and resources. These supervisors address problems promptly.

- Successful managers have the trust and credibility of their workers. This is a difficult trait to define. But commitment to telling the truth, effectively solving problems, and working for the benefit of the company earns trust and credibility.

Supervisory Story

My best supervisory experience was with my first manager, Claire. I was just out of high school and got my first job at a restaurant waiting tables. Claire knew how scared I was. I will always remember her letting me follow her around, as I watched and learned. I was worried about dropping things because I was pretty clumsy as a teenager. But I was surprised at how much skill it takes to talk to so many different people, remember orders, and get them right. The first day I was overwhelmed and almost quit. Claire encouraged me and mentioned some things that I did right. Then she gave me some simple tasks that I could do myself, like serving salads. She made me feel like I could do something useful. When the cook harassed me for being a rookie, Claire stepped in. I felt that I was her personal project and that she was determined to make me a success. I had faith that she could help me. Before too long, I was earning good tips and customers were asking for my tables. Claire seemed to enjoy my success. I would have done anything she asked. I admire and respect her to this day. I knew that when I became a supervisor, I would try to be like Claire.

Discussion Notes: The first thing Claire did right was to recognize that every new employee is scared and needs help to be a success. A new recruit will be discouraged if the supervisor does not show a willingness to help. Claire's efforts to help the new recruit quickly paid off in good performance and loyalty. Claire inspired cooperation and motivation from her workers because of how she handled them on their first day of work—and all of the way to a successful promotion. Take note.

Supervisory Story

I remember my junior high basketball coach, Mr. Dindle. He didn't use many words; he didn't need to. Somehow, everybody on the team knew what was necessary and just did it the right way. When Mr. Dindle did talk, he spoke of team spirit and doing our best. When we messed up, he would frown and give his hand signal for *do it again*. When we got the play right, he just smiled and nodded his head. Mr. Dindle thought we were the best team he had ever coached and we wanted to prove him right. Once, a player failed a math test and was taken off the roster. Mr. Dindle chose three of us to be tutors until he could pass the test. We knew that Mr. Dindle would do the same for any of us.

We faced one opposing team that was aggressive and used injuries as a strategy for winning. Mr. Dindle called us into the locker room before that game, taught us defensive moves, and how to alert the referee to fouls. He warned us never to lose our tempers, but to look for ways to use this team's aggressiveness to our advantage. Despite my best effort, I was injured and limped off the court with a sprained ankle. Mr. Dindle protested so loudly that the referee threw him out of the game. My teammates and I were amazed that a quiet person with a well-controlled temper could protest so loudly. Mr. Dindle spent the rest of the game wrapping my ankle in the locker room. He drove me home that day. We lost that game, but I never forgot how Mr. Dindle cared about his players. I always try to emulate him with my team at work.

Discussion Notes: You don't have to be dynamic or charismatic to lead people. Mr. Dindle is an example of a quiet leader who cared about his players. They knew his intentions and listened to his every word. They trusted him. You have to be yourself. Find your own way to support and help your team. People will overlook a lot of your faults if you have the basics right.

Supervisor Criteria

When management considers a person for a supervisory position, they look at these criteria:

- Energy and good health
- Ability to get along with people
- Job know-how
- Self-control under pressure
- Dedication and dependability
- Ability to stay on course and achieve goals
- Ability to learn
- Problem-solving skills
- Leadership potential
- Trust of management and staff
- Ability to handle multiple tasks and information

How many of these traits do you have in good condition? Put a check beside the ones that you think you have and a question mark beside the ones that you need to improve.

You probably didn't know that the people who talked you into becoming a supervisor thought that you had most of these traits. They probably told you that you were a good worker and would make a good supervisor. The most visible aspect of being a supervisor is teaching people to do the job, so many people think that job knowledge is the most important criteria. It is true that workers will respect you if you can both do the job and teach it to them. They also appreciate that you can step in at any time and do their job as well or better than they can. But, beyond that, the way you interact with employees is the most important supervisory skill. You can make your team's day miserable or happy, depending on how you treat them. Some workers' lives are pretty miserable, and working for a good supervisor is the best part of their day. Working for a good supervisor gives them stability, positive experiences, and some relief from having to deal with life's difficulties alone. You are an important part of their support system. When I ask supervisors how much of their time they spend on people problems and issues, they typically say 90%. That means that good people skills will get 90% of the supervisory job done well, and poor people skills will fill 90% of your day with problems.

Take a minute to list **your** goals for learning to be a better supervisor.

If people skills are so important, how do you begin to master them? We will begin by studying the Myers-Briggs Type Indicator®.

What is the Myers-Briggs Type Indicator®?

The Myers-Briggs Personality Type Theory has long roots in history. The ancient Greek, Hippocrates, the father of modern medicine and the Hippocratic Oath, taught that there were four body fluids or *humours* in the human body. The degree of balance between these four *humours* determined a person's personality and health--choleric, sanguine, melancholic, and phlegmatic. Illness was theorized to be a side effect of an imbalance of the *humours*. In the Middle Ages, the common thought again was four personality types that determined a person's predisposition to disease.

In the 1800s, Sigmund Freud spent considerable time studying personalities. As a psychiatrist, Freud had the same problem you have: How do you get people to change? He determined that there are traits and forces within the personality that cause behavior. In the 1900's, Freud's student, Carl Jung, wrote volumes advancing Freud's work. His theories on human behavior are quoted often in books. In fact, some of the names currently used for personality types come from Jung's work. But it wasn't until the 1950s when Katharine Briggs and her daughter Isabel Myers developed a questionnaire and entered millions of test results into a computer database, that personality types were verified. They performed statistical validations that verified and advanced the theories of Freud and Jung. The Myers-

Briggs™ (or MBTI®) has identified 16 Personality Types with their component parts. This method is now widely taught as a way to understand personality.

Myers-Briggs' research has identified definable personality traits that hold true in all cultures, across genders, and throughout the ages. These traits are clearly visible in us by age five and, although we may learn to modify them, these traits remain with us throughout our life. Think about that for a minute. Once you learn these traits, you will better understand every person you will ever meet, or have ever met, even those in foreign countries. It will help you to understand people of different ages and gender. That's a useful tool, don't you think? As a supervisor, you manage a wide variety of people—this tool will be a great help to you.

I developed the following checklist after studying the Personality Type System. Let's begin by doing the checklist.

Survey of Your Personality Traits

Name:_____ Date:_____

Directions: Read each item and place a number **0-2** in the Score column. **Zero** indicates those statements that you think almost never apply to you. **Number 1** applies to you some of the time. **Number 2** applies to you most of the time. Add your totals for each group.

0. Almost never applies to me.
1. Applies to me some of the time.
2. Applies to me most of the time.

			Score 0-2
1.	Prefer to work independently by myself		
2.	Do not like interruptions. I have to concentrate		
3.	Don't like people coming into my space unless expected		
		Total for I	
4.	Want to interact with people to get my work done		
5.	Want to express what's on my mind right now		
6.	Like to share my space and things with others		
		Total for E	
7.	Prefer to focus on facts and details		
8.	Like things that I know are true because they already happened		
9.	Accuracy and precision are more important to me than good ideas		
		Total for S	

10.	Good at solving problems quickly	
11.	Love to imagine possibilities and work them out in my mind	
12.	Find decision making easy and don't mind a few risks	
	Total for N	
13.	Find myself focusing on how I feel about people and events	
14.	Need to have harmonious relationships—and avoid conflict	
15.	Prefer cooperation and likes to help people	
	Total for F	
16.	Like setting clear goals and strategies to achieve success	
17.	Like to debate and test people's commitment—don't mind arguing	
18.	Insist on objectivity and consider myself tough and strong	
	Total for T	
19.	Prefer to have a lot of options from which to chose	
20.	Like having several projects going at one time—don't like schedules	
21.	Enjoy creative and innovative work and dislike repetition	
	Total for P	
22.	Prefer structure, rules and discipline as a way to get things done	
23.	Like to organize and to get a lot of work done in a given time frame	
24.	Like to follow tried and true rules rather than change things	
	Total for J	

After you total each section, place an X on the dotted line about where your score would fall. You will have two Xs on each line. See which trait you scored higher on, Extrovert or Introvert. If you scored higher as an Extrovert, subtract your Introvert score from your Extrovert score (or vice versa if you scored higher as an Introvert). This is your type score.

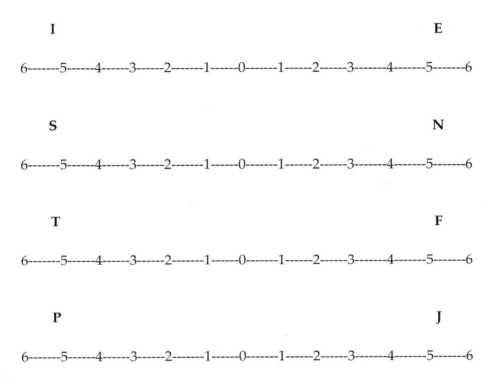

I   E

6-------5------4-----3------2-------1------0-------1-----2-----3------4------5------6

S   N

6-------5------4-----3------2-------1------0-------1-----2-----3------4------5------6

T   F

6-------5------4-----3------2-------1------0-------1-----2-----3------4------5------6

P   J

6-------5------4-----3------2-------1------0-------1-----2-----3------4------5------6

Example:

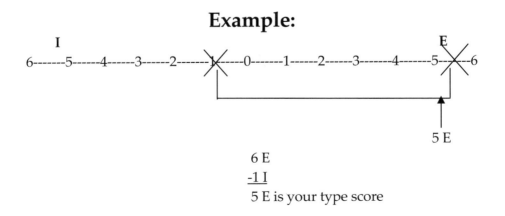

I   E

6-------5------4-----3------2-------X------0-------1-----2-----3------4------5--X--6

5 E

6 E
-1 I
5 E is your type score

Introvert	**Extrovert**

6-------5------4------3------2-------1------0-------1------2------3-------4-------5------6

Introvert	Extrovert
Thinks in terms of territories	Sociable, no boundaries
Concentrates on the task at hand	Interacts with people
Lives in an internal world	Lives in the external world
Goes into depth on a topic	Goes for broad surface information
Intense	Extensive
Has few relationships	Has many relationships
Loses energy when with people	Gains energy when with people
Gains energy alone	Loses energy alone
Self-reflective	External, little self-reflection
Prefers to listen, then talk	Prefers to talk, then think
Slow to make decisions	Quick to decide
Thinks independently	Uses group thinking
Hates being interrupted	Likes interruptions
Good at one-on-one situations	Good with group situations
Keeps secrets	Tells all
When disagrees, gets quiet	When disagrees, talks more
Seems distant, takes time to respond	Seems friendly, outgoing, responsive
Serious	Engaging, often humorous
Talks conclusions, not thoughts	Talks thoughts, not conclusions
Very time efficient	Takes more time
Avoids attention, freezes up	Likes attention
Tends to be passive	Tends to be aggressive
Good listener, poor talker	Poor listener, good talker
Needs quiet to work	Likes noise and activity to work
Often underrated by others	Often overrated by others

Best Case

Thoughtful, efficient worker who can make independent decisions	Likable worker who builds teamwork

Worst Case

Uncommunicative, stubborn, slow, suspicious	Disruptive, superficial, aggressive

Weaknesses

Doesn't communicate well enough
Others think the Introvert doesn't like them
Avoids others and group situations

Disrupts and seems aggressive
Tells things that shouldn't be told
Makes impulsive decisions on poor information

How to Use the Range of Traits Page

Notice that on the left-hand side we have the Introvert—your total for I, and on the right we have the Extrovert—your total for E. As I describe these traits, keep in mind that I am describing the extremes (that would be a score of 6). I will describe these extremes to give a clear idea of these traits and to add a little humor regarding human nature. Keep in mind that if you have scored as an I or an E, you are not going to have all these traits nor are you are going to have all of these traits in the same strengths. I would recommend that you put a plus sign or a minus sign showing how strong or how weak you feel that you are in these traits.

Has few relationships
+Loses energy when with people
+Gains energy alone
Self-reflective
-Prefers to listen, rather than talk

+Has many relationships
Gains energy when with people
Loses energy alone
External, little self-reflection
-Prefers to talk, rather than listen

The number that you scored on your checklist will give you some idea of how strong or weak you are with regard to the Introvert-Extrovert range. A 0 would be neutral—in the middle. A 2 would be a little stronger, either on one side or the other, 3 or 4 is very strong, and 6 is an exceptionally strong score. **Notice that the traits on one end of the range are opposite to the traits at the other end**.

What Do The Terms Extrovert and Introvert Mean?

Territory: The Introvert has a sense of ownership of the space where they work, think, and live. This space can be their personal space about an arm's length from the body, or it can be a workstation, desk, department, room, vehicle, or job. Introverts prefer to work in their territory that consists of a rich world of thought and does not extend into anyone else's territory or thought. Others who enter into their work or personal area are regarded as intruders and are expected to recognize that they have just entered private territory. If any of you remember the old television program *WKRP in Cincinnati*, there was one character, Les Nessman, who did not have an office. Like many of us, he had a desk in an open area that everybody shared. Being an

Introvert in an Extrovert situation, he was uncomfortable and wanted a defined territory. He put a piece of tape on the floor around his desk. If coworkers came to talk to him, they had to pretend to knock at the invisible door before crossing over the tape.

That's much the way Introverts would like you to respect their space and possessions. They don't like it if you get into their car and change the radio, the mirror, or their seats—this is their private world. They regard office materials in their area as their personal property. If you come to their desk and pick up a piece of paper, a pen, or a tool, they could take offense.

On the opposite end of the range, an Extroverts' sense of territory includes the whole world. They consider everyone's territory their own and, essentially, they have no boundaries. Extroverts are comfortable allowing everyone into their area. They share their space and equipment, and feel free to enter into anyone else's territory without permission. Because they don't see any boundaries or any prohibition to sharing, Extroverts are considered to be open, friendly, and sociable.

But Introverts may consider the Extrovert's lack of awareness of boundary as rude, inconsiderate, and disruptive. The good part of being territorial is that the Introvert owns the territory, takes care of it, and makes it their own. They will take responsibility for their department, a crew, an office, a client base, a project, a truck, a workspace, etc. The Introverts' downside is that they can diminish communication and keep people out, creating competition and conflict.

The good part of the Extrovert's approach is that they include everything and everyone in communication, as they move freely throughout the whole organization. The bad part is that they don't focus on one area enough to get a good result and, of course, upset the Introverts who consider them disruptive and nosey. Neither approach is right or wrong but each has unique strengths and weaknesses.

Talkativeness: One of the most important things that Introverts do in their territory is to think. They talk silently to themselves, thinking deeply about things, but do not necessarily say aloud what is going on inside. In fact, you might not even realize that he or she is thinking at all. Because they do not respond immediately when spoken to, one might assume that they didn't hear or understand what was said or worse yet that they ignored the comment on purpose. However, the reality is that Introverts live in a rich world of thought, considering everything that goes on around them. When they do discuss an idea, they give you their thoughtful conclusion. What they usually won't share is the thought process they followed in order to arrive at it. This often leaves people hungering for more input. As a result, people have to ask questions and wait for a response.

> I have an Introvert worker. He never says anything, but he gets the work done. I wonder if he's said anything in six months. I thought he was pretty weird, but maybe not.

Extroverts are absolutely the opposite. They will share all of their thoughts as they are thinking them. In essence, they are thinking aloud. But when you deal with an Extrovert, you must recognize that they do not necessarily arrive at any conclusions. They may be merely processing their thoughts while they are talking with you. This can create problems for Introverts who assume that the speaker is giving well-considered conclusions—that they really mean what they say. For example, if your boss is an Extrovert and you are an Introvert, you might think that your boss is directing you to take action on something. What your boss is actually doing is just thinking aloud and wanting you to share your thoughts to gain a consensus.

Typically, in a conversation like this, there is a lot of misunderstanding. An Extrovert might say, *I'm thinking about doing this*. The Introvert might interpret that statement as a decision and would start making changes. But the Extrovert was really just inviting the Introvert to begin discussing the issue to help him to arrive at a conclusion. The Introvert might become quiet and confused. The Extrovert, because he didn't get input from the Introvert, might also be perplexed. The Introvert might go off and start taking action on what the Extrovert said—something the Extrovert would not expect. These miscommunications are not the result of ill will, but can occur simply because people can have natural, but opposite traits. When working with an Extrovert, it is wise to ask them if they are now making a decision or are still discussing the issue.

There is a story of a general in the army who was standing on a hill watching the platoon dig a trench. He mentioned to the lieutenant standing beside him that maybe the trench would be better to the left. The lieutenant signaled the platoon to start a new trench to the left. The general was surprised and asked, *Why did you do that?* The lieutenant said, *Because you said to*. The general was merely thinking aloud about the location of the trench and wanted the lieutenant to discuss it with him.

I am an engineer, and I learned in class that my boss is an Extrovert. This saved me hours of time. I just keep talking to him until I am sure that he is ready to make a decision—that's when I take action. Before I was wasting time making drawings and just redoing them.

Where Do These Traits Come From?

Let's pause for a moment and talk about how these traits develop. Research shows that these traits are pretty-much set by age five and are not going to change much as we grow older. But we can make modifications. As we become wiser, have more life experiences, gain training, or receive guidance, we learn to adjust our traits. We can make these adjustments by trying to understand them and their impact on other people. We can change how we interact based on our understanding.

> When I learned this in class, I doubted that it could be true with so many people. But it was! What I learned from this program is to stop and think more before I interact with someone. I think about how I am with people and what type of personality they are. I get better responses from people now.

Energy: Returning to our Introvert-Extrovert range, remember that when Introverts have to speak to a group of people, they expend a lot of energy communicating what is going on inside their mind. Words don't come easily, and they have to figure out what they are going to say and how they are going to say it. They consider all of this deeply. It takes a lot of time and energy, and they become fatigued around people when they have to speak.

Extroverts, however, thoroughly enjoy talking. They gain energy discussing their thoughts with others. The longer they talk, the more energized they become. The joke is that if you have a party, the Introverts will come on time and have a good time for about half an hour, then slowly become quiet as their energy level declines. They look forward to going home as an opportunity to be alone and reenergize. The Extroverts, on the other hand, arrive late, and become happier, more excited, and more energized as they socialize. They dread going home—being by themselves is a let down from the high energy they have been enjoying at the party.

Once again, I am describing the extremes. If you are a mild Extrovert, this trait won't be as pronounced. You may do a little bit of this, but maybe not to the extent that I am describing.

Another way that this use of energy shows up in Introverts and Extroverts is when they come home from work at night. The Introvert looks forward to being alone for a little while to recharge. When an Extrovert comes home from work, the first impulse is to talk about everything that comes to mind. The possibility for conflict and misunderstanding occurs when the Introvert needs to be quiet and alone and the Extrovert needs to talk and to be together. These conflicts can be hard on a marriage, friendship, or family.

Luckily, there is a way to have perfect teamwork. Give the Introvert a half-hour or so to read the paper, go to the garage and tinker, start the laundry, or a similar solitary activity. When the Introvert comes back recharged and interested, the trait of being a good listener comes into play. The Extrovert can then enjoy talking about the day to an attentive listener.

Introverts invest time and energy in listening. When you say something to an Introvert, they start thinking about what you said, but may not comment on it for a while.

Introverts do not like to be put on the spot to give a response while they are still putting energy into thinking and deciding how to verbalize their conclusions. If you tell them that you will get back with them in a day or so to get their thoughts, you will get a good response.

On the other hand, Extroverts can speak with great ease. They are open, friendly, talkative, and sociable. To ask them what they think on the spot is asking them to do something that they enjoy and can do easily—they enjoy talking and interacting. Conflict between these traits is common. It can be very painful and disruptive. But with a little understanding and skill, both traits can function comfortably.

> You just described my last divorce. Is it really that simple?

How These Traits Affect Teamwork

Trust: An essential component of teamwork is trust. The difference in how Introverts and Extroverts think and express themselves can easily threaten trust.

Introverts puts a great deal of thought into what they are going to say and only express their resulting conclusions. Extroverts tend to speak their thought aloud while they are thinking and possibly never arrive at a conclusion.

An Introvert may listen to an Extrovert and wonder why the person is taking the time to speak such poorly thought out ideas that don't end with a good conclusion. They may think that Extroverts are airheads, thoughtless, aggressive, and not to be trusted. An Extrovert might ask an introvert a question and expect to hear all of the Introvert's thoughts aloud. But the Extrovert only gets silence. As a result, the Extrovert might speak louder or change the words, thinking that the Introvert hasn't heard them or is not very smart. Their worst conclusion might be that the Introvert is ignoring them and being unfriendly.

The irony is that each person might believe that the other is not smart or not really interested in the conversation. This could possibly result in a considerable breakdown in communication and trust. I've seen teams and departments with people who will not talk to one another because they misunderstand these completely natural traits. Trust and communication can be restored if each party stops putting derogatory labels on the other and looks for ways to use the strengths rather than stumble over the weaknesses.

Meetings: Here is a good opportunity for I-E teamwork. Extroverts are successful at opening up topics for discussion, getting people to talk, and getting issues out on the table. In group situations, Introverts are going to lock up and be afraid to respond immediately. They need sufficient time to think through the issues. While the Extroverts are talking, the Introverts have time to think and decide on a good response. Towards the end of the meeting, the Extroverts can ask each Introvert what they think. Introverts will do a good job of drawing conclusions, summing things up, and adding thoughts that have not yet been considered. Following the meeting, the Extroverts could do a good job of disseminating the results of the meeting in conversations throughout the day. Introverts could concisely summarize things in an email. All of this cooperation requires understanding and respect for the contributions of each.

> I realized that I had to work harder to get my ideas across. I have more confidence that I can successfully communicate with strong personalities. Before, I just gave up and walked away.

Communication: Because Extroverts are so social and speak out with ease, they have a habit of going along with the group thought. Introverts, on the other hand, are more independent in their thought processes. Because of this, they are sometimes out of sync with what everyone else is saying. This can be good because alternative thoughts need to be addressed in any good discussion. But it can also be bad because Introvert thought is often ignored or considered disruptive. To make matters worse, Introverts often do not fully explain their thoughts, as it takes so much energy, or they feel that the Extroverts are monopolizing the conversation. Introverts don't enjoy socializing, and it is tempting for them to mentally drop out. As you can see, communicating is a challenge for Introverts and listening is a challenge for Extroverts.

A supervisor who is an Introvert is often well organized and thoughtful, but fails to explain the plan well enough to get others on board. Extroverts, as supervisors, are good at talking, but are often not organized or thoughtful enough to have a good plan to explain. It would be ideal if we all had both organized thought and talkativeness, but we don't. Inevitably, we are strong in one or the other. But if we can achieve teamwork between Introverts and Extroverts, we can have both.

Interruptions: Another interesting work trait is an Introvert's aversion to being interrupted. Remember, an Introvert enjoys being alone, while using a great deal of energy in the thought process. As a result, the Introvert dislikes having that process interrupted. In fact, Introverts often walk around with eyes averted, a signal to others not to interrupt the laborious thought process. People quickly learn to leave the Introvert alone. It is very easy to get out of the information loop and, perhaps unintentionally, to communicate to people that you don't care.

> It really makes me mad when people just barge in and start talking. Don't they realize that I'm working here? To be honest, sometimes I'm rude to them so they get mad and leave me alone.

On the contrary, the Extrovert loves to talk to everybody and is inevitably the creator of the dreaded interruptions. Often, these interruptions are for socializing or collecting information rather than for purposeful communication, so people learn to ignore much of what they say. Introverts consider socializing a waste of time and energy and resent time taken from the important task of thinking silently to themselves.

Type Bias: Since we all have a tendency to think that our traits are right and others are wrong, there is the opportunity for Extroverts to think that Introverts are uncommunicative, unfriendly, and just plain weird. There is also the opportunity for Introverts to think that Extroverts are aggressive monopolizers of airtime, as well as thoughtless and rude intruders. Notice that each thinks that the other is stupid and disruptive—their way is correct.

Your first task is to begin to accept that your way is wonderful, but not right in all situations. In addition, you do not possess all of the skills to be the perfect communicator. None of us does. The truth is that our opposite type has all of the traits that we lack, and we have all of the traits that they lack. In other words, the person who is most annoying and different from you is the very person that you need the most and vice versa. The irony is that the precise tasks that Introverts hate to do are the very things that Extroverts love to do. It is as if one whole personality was divided into two—neither is complete, right, or perfect. In truth, the only way to be complete and right in every situation is to achieve teamwork between opposites.

Work Assignments: As a supervisor, you can quickly identify the Introverts and Extroverts on your team. If you are an Introvert, you may be tempted to think that the Introverts are better. If you are an Extrovert, you may be tempted to think that Extroverts are better. But the truth is that each has their distinct work traits that can help you to achieve your performance goals.

For example, Introverts work well by themselves in a quiet environment and don't interrupt or talk to others. Extroverts work well in a noisy environment with lots of interruptions and people. Introverts could do the quiet work in your department that requires intensive concentration and in-depth thinking. Extroverts could do the work that requires lots of interaction with people, constant interruption, and quick responses. Neither would have to do what they hate and are poor at, but both types of work would be accomplished.

Working on projects, for example, provides Introverts and Extroverts with an opportunity to cooperate with each other. Introverts could do research and analysis, while Extroverts could do presentations and persuade people to participate. When people understand and feel comfortable in their role, they are willing to let others do their part, resulting in a good outcome for the team. The work is more efficient, higher quality, and satisfying. A team that knows how to function this way will look forward to doing more work together. Their trust and confidence builds and they become a reliable team. Working like this is actually fun.

> I've never been very social myself, and I have always admired people who can talk in just about any situation. They seem so confident. They can even talk in front of groups. My boss is like that. I am always relieved when he starts the conversation.

Opposites in Relationships: There is definitely a tendency for opposites to be attracted to each other. Introverts often so admire the social skills of the Extrovert that they form friendships and even marry one. They enjoy the sense of completion that they experience in being together. Extroverts admire the independence, thoughtfulness, and listening skills of the Introvert so much that they are attracted to relationships with them, as well. The challenge is for the two opposites to avoid the relationship breakdowns that annoyance and misunderstanding can create.

This is where tolerance comes in. Even if there is no intention of ill will, the annoyances and negative assumptions can be counterproductive. While Introverts are just being Introverts and Extroverts are just being Extroverts, it is so easy to write off the opposite with a critical word or avoidance. If you are in a relationship with someone who is your opposite, you will need to exercise tolerance and understanding in order to work as a team—in peace and harmony.

If you see room for improvement in your tolerance, understanding, and teamwork, then you are a lucky person. This may be the opportunity of a lifetime to finally know what is causing you problems and what you need to do about it. Keep in mind that each party makes teamwork easier when they are willing to moderate their traits just a little to allow cooperative effort. You need to know your traits, how they impact others, and be willing to make adjustments so that your opposite can use their strengths for the common good.

Extrovert-Introvert Exercise

Here is an exercise that will help you get in touch with your opinion of the opposite end of this range.

1. What most annoys or bothers you about people who are opposite of you? If you are an Introvert, what are the things that Extroverts do that most annoy you?

2. What are the traits that you most admire and appreciate about the people at the opposite end of the range?

3. What are you willing to do to make teamwork with the opposite range better?

Here are some responses that people have shared with me in workshops:

What most annoys Extroverts about Introverts

- They don't respond when you talk to them. We think that they are rude.
- We can never tell what they are thinking. We have to guess.
- When they get mad, they just get quieter. It's hard to have a good fight.
- They are hard to work for. They're poor communicators.

What most annoys Introverts about Extroverts

- They talk too much. We can't get a word in edgewise.
- We wish they would just leave us alone.
- Most of what they say isn't worth listening to.
- They are hard to work for. They don't listen to us.

What Extroverts admire about Introverts

- They amaze us with what they think. They think better than us.
- They listen to us and other people. This means much more information.
- They make good friends, but we have to work at it a bit.
- They are good to work with, just don't make them talk in groups.

What Introverts admire about Extroverts

- They handle social situations so well. No awkward silences.
- They have so many friends. Everybody likes them.

- They can talk in front of groups so well. They are persuasive.
- They are good to work with. We think; they explain.

What Extroverts are willing to do to help teamwork with Introverts

- Don't make fun of them. Respect and listen to what they have to say.
- Give them time to think before asking for a response. Wait.
- Ask them questions to get them to talk and to explain more.
- Include them in socializing and work. They will make us better.

What Introverts are willing to do to help teamwork with Extroverts

- Don't make fun of them. Make an effort to talk to them.
- Be patient. Have a bit of humor. Make an effort to socialize.
- Don't take all of their words too seriously. Sometimes it's just talk.
- Let them in our space. They are just being friendly.
- Use their ability to sell an idea or persuade people with talk.

Here is an assignment for you

Identify five people who work for you or, if you are not currently a supervisor, select five co-workers. Try to identify them as Introverts or Extroverts. You may think that this is a hard assignment, but it is easier than you might think. List their names below and the traits that lead you to believe that they are one or the other.

Person #1:

Name:	Introvert or Extrovert (circle one)
Traits:	

Person #2:

Name:	Introvert or Extrovert (circle one)
Traits:	

Person #3:

Name:	Introvert or Extrovert (circle one)
Traits:	

Person #4:

Name:	Introvert or Extrovert (circle one)
Traits:	

Person #5:

Name:	Introvert or Extrovert (circle one)
Traits:	

This is the end of Class One. Do not immediately go on to the next class. Take what you have just learned and try to apply it to your work setting. In particular, do a good job of identifying the Introverts and Extroverts that you work with. See you next class.

Walkaround

When I present this program on-site with companies, I do individual *walkarounds* with each supervisor in their work area, helping them to solve their supervisory challenges by applying the skills that I am teaching. The following is a *walkaround* for a supervisor who is fairly new to supervision, but wants to be a career supervisor.

Cameron got his opportunity to be a supervisor after only two years working at the company. He and his wife Sherry were very happy for the recognition, better pay, and inclusion in the company pension plan. When I visited Cameron on third shift in the maintenance department, I found him in his office going over email. He wanted to find out what was done on second shift that was going to be important for him to know. He had already had a short shift meeting with his four mechanics and had given them their assignments. I had heard many good comments about him, but also several serious concerns from management and the other supervisors.

The first issue that we discussed was the four mechanics. He had identified which were Introverts and Extroverts. He considered himself an Introvert.

Eric: Extroverted and bossy. Eric aspired to be a supervisor and was annoying everybody by telling them what to do and how to do it. Cameron had concerns that Eric might be trying to outshine him and take his newly won position. Other than that, Eric had a lot of good experience and probably had the makings of a supervisor. Problem: How to get Eric to use his leadership skills without annoying people and challenging Cameron's authority.

Glenn: Introverted and discouraged. Glenn had moved from first to third shift due to a layoff situation two years ago. He'd never been given a chance to get back on first shift. His wife was putting a lot of pressure to get him back to first. But it seemed that the company was using first shift to train new hires and leaving the experienced people on the other shifts. Problem: How to keep Glenn interested and motivated on third shift so he doesn't quit.

Salvatore: Sal was the electrical mechanic of the shift and was a miracle worker for solving problems. He was a good natured Extrovert and had good attendance. No problem here, but the goal was to fully utilize his talents and to recognize him so he stays motivated.

Marlene: Most of the cleaning in the plant was done on third shift. Marlene was the cleaning crew supervisor. She reported to Cameron but got her daily work list from the plant manager's office. Cameron learned that she had endless problems with her four people not showing up or slacking off if Marlene wasn't watching. She came to Cameron for help, but he was not sure what to tell her since the crew consisted of all women. Problem: How to help Marlene (who is an Introvert) motivate her crew.

When I asked Cameron what problem he wanted to address first, he unexpectedly said, *How do I talk to Dusty, the Maintenance Superintendent, on first shift?* Cameron thought that his job was in jeopardy because Dusty was unhappy with his work. Indeed, this was the first and most important problem to address.

As we discussed the problem with Dusty, it became clear that Dusty was under a lot of pressure to get things done, but he had trouble getting his first shift crew to complete their work. The pressure then rolled into second shift, where Leroy struggled to stay on top of a long list of problems and incomplete tasks. That left third shift with the residue of the day's problems, as well as a mountain of preventive maintenance work orders. Dusty would come in early and check with Cameron at the end of third, but he was never pleased—even though Cameron felt that he had accomplished more than first and second combined. Cameron's secret fear was that he would be blamed for the whole maintenance department failures. After all, he was the rookie supervisor and no one was on third to see what a good job he did. As I thought of the criticisms that I had heard about him, I would have to agree that the scapegoat process was developing. On the other hand, I also saw that some of the criticisms were accurate—Cameron was poorly organized and let Eric walk all over him.

I told Cameron that I would like to help him first improve his crew's performance and then we could work on getting Dusty to see what he could do to improve first and second shift so that he could win Dusty's confidence. Cameron thought that this would work and said that his biggest crew challenge was Eric.

I commented that Extroverts were wonderful people, but they had a tendency to oversell themselves and not think things through well enough. But if Eric wanted a shot at being a leader, why not channel his energy in a productive way and sell himself to Cameron as a supervisory candidate. Cameron would be, in essence, on his side, helping Eric to develop his leadership skills so that he would be a good candidate when a supervisory position became available. In the meantime, Cameron would get a lot of good work from him and less disruption and conflict. Whatever we decided to do, we also wanted to give Glenn and Sal some recognition, motivation, and better organization.

We talked a little longer and decided that Cameron would have a conference with Eric and ask him why he wanted to be a supervisor. He'd offer to help him develop supervisory skills and recommend him when and if a position opened up.

But I also wanted Cameron to work on his own organizational skills. I asked him how he decided each mechanic's assignments. Cameron said that each had their favorite jobs that they liked to do, so he just gave them an update each day on those jobs. I asked him if he also checked email to find more urgent jobs that needed to be assigned. He said yes and thought about that a long time.

I waited patiently (as is always beneficial with an Introvert) and suggested that he work out a better way to organize the jobs for the day—so that he could more efficiently use his workers' time and abilities. Again, after a long silence, he jotted down three things on a notepad: check email, check with the production supervisor, then assign work. I was impressed with his thought, as he had not mentioned the production supervisor before. But it made perfect sense to get all of his priorities before he organized the work. I suggested that he work on this for a week or so. I promised to check back to see how it was working. He smiled, shook my hand, and thanked me for so much help. I told him I thought he had done most of the work himself and he would probably be very successful in his improvement efforts.

Study Questions

1. What are some of the characteristics of a good supervisor that you saw in Cameron?

2.   If you look at the issues of gaining respect and trust as part of the challenge of a rookie supervisor, how do you think he should proceed with each of his four workers?

Eric:

Glenn:

Sal:

Marlene:

3.   Cameron might not want Dusty to come to his shift and possibly see much to criticize. How could he get in better standing with Dusty so that he didn't have to feel that his job was in jeopardy?

4.   What advice would you give to Marlene to help her better manage her crew?

"Be like a postage stamp, stick to one thing until you get there."
Josh Billings

Class Two

Welcome to Class Two, where we will be discussing the terms Introvert and Extrovert and how to apply this knowledge of people to solve some of the problems that any supervisor encounters on the job.

Supervisory Problem Solving Skills

General Principle: Extroverts work better in jobs that require a lot of interaction. Their energy and productivity declines if they are isolated. If they seem to be unproductive or trouble makers, consider giving them a task or responsibility that requires some interaction. If they are already too interactive, you might coach them to moderate this trait and be more thoughtful. You can often see quite a dramatic turnaround in a person with this approach.

General Principle: Introverts work well in an independent, isolated situation. They don't bother others, but they also can get pretty far out of the loop. If they are in a work situation that requires a lot of interaction, they will get very tired and try to find ways to avoid talking to people—maybe being deliberately offensive in order to drive people away. Try changing their duties so that they have quiet work with intermittent times for brief communication. Or you might coach them to be a little more communicative.

Troublesome behavior in a worker might be the result of them just being a strong Extrovert or Introvert. Remember that, unless people are a six on either end of the range, they have some of the traits of both ends—but more of one than the other. You can coach them to be a little milder in one trait and a little stronger in the opposite. This might show you some improvement in their effectiveness. The distance we have to travel is usually only a few inches—not a mile. In another class, we have counseling sessions where we will attempt to coach a worker to modify his traits.

How to do a case study

Now is your first opportunity to apply what you have just learned about the range of people's personality and behavior. Let's see how this range might show up in the workplace where you would be confronted with the task of resolving a supervisory problem. As you read the case study, look carefully for how the Introvert-Extrovert traits are demonstrated in the behaviors of those involved. See if you can understand how these traits are causing problems. Keep in mind specific people whom you know and supervise, and try to determine which traits are generating their behavior.

There are some questions at the end of the case study. See if you can explain the problem and provide some possible solutions.

Good luck. I'll include some of the comments from other participants, but don't jump ahead. Try to figure it out for yourself—so you can use it for yourself on the job.

Case Study: Introvert-Extrovert

Kate and Sam

Kate had always wanted to be a supervisor. She loved the sense of responsibility and interaction with people. She was offered the job of lead operator at the paper plant and was happy to accept. She hoped that it might lead to a supervisor's position. Her supervisor, Sam, had recommended her and was prepared to teach her all that she needed. He wanted to support her authority with the five-person crew.

Things went well at first, but within a few weeks, some problems began to occur. Sam, a quiet and thoughtful person, began to be annoyed when Kate shared his supervisor's desk. He was irritated that she didn't put the reports in the right file, used up all of his pens, and left pop cans and wrappers all over the desk. Sam was an organized and neat person. He hadn't anticipated that sharing his work area with a lead person would be such a problem.

On the other hand, Kate was confused with the direction that Sam was giving her. He would say, *Run the quality report before 10:00,* and then walk away. Kate was not sure which of the many quality reports he meant and exactly how to complete the report. She also felt that Sam did not like her because he never spent time just talking with her. She began to lose confidence in herself and in Sam. After all, if Sam did not take time to explain things to her, maybe he did not think that she could do the job. And if he did not talk to her, maybe he was not interested in helping her to be a success. She felt all alone and unsupported. The day that

Sam complained to her about the pop cans and wrappers, she concluded that he didn't want her around. She resigned the lead operator position.

Sam was mystified as to why she resigned. After all, he showed his confidence in her by leaving her alone to do the job her way—just like he liked to be left alone himself. Kate was never able to become a lead operator again because everyone questioned her ability and desire. This was a bad turning point in her career, and both Sam and Kate regretted how it turned out.

Discussion questions

1. Who was the Introvert or Extrovert? How do you know?

2. What did Kate need from Sam to feel supported and motivated?

3. Why didn't Sam provide this support? Was he deliberately causing her to fail?

4. If Sam and Kate had understood their differences things could have been better. What could Sam have done differently? Kate?

Responses to discussion questions

Sam obviously is an Introvert. He is territorial about his workspace, frugal with words, and underestimates the importance of thorough communication. He assumes that everyone is an Introvert and would like to be left alone to do the job—just as he does. That is why he is leaving Kate alone. He does, on the other hand, put a lot of thought into what he does and has earned the respect of his crew. He always has the right answers and is trying to help Kate advance.

Kate obviously is an Extrovert. She wants to be a lead person and her communication and energy would be a great addition to Sam—who is too quiet. She is not as thoughtful as Sam is but, if he would give her an adequate explanation of what he wanted, she could communicate it to everyone else. She needs to have a lot of talk to feel included, appreciated, and supported. Sam has missed this point completely and just leaves her alone. That's when she starts to lose her confidence. To feel included, she also needs to feel comfortable in his space, but this is the critical rub. He can't tolerate anyone in his space and complains to her. She interprets this as rejection and a lack of confidence.

The bottom line is that neither person understands what is going on and both take a step backwards in teamwork—though neither person is trying to sabotage the other. What started as a positive development has become a negative situation that may be difficult to overcome. Kate may never try again to advance, and Sam may have lost the confidence of his people to promote and train others.

With a little bit of understanding, Sam could have used Kate's Extraversion to communicate his desires to his workers. He would have had to spend more time explaining things to her—and socializing—as well as tolerating her in his space. It would have been well worth it. After she gained her confidence, he could have taught her to be more concise in her meetings with him and to keep their workspace less cluttered. If she had made even a modest effort to respect Sam's space (and not take offense when he wanted to be alone), true teamwork could have developed.

This is a complicated but fairly common interaction. Can you see how it all flows from people just being themselves? There is no need to say that one is right or wrong. And the worst of it is to be unaware of what is happening. If the traits are understood, just a few small modifications can create a positive outcome.

1. Do you have an I-E situation that you want to address in your workplace? Describe it here and identify what changes would insure success.

2. Knowing that you are either an I or an E, what changes could you make to be easier to work for?

Case Study: Introvert-Extrovert

Terry—Maintenance Supervisor

Terry had been a maintenance lead person for several years at the power plant. He was an outgoing person. The crew of three maintenance mechanics, Al, Andy, and George, had learned to get along with his overbearing style. But they were none too happy to see him promoted to supervisor.

Al was most like Terry in that he loved to talk and tell stories. In fact, when they got together, little work actually was done. But they felt that they understood each other and had formed a good friendship. Unfortunately, now that Terry was a supervisor, he was being held accountable for downtime and outages and was faced with the problem of having to get Al to produce more work. He tried to give Al some orders, but Al figured that he was untouchable since they were such good friends. The rules just didn't apply to him the way they did to Andy and George. Al was confident that Terry would never discipline him or fire him. After all, he would just remind Terry that he had also spent many a work hour talking about everything and getting nothing done. Al was fast becoming a motivational problem.

Andy was a different story. He thought that Terry's talkativeness was aggressive in nature—Terry was always hounding him with unnecessary details. In fact, Terry just plain wore Andy out with too much talk. So Andy made it his business to avoid Terry as best as he could. He talked to him as little as possible and was hard to find all day. When Terry did find him, Andy was resentful, impatient, and silent. Terry had no idea why Andy was so angry, so he tried to talk to him more. The more Terry pursued Andy, the more Andy hated his very presence. Andy was thinking of quitting and finding another job, but the benefits were good at the plant and he needed the job. But his heart was not in his work, and he resisted Terry. He was a motivation problem.

George had a lot of seniority at the plant. From his years of experience, he knew where everything was and what did and didn't work. He was a valuable resource of information. George did not find Terry too talkative, but he did resent that Terry did not really listen to anything George told him. After all, George knew the right way to do things. He told Terry what to do in very brief statements, such as, *Bolts won't work. You have to weld it.* Often Terry didn't even hear what George said and he certainly didn't understand why bolts wouldn't work. In addition, he felt that George's blunt statements were undermining his authority. Because Terry was a new supervisor, he felt he had to assert himself. He often talked over George's comments. In essence, they were both talking at the same time, and neither one was listening. After a while, George just quit talking altogether and joined Andy in avoiding Terry. He was now also a motivational problem.

Discussion

1. Identify the Introverts and Extroverts in this situation.

2. Explain how Terry was creating problems for himself.

3. What changes could Terry make that would improve the situation?

4. Work out a plan that Terry could use to interact better with each crewmember.
Al

Andy

George

Discussion on the case study

In some ways, this situation is the reverse of the first case study, with the supervisor, Terry, being the Extrovert. Al is also an Extrovert and is using his social interaction with Terry to get preferential treatment. Andy, being the Introvert, views all of Terry's talk as aggressive. Rather than confront Terry and try to form a good team, Andy just gives up and avoids Terry — as many Introverts do. George is an Extrovert, but a knowledgeable one. He hangs in there for a while, trying to help Terry by telling him the right way to do things. He might have been abrasive about it, but what he was saying was worth hearing. Unfortunately, listening is not one of Terry's strengths; so, he just subdues George with the power of his position. George then goes the same route as Andy, and neither one is cooperating with Terry. As a result, Terry now has a favoritism problem and two people who won't talk to him. A lot of damage can be done by just not listening to people, don't you think?

An alternative approach to this situation could have been for Terry to sit down with Al and, in a friendly manner, ask for his cooperation. He could explain that he intends to give out jobs fairly to everyone. He could have asked Andy some questions, listened to his problems, and offered to help him. Andy would have opened up to him. Being an Introvert, he would have been a quiet, independent, and thoughtful worker who took little time to manage. If Terry had listened to what George was saying and gotten him to train some of the others, he could have capitalized on all of George's experience. This could have prevented many mistakes. In addition, George would have felt validated. When Terry then had to counsel George to be less abrasive, he might have listened and tried to be less of a pain.

This was a much more difficult problem, but I bet lots of you reading this have seen situations like this. It makes you appreciate how difficult it is to become a good supervisor. Now you are beginning to understand why these things happen and what to do about them. Notice that in order for these solutions to work, Terry would have to understand himself and the others—and be willing to make a few small changes in his own behavior.

Hint, hint: you may have to do the same thing.

Here's one last I-E case study just to polish your skills:

Case Study: Introvert-Extrovert

Randy, the Introverted supervisor

Randy was the supervisor in the shipping department for six months. He had worked in the department for three years before being promoted. Everyone felt that he was a good worker—he was organized, efficient, and stayed focused on his job. He was glad to get the pay increase and worked hard to do a good job. He put a lot of thought into what he was going to do every day. It was his habit to talk to each worker individually each morning to establish a brief outline of the work for the day—and to answer questions. Randy had always been a quiet person and talking to people was a bit of a challenge for him. After talking with each person, he would work in his office or in the warehouse for the rest of the day, organizing and cleaning up. He felt that he was doing a good job of being a supervisor. But his workers felt the opposite. The company was experiencing a rapid rise in orders, as the economy was booming. This caused stress on the workers because they were asked to work overtime and increase their efficiencies. They seemed always to have a complaint, and Randy could never be found.

The manager that Randy reported to was Carolyn, who was an Extrovert. Carolyn liked Randy but did not understand him. She liked to come into the department and talk to everybody several times a day. Often she could not even find Randy. The workers often asked her questions and vented their frustrations to her. She loved to tell them all about the customers, the products, and what was going on in other parts of the plant. The workers liked to see her come—they basically just ignored Randy. When Carolyn made a suggestion, the workers took it as an order. When Randy checked, he noticed that they were doing things Carolyn's way—and that actually caused rework. This really made him mad. This was his department. Why was she interfering? Didn't she see how well he had thought out his plans? She was countermanding his directions. Didn't she have confidence in him? He thought he must be doing something wrong, and maybe he was going to be fired. Randy was reluctant to talk to Carolyn. But eventually she called him into her office to talk about his performance as a supervisor.

Discussion questions

1. How are the weaknesses of being an Introvert causing Randy problems?

2. How are the weaknesses of Carolyn being an Extrovert causing Randy problems?

3. What do Randy and Carolyn need to do to improve the situation?

4. What would happen if the problem was not recognized and nothing was done?

Discussion of case study

Carolyn does not intend to detract from Randy's authority or self-confidence, but her natural communication is doing just that. Randy is not outgoing enough to discuss the problem with her before it goes too far. If Carolyn had made the effort to find Randy and coach him on better communication skills—and possibly listening to him better herself—she could have prevented the problem. She would have a competent supervisor rather than a painful performance review.

By now you are becoming much better at this. Take a moment and list three things that you have learned about the Introvert-Extrovert Range and how it affects people's behavior:

1.

2.

3.

Now take a minute to write your own case study of a problem that you observed or were involved in where the Introvert and Extrovert Range was either unsuccessful or successful.

Your Introvert-Extrovert Case Study

Essential Listening Skills

While we are talking about Extroverts and Introverts listening to each other, I would like to introduce you to one of the most powerful listening skills that you can use as a supervisor. I call it *Peeling the Layers of the Onion.* If you have ever tried to peel an onion, you know that the outer layer is papery, dry, and brown, and the inner layers are white, juicy, and emit a spray that causes tears. People are somewhat like that onion. Most of their conversation is on the outside, where they can defend their inner most thoughts from others. If you can get past the outside layers, people will tell you what is really going on and maybe express some emotion—like anger, sadness, or fear. This emotion is your sign that you have gotten inside. Don't be afraid of it.

In so many conversations, we are only dealing with the outside layers of others. As a result, we have little or no clue why people act the way they do or what we can do to help. Because you are going to be a helpful supervisor, you will need to get down to the inner layers. Otherwise, you will come up with a solution or action that is ineffective and you won't understand why it doesn't work. Getting to the core of a problem early will save you time and frustration.

The technique is simple and easy to use. Begin with an open ended question that cannot be answered by a yes or no or a factual statement. Example: How are you doing? What's going on today? What do you think about this? How did that happen?

These questions require the talker to say more. They invite them to talk freely about what is going on inside. The first question might be ignored or rebuffed. If so, ask another one and another until you get down a layer. Once at that layer, ask another question. Go down another layer—until you get to the bottom. If there is some emotion expressed, so much the better. At least you know what the real problem is and can decide what you can do about it. This is better than taking a half truth, only to spin your wheels until you find that it leads you nowhere. We will be referring to this skill frequently in our case studies and roleplays, so you will have many examples of how to use it.

Here is a short example of how to peel the layers in a conversation between a supervisor and a worker.

Supervisor: *Todd, how is your day going?*

Todd: *OK, I guess.* (Notice the tough outer layer. If the supervisor stopped here, he would never know what is really going on in his department.)

Supervisor: *What's different about today?*

Todd: *Not much, I guess.* (Another tough layer.)

Supervisor: *Everyday has some good and some bad. How's yours today?* (Notice that the supervisor asked essentially the same question three times now, using different words.)

Todd: *Well, I can sure tell you the bad.* (Things are getting juicier.)

Supervisor: *I'm here to help, tell me more.*

Todd: *Promise that you won't put me on disability?* (This sounds like fear for his job.)

Supervisor: *Whatever it is, I'll try to help.*

Todd: *I hurt my shoulder playing softball over the weekend, and man is it sore. Lifting boxes over my head is killing me, but I can do it. I want to keep this job.* (No need to go for more layers. This one seems like the real problem. Move on to finding a solution.)

Supervisor: *I want you to keep this job too, so let's see if we can keep you working until your shoulder heals up. How high can you lift without pain? Maybe we can get you a ladder so you don't have to lift over your head.*

Todd: *Actually, I was thinking that a wooden crate would work. I'll probably heal in a couple of days if I stop lifting over my head.* (Confirmation that the worker gave the supervisor a workable solution that will satisfy both him and the worker.)

You will see the peeling the layer process repeated in many of the exercises that will follow, but here is a roleplay that dramatically illustrates the need to peel the layers.

Peel the Layers Roleplay

Jerry, an Introvert has been a good, steady five-year employee. He is quiet and keeps to himself, but generally gets along with others. His attendance is good. He is of average skill and intelligence and seems to be a devoted husband and family man. He is, unfortunately, somewhat gullible and believes everything that co-workers tell him. All of the sudden, his attitude and performance have changed. He is defensive, sullen, and quiet. He seems unmotivated and his work is declining in both quantity and quality. You call him into your office to talk.

Supervisor: *Jerry, I've noticed that you are not your usual self lately. What's up?*

Jerry: *What's it to you?* (Tough outer layer and the temptation to be rude back to him.)

Supervisor: *Hold on. I just asked you a simple question.*

Jerry: *Well, just butt out.* (Seems to be getting tougher here. Hang in there.)

Supervisor: *Okay, but it's not like you to be this way. There has to be something wrong.*

Jerry: *Well, you'd be bothered too. But what do you care?* (Not much progress, but keep peeling the layers.)

Supervisor: *Jerry, we've worked together for a long time, and I've always tried to help. Is there something that I can help with?*

Jerry: *You a miracle worker?* (Finally, just a hint of opening up.)

Supervisor: *Nope. No miracles, but maybe a little help. What's the situation?*

Jerry: *If I needed some time off you probably wouldn't give it to me, would you?*

Supervisor: *The company has policies for some time off depending on the situation. There's sick leave, vacation, personal days, and family medical leave. Do you need some time off?*

Jerry: *What did you say about family medical leave?* (A direct hit.)

Supervisor: *Well, if an employee has a family member with a serious medical problem, they can take unpaid time off and be guaranteed their job back. Is this what you need?*

Jerry: *The guys said that medical leave is BS. Nobody ever got that kind of thing approved.*

Supervisor: *Not true. In fact, I approved two instances of it in the last two years.*

Jerry: *Really?*

Supervisor: *Sure. Jerry, is there a medical problem that you need some time off for?*

Jerry: *Well,* (long pause) *my wife was diagnosed with breast cancer, and I may need to take care of her. I want to be with her every minute, but I need the insurance.*

Supervisor: *Wow, that is really serious news. I can see why you would be upset. I understand that you would want to be with her.*

Jerry: *What if she dies?* (Here's the real emotional part.)

Supervisor: *Well, what if she doesn't. That's the good thing about the insurance coverage here at the company. You can get the best treatments and maybe get a remission.* (Jerry might be taking too dim a view, so offer some hope.)

Jerry: *I have to keep my job, but the guys said that the company wouldn't give me time off for anything.* (This explains why he was so defensive.)

Supervisor: *Jerry, you are listening to misinformation. I am the only one who can start the paperwork for you. I assure you that I will help you work this out. Will you trust me to help you with this?* (Notice the word trust.)

Jerry: *Somebody better.* (Tears are running down his face.)

Supervisor: *Jerry, this could happen to anyone of us. We will all be supportive of you and your wife as best we can. Let's talk about what time off you might need.*

Roleplay Comments

What if the supervisor had become angry at Jerry's rude initial comments and told him to straighten—or worse yet to get out of his office? What if the supervisor had given up half way through and referred Jerry to human resources? In both cases, it would have only confirmed Jerry's conviction that the supervisor and company didn't care about his emotional problem. Congratulations to the supervisor who hung in there through all of the layers until he got to the core of the problem—and offered an effective solution. This talk will improve Jerry's attitude and performance, and raise his respect for the supervisor and the company. The help he received will also make the situation a lot easier for him to manage. This supervisor will have a better motivated worker who appreciates his job and his supervisor.

Take a moment for personal reflection

These personality traits and communication skills affect our behavior at work and at home. Here are some typical Introvert-Extrovert situations that can occur at home that cause conflicts and maybe even divorce. With a little understanding and effort, some of these conflicts are avoidable. Because you have to be either an Introvert or an Extrovert, you will see yourself in parts of these situations. Watch for how to use the skill of peeling the layer of the onion.

I-E Situation at Home:

Situation One

An Extrovert is talking on the phone with a friend, the Introvert. She discusses everything that comes to mind, including something that the Introvert considered confidential. The Introvert would consider this a deliberate violation of a loyalty, but the Extrovert probably gave little or no thought to it in the excitement of talking.

Situation Two

An Extrovert is thinking about what to have for dinner and mentions sandwiches. The Introvert assumes that the Extrovert has made a decision that there will be sandwiches for dinner. The Introvert wanted pizza and sees a conflict. Actually, the Extrovert was only throwing out ideas for discussion.

Situation Three

An Introvert has thought about the plans for the weekend and has come to a decision. He announces the plan to the family. Everyone sees conflict because they did not have an opportunity to discuss the plans before the decision was made.

Situation Four

Several Extroverts are talking about going shopping. After going around the topic several times, the Introvert tunes out the discussion and reads the paper. Eventually, the Extroverts reach a decision and get ready to go. The Introvert says, *Why are you going there now?* The Extroverts see conflict because the Introvert is so out of touch, obviously had an objection, but did not voice it during the discussion.

Situation Five

An Extrovert is upset about a situation at work and talks about it at great length. The Introvert says little and gives no helpful response. The Extrovert sees conflict because the Introvert seems not to have heard or cared. Actually, a day later, the Introvert comes up with a helpful suggestion that demonstrated a lot of thought. By that time, the Extrovert is thinking about something totally different.

Situation Six

An Introvert is talking to another Introvert about a problem. The other Introvert does not respond at all. The first Introvert assumes that the second Introvert is mad, and retreats from any other discussions. Both are confused as to how the other feels. Communication has completely stopped.

Situation Seven

Two Extroverts are talking about politics. The longer they talk, the madder they get that the other disagrees. Neither stops to think, so the emotions run high until voices are raised, feelings get hurt, and the argument expands into religion and child rearing.

After a few years of these types of conflicts, what happens to a marriage? Even though you can see that the Extroverts are only being Extroverts and Introverts are only being Introverts, there will often be conflicts. What can people do to build better marriages and families? As you study these traits, you will come to see that the first step is to understand yourself—and be willing to adjust a little by moderating your traits. The second step is to understand the traits of the other—and not assume bad motives. The third step is to find ways to make the traits work to mutual benefit. All of these steps require patience, tolerance, and a commitment to a positive outcome. As you learn these traits and how they apply to supervision, you can apply them to your other relationships.

Write your own case study of an I-E combination at home

I-E Situation with children

Probably one of the most critical issues in families is how children grow up to accept themselves and become productive adults. Consider the fact that you may have both Extroverted and Introverted children. In most families, one of the parents will dominate in terms of their influence over the children. Dominant parents may tend to favor children with personality types similar to their own. Whichever type is in favor in a family will have a tendency to influence the children to be like that type—even if it is opposite of the true identity of some of the children. How many of us have heard the words, *You'll never be a success unless you learn to be more outgoing. You should be more like your father.* This is the Extrovert's message to a minority Introvert. The reverse might also be said, *You talk too much. Your teacher said that you disrupt class by talking all of the time. Why can't you be more like your mother?* This is the Introvert's message to the minority Extrovert child.

If you have grown up with some of these negative messages, please understand that no one meant any harm. They were just doing what they thought was best. But do take a moment to erase such negative ideas from your mind. **You are okay just the way you are**.

Not perfect, but okay—acceptable, normal, well equipped to succeed, etc. I hate to think of how many of us suffered with painful feelings about our natural traits because of this unintended criticism. I hope you can put such criticism aside with regard to your own upbringing. And, more importantly, don't pass this criticism onto your children with negative messages about their natural traits.

If you have figured out that it doesn't matter which type your children are, you have come up with the right conclusion. What does matter is that each child is taught to respect who they are and learn to overcome weaknesses, while capitalizing on strengths. This can be expressed in subjects or activities in school, friends, relationships, and career choices. It would be counterproductive and painful to take a perfectly good Introvert and expect them to become a talk show host. The same holds true for an Extrovert confined to working alone at a drafting table. As a parent, take time to thoughtfully consider your children's strengths and weaknesses. Look for positive ways to build their self-confidence and success in the world.

Try these messages on for size

You are not a big talker like your brother, so don't feel bad about yourself. The good thing is that you are thoughtful and people value what you say. As you grow up, you will learn how to speak effectively to different people and groups so they can enjoy hearing your thoughts as well. We'll help you along the way.

We got a note from the teacher about you disrupting class by talking to others too much. We think that your outgoing and friendly nature is one of your best traits, and it will help you in life to be a success. But in class, there are many children who need to talk. So, you need to talk less and listen more to the children and the teacher. We will help you, but would you try to work on this in school?

Children Types

Take a moment to list the children in your life, their personality types, and how you can better help them with their task of growing up happily.

Supervisory Roleplay

Our experience has shown that, once you understand these principles, you have taken one giant step up on effective interaction with all kinds of different people in all areas of your life. Now, the next step—finding the right words. We have developed the technique of role-plays to give you an opportunity to find the words that are going to work for you as you help people to perform better. We will give you some examples of words that others use, but you have to try them out and make the words your own. If you do a good job of this role-playing exercise, the words will just pop out of your mouth with ease and effectiveness when you need them. After you find the right words for you, they can be used over and over again. Don't skip this step. It may be difficult, but it is the only way you can be sure that you can respond in situations when you don't have a book in front of you. Ready? Here we go.

Situation: An Extroverted supervisor is upset that his crew keeps making the same quality error. He decides to talk to two of his crewmembers, one an Introvert and the other an Extrovert. How would he start the conversation with the Introvert? Here's one possibility:

Supervisor: *I'd like to get some thoughts about our quality problems on part 6991. Would you think about it some and meet with me tomorrow morning?* (Good way to get a good response from an Introvert who would freeze up under an immediate discussion.)

Introvert (the next morning): *Well, I've tried to think of everything, and I've concluded that some people get it right and others don't.* (Notice the short pithy conclusion that does not really explain all of the thought that went into it.)

Supervisor: *What do you see going on?* (A good question to draw out more information.)

Introvert: (There was a silence of about one minute that the Extrovert thought was an eternity. But the supervisor kept his patience and waited respectfully until the Introvert spoke.) *I think that the work instructions are wrong.*

Supervisor: *Wrong? What do you mean?*

Introvert: *Well, I've been following them to the letter, but other people say to do it a different way. In fact, some people are doing it one way and others are doing it another.*

Supervisor: *What makes you think that the work instructions are wrong?*

Introvert: *Well, when I do it the way some of the others say to do it, there are fewer mistakes.*

Supervisor: *Why haven't you mentioned this or asked me about it before?*

Introvert: *I try to just do what you say and not make waves.*

Supervisor: *I don't consider asking questions like that to be making waves. In fact, I expect people to bring up such issues. (Encourage the Introvert to communicate more and better.) That way, we all help to do it better. I'll look into the work instructions and try to find out who's doing it the right way, but I'd like to talk to you again to get it clear between the two of us what is the right way, Okay?*

Introvert: *Great, sure. I won't get into trouble with the others, will I?*

Supervisor: *No, I'm going to talk to everybody the same. Okay?*

Now here is the same conversation, but adapted toward the Extrovert

Supervisor: *I'd like to get some thoughts about our quality problems.*

Extrovert: *I've been talking to George about just the same thing. He thinks that he has a better way to do the process. Also, Sally has said that she has trouble getting her machine changed over for this part. But, really, I. . ..* (Notice the immediate flood of information gathered from conversations with others.)

Supervisor: *Hold on. Slow down. I really want to hear what you have to say, but you have to take your time and just give me the most important parts first. Okay?*

Extrovert: *Yeah, okay. Are you talking about part number 7445?* (This is a good question because Extroverts often talk about one thing when you think they are talking about something else. Not listening very well causes this.)

Supervisor: *No, actually that one has been running pretty well. It's 6991 that has my attention. It seems that sometimes we make mistake and sometimes we don't. I can't figure out why. What do you see?*

Extrovert: *Well, that part is confusing. We've been running it for years and the customer has made many changes. Some people who have been here a long time do it one way, and others read the work instructions and do it another way. A good example of that is . . ..*

Supervisor: *Hold on. Did I hear you say that the work instructions are different from what the experienced people know to do?* (Don't let the Extrovert run on which would only cause confusion. He made a great point here.)

Extrovert: *Yeah, didn't you know that?* (Being such a good communicator, the Extrovert assumes that everybody else is a good communicator as well.)

Supervisor: *I guess I'll have to look into this a little deeper. Thanks, you have been a big help. I can see that you talk to everybody and have a good idea of what is really happening on this part. After I get this straightened out, would you help me explain it to everyone so we all do it the same?* (Capitalize on the communication ability to disseminate information.)

Extrovert: *Yeah, I'd love to. I can talk to George, Sally and . . ..*

Discussion

Notice that the supervisor did not jump on the Introvert to talk on the spur of the moment. By announcing what he wanted to talk about in advance, the supervisor allowed the Introvert to collect his thoughts and develop a good response. The whole conversation was short and focused. Also, notice that the supervisor waited respectfully for the Introvert to talk. This proved to the Introvert that he truly wanted to hear what he had to say—it gave him airtime to speak uninterrupted, something that Introverts like.

Also, notice that the Extrovert rushed into the conversation with a lot of words and assumed (incorrectly) which part number had quality issues. The supervisor appropriately slowed her down in a positive way and restarted the conversation with more focus. Because the Extrovert talks to everyone, the supervisor realized that he had a good source of information, as well as an efficient and effective way to disseminate the correct information.

Both the Introvert and the Extrovert said essentially the same thing, but in two different ways. Your job as a supervisor is to be versatile in your approach so that you can get the best from both. It really is easy. You just have to know the personality style of the person to whom you are talking—and adjust your actions with that in mind.

Do-it-yourself role-play

You are the supervisor and have an employee who keeps leaving her workstation to talk to others. She is a wonderful person, but her production is suffering. Her workstation is close to the break room and time clock. You have another employee who is responsible for refilling supplies at each station, as well as giving break relief. No one likes her. She never has much to say, and workers are gossiping behind her back about her being a loner. Now that you know something about Introverts and Extroverts, what do you think would be a good solution and what would you say to each? Don't look at the suggested answer just yet. Give yourself time to figure this out for yourself.

Finding the words

Take this space to write out the words that you would use to talk to the Introvert and then the Extrovert. Try to predict how they might respond and prepare an answer that will get you to the solution that you want to implement.

Supervisor talking to the Introvert:

Supervisor talking to the Extrovert:

Suggested answer

Switch the two employees' duties. The Introvert is not as likely to interact with people near the time clock and break room. But because she is in the midst of things and not acting like a loner, people will not be as likely to criticize her. The Extrovert would love to talk to everyone as she replenishes each workstation and gives breaks. But people will not want to talk long, as they will want to get to their break. Actually, the Extrovert might be doing a good service by updating people on changes in production and break rotations as the day goes on. Your role-play words should be positive and professional. Explain your reasoning in greater detail to the Introvert—she may not be as likely to ask questions. Keep the Extrovert focused on the conversation, and make sure that she heard what you wanted to say. Actually, you have an opportunity to make both employees more productive—a pretty good outcome for just taking a little time to consider each person's style strengths and weaknesses.

End of the Second Class Suggestion

Before you go on to Class Three, put this book down for a day or two. Work with these insights until you are confident that you understand and can apply them.

Second *Walkaround* with Cameron

A week after our first talk, I revisited Cameron to see what progress he had made on his improvement plan. He said that he had talked to Eric, who was surprised and pleased to know that Cameron would support his being a candidate for promotion. Cameron took that opportunity to ask Eric for cooperation in being less abrasive with coworkers. He pointed out that being a supervisor is not the same as being bossy. Eric said that he would think about it and actually was doing a little better.

The second part of the plan was for Cameron to get better organized about his work assignments. He pulled out the page in his notebook listing the three steps: Check email, check with production, make assignments. On the pages following were long lists of work assignments, with the names of his crew assigned after each item. I was impressed and asked him how it was being received. He said that it blew up in his face where Glenn and Sal were concerned. They had their favorite jobs and did not like to be assigned work left over from other shifts. Cameron was surprised. He thought Eric was going to be the main problem, not Glenn and Sal. When I asked what he wanted to do, he said he wanted to use the better-prioritized list. It would certainly prove to Dusty that he could get the work done. The problem was how to get people motivated to do what he needed them to do. This is the main goal for almost any supervisor, so it was worthy of some effort.

We decided to discuss Glenn first, but all Cameron seemed to know about Glenn was that he wanted off third shift. I suggested a *peel the layers* discussion to see what might surface that would shed some light on the motivation problem. Cameron felt comfortable with the idea after we roleplayed the situation a bit to find the right words.

The situation with Sal was entirely different. Cameron was aware that Sal considered himself to be a highly skilled electrician. Sal felt he had the privilege of doing what he wanted to do—after all, he could get a job anywhere at any time. Cameron recognized that this was true and wondered what he could say to counter that argument. We discussed that there was really no alternative than to stand up to Sal and hope that he likes working here well enough that he doesn't quit. Again, we roleplayed the words to say to Sal that would not be offensive or de-motivating. Sal needed to perform the tasks that the company needed—when it was needed. Cameron was leery of this conference, so I asked him to talk to Steve, the production supervisor. Steve had a similar situation and it worked out okay.

We then talked about Marlene. Nothing much had changed, but Cameron had been asking her more questions about her crew and their problems. He was thinking that Marlene was siding with the employees too much, agreeing that theirs was a lousy job, but what could she do about it. This type of talk reduces a supervisor to a buddy and causes a lack of respect and authority. I suggested that Cameron talk to her about being more positive about the job. She needed to remind people that they make good wages and benefits and, if they worked together, they could make the work easier. This suggestion was the easiest of the three. I encouraged Cameron on his progress. I also shared with him that I had heard another supervisor compliment his work. I promised to be back in about a week.

Study Questions

1. Why do you think that Glenn and Sal objected to the changing work requirements?

2. How had Cameron created some of the problem himself?

3. Would it have been a good idea to treat the problem with Glenn and Sal with the same approach? Why or why not?

4. It doesn't seem that Cameron is making much progress, but actually he is. What progress can you identify?

> *"If you think that education is expensive, try ignorance."*
> *Derek Bok*

Class Three

By now, you have already started down the path of being a good supervisor. Now let's take the opportunity to think about how supervisors are selected or promoted—how they grow into this complex and rewarding job. The following is a partial list of what management considers when selecting a person to be a supervisor:

Criteria for Supervisors

- Energy and good health
- Ability to get along with others
- Job know-how
- Self-control under pressure
- Dedication to the company
- Excellent attendance and dependability
- Ability to set goals and standards
- Ability to organize and discipline
- Ability to learn quickly and adapt
- Good problem-solving skills
- Leadership potential
- Trust of management and workers
- Ability to multi-task and prioritize

Does this amaze you? Did you know that you had such credentials? Keep these in mind as you think about suggesting others for promotion into supervision.

After you become a supervisor, you start down a long road that can best be described as a transition followed by an evolution.

Your Transition into Supervision

From:	To:
Skilled Worker	Supervisor/leader
Follow directions	Give directions
Get along with few	Deal with everyone
Represent yourself	Become management
Subject to rules	Set example
Receive discipline	Give discipline
Do one job	Manage many jobs
Speak your mind	Be professional
One boss	Management team
Motivate self	Motivate others

Most of us come to supervision because we have been good workers and have shown some leadership potential. But once we get there, it is a big step to take from where we came to where we are going. Before, you only had to follow the directions of others to not lose your job. Now you have to give good direction to many others—and be right most of the time. Before, you could talk to just co-workers, but now you have to talk to all workers, no matter how difficult or strange they might seem. Now there are other management people and supervisors to address on a professional level. You are challenged to learn how to get along with many different types of people. This book will help you do that.

The idea of always maintaining self control may seem difficult. You will sometimes get frustrated. But with self control, you will be able to keep thinking in a professional manner when you do get frustrated—despite the pressures of the moment. People are depending on you to give good direction even when the going gets rough. Will you ever lose your temper? Probably, but don't unload anger onto employees if you want them to cooperate with you later. You might even cuss or swear. That's part of the work environment in many workplaces. But don't ever cuss or swear at an employee. You are speaking to a fellow human being—and how you treat them is how you will be treated. What goes around comes around.

Let's take a moment to appreciate the magnitude of your new role within the company. As a worker, you could recognize and achieve goals. As a supervisor, you have to use that ability to achieve measurable goals for your team, for which you will be held accountable. This means that you will have to organize people, time, tools, and tasks. A supervisor can't just walk away from people or situations because they're difficult. You have to come up with answers, direction, and results.

You need the ability to set an example and discipline other people, based on your example of self discipline. You cannot discipline someone about attendance, for example, if you are late for work.

You must have the basic intelligence to *think on your feet*. Supervisors are usually intelligent. Not only do they have to learn a lot, they have to be adaptable and flexible. You must have problem-solving skills even when problems come all at once. You must be able to prioritize problems and create a strategy that can solve several problems at one time.

The tone of your language counts now more than ever. Now you have to be a professional. You can let off steam, but be sure that it is done in a way that does not intimidate, demoralize, or humiliate. You must not demean anyone. Think about how it felt when one of your bosses was demeaning to you! You have a lot of authority and power as the boss, and it must always be used to help. You could make the employees' day a good one or an exercise in misery that they are forced to endure in order to save their paycheck.

As an employee, you only had one boss—now you have a whole management team. You have to figure out how to respond to each person and how to get them to respond positively to you. This requires people skills. Not only do you have to interact with management, but you have become management. Even though you might not agree with every management decision, you have to support it. This is an area where many supervisors fail to meet the challenge of being a supervisor. I have heard supervisors say, *I don't agree with this, and I think it is wrong, but I have to do it because my boss told me to—so I am telling you to do it.* This approach effectively cuts a supervisor off from the full authority and power of management. You might think that the people will think better of you, but they will actually consider you weak and will likely question why they should do what you tell them to do.

As a supervisor, motivation becomes a key issue. Before, you only had to motivate yourself to get out of bed and go to work. Now you have to motivate the whole crew. You may manage a crew of 5 to 50 workers, and some of these people might be hard to motivate. Before you could let the boss worry about the customers, the profit, the other workers, etc. Now you have to plan how you're going to direct your crew and accomplish your goals. You take on these burdens to not just try, but to fully achieve the goals—because they have become your own goals.

Turn back the hands of time and think about how it was before you were made a supervisor. Perhaps you had the experience of people seeing you differently when you put on that white hat?

It's surprising how your position changes people's perceptions of you, especially when they are older than you. *I've been here longer than you. How did you get that position?* or *Who do you think you are?*

One participant recalled that it was a strange feeling when his former supervisor stepped down and became an employee again—and the participant stepped up to manage/supervise the former supervisor!

Another participant described that it was a struggle to be a lead person and not have authority over subordinates. She is even required to deal with management, but she is not a supervisor.

> The internal department authority wasn't difficult for me, but outside the department was a bigger problem. People wanted to test my confidence.

> Being a lead person is harder than being a supervisor, because a lead person doesn't have the authority, but does have much of the responsibility.

Some people can continue to be your friends after you become their supervisor and some cannot. Some supervisors don't want to lose their relationships with friends, so they talk to them differently than the other employees. This can lead to the impression of favoritism and, in turn, resentment, poor motivation, and poor productivity. The supervisor has to make a commitment to be either a skilled worker and buddy or a dedicated supervisor. You can't be on middle ground and succeed. An analogy would be to picture a boat at a dock with someone having one foot on the dock and the other foot in the boat. When the boat starts to leave, there is no safe place in the middle. Get in the boat and go with being the supervisor all of the way or remain an hourly employee and leave the supervision to others. Between the two roles is a no-man's land where you cannot succeed as either and may not be able to go back to your former role. Typically, if you fail to fully make the supervisory transition, you will have to change jobs and start over again somewhere else. This is a high price to pay, so think about this issue honestly and wisely.

> I don't work to make friends. Don't get me wrong, if it happens, it's a bonus. But I don't work to make friends.

Once you become a supervisor, you begin to evolve through several recognizable stages—Rookie Level, Moderate Level, and Advanced Level supervisor.

The Evolution of a Supervisor

Rookie Supervisor

- Still doing the work themselves
- Not training well
- Higher turnover, which causes mistakes and more training
- Has trouble dealing with people problems—and people know it
- Struggles to make right decisions and, consequently, performance goes up and down
- People may bid out of their department
- Tries too hard and takes a lot of stress home

Most rookie supervisors want to show the workers that they could do all of the work themselves and do it as well as any of the workers. This can help to earn the respect of the workers, but it could be a deadly trap if you end up doing the work yourself. The first task of any supervisor is to motivate the workers to do the job the way the supervisor wants it done. Some workers will cooperate because they are good workers, others will cooperate if you insist, and still others will give you a run for your money to see just how strong you are. It is tempting to use the power or authority of the job to motivate. After all, you are the supervisor and can fire people. Right? This amounts to using the nuclear arsenal before you have tried diplomacy.

Motivating people to consistently work with high performance is not easy. If a supervisor has little skill in this area, the net result will be that the workers do not work well—or at all. And the supervisor, trying hard to be competent, begins to take on more and more of the work. In addition, people who are not properly motivated or disciplined are disruptive. They may create problems that can't easily be solved. This disruption prompts others to leave your department. Replacement workers need to be oriented and trained, which takes more of your time and energy. Also, mistakes are being made that will take you more time to rectify and result in further training. Are you getting the picture? The rookie is burning the candle at both ends and still not making any progress.

Imagine the stress and frustration. If you were such a supervisor, think about how exhausted you might be going home. Imagine how grouchy you might be to your family. It is a pretty miserable place to be and won't last long. Your boss will begin to notice that production and quality are declining. Here is a story about just such a supervisor:

Case Study—Irvin, the New Supervisor

Irvin always knew that he wanted to be a supervisor. Over his ten years of working for The Baskin Book Company, he had held a job in every department—from production to order entry. This year, in recognition of his skills and dedication, Irvin's boss made him the supervisor of the shipping and receiving department. Irvin was proud of his promotion; he thought it would enable him to bring the highest standards to the whole shop, not just to his own work. But, within three months, Irvin was uncomfortable in his new position. Irvin had always enjoyed the friendly banter and loyalty of his co-workers, but this easy relationship disappeared since he was made boss. His old friends, wanting to get out of the hard work, were taking advantage now. The work schedule was suffering, and Irvin was working harder than ever to keep up. After all, he could do any job in the department better than they could. He would say, *Stand aside, I'll show you.*

Actually, Irvin was so busy that he often forgot to talk to the more productive workers. He even forgot to hold daily meetings. Often, his employees weren't sure what they should be doing—they wasted a lot of time. Irvin knew that meeting the schedule should be the first priority, but he was privately worried about the paperwork piling up on his desk. Inevitably, Irvin ended up doing much of the work himself in order to get back on schedule. It all came to a head when Irvin's boss expressed his growing dissatisfaction with his work.

1. What do you think Irvin is doing wrong, and what should he do differently to succeed?

2. In your opinion, what are the challenges of a rookie supervisor?

Discussion

Many supervisors who read this case study tell me that they doubt that Irvin will ever be able to reverse the situation. They feel that once a negative precedent is set, it is hard to make a totally positive change. They feel that the motivational and management skills that Irvin needed would take a long time to develop. Fortunately, most of us do not start out like this. Most of us come to the job with some skills and have the opportunity to improve them. Those skills are exactly what this book is about.

This brings us to the Moderate Level Supervisor where most of us are to be found.

Moderate Skill-Level Supervisor

- Makes people do the work, but helps
- Better at motivation—less turnover
- Doing less training, but doing it better
- Gets new people off to a better start, so fewer discipline problems
- Resolved some difficult people problems, and people know it
- Performance has fewer variations
- Has time to think about goals and solutions to problems
- Has time to organize and bring issues to management's attention
- Talks to co-supervisors for suggestions and cooperation

The moderate level supervisor has learned enough about motivation to get most of the people working productively. Without the stress of turnover, the supervisor has time to organize, communicate, and train. These critical activities greatly increase productivity because people know what to do and make fewer mistakes. The result is fewer turnovers, less time spent training new workers, and fewer mistakes. This is a big improvement over the Rookie Supervisor's situation. How does the Rookie move to the Moderate Level? Here is a case study:

The Life of a Supervisor – Case Study of Al

Al worked at Energy Products for five years and hoped to qualify for the supervisor position when his boss, Gwen, retired. When he was first offered the job of supervisor, he had been pleased that management had recognized his good attendance record and how well he knew every job in the department.

He will always remember his first days as a supervisor. With his new authority, he told the crew what to do and how to do it. His former co-workers just laughed at him and proceeded to hide critical tools and paperwork from him. Al was disappointed and angry, but was determined to get his department to perform. So he dove into doing the work the way he knew how to do it—just to show them that he knew what he was talking about. It wasn't long until the workers were clocking out on time and Al was working overtime to get the work out. After his wife complained about the situation, he began to look at the problem and wonder what he should do.

Fortunately, Mike, an experienced supervisor in another department, started having talks with him on breaks. One day over lunch, Mike put up his hands and said, *I only have two hands and, all together, my crew has 24. My job is to get them to do the work. Twenty-four hands can get a lot more work done than two.* Mike explained how each worker had different reasons for working. He gave Al insight into how to appeal to each one to do the work. He talked about the value of giving praise and restrained and wise discipline.

Al found that Mike's advice worked pretty well, so he began to improvise with some ideas of his own. There were some tough situations and setbacks, but Al eventually developed his own style. In five years, he perfected his style until he had a well-trained and experienced team who did all of the work reliably and consistently. He knew that he had learned something valuable, and that he could transfer those skills to any new position easily.

> Now that I understand myself better, my people comment that I'm more open and approachable. I'm finding out a lot that I didn't know just because they are talking to me more.

Discussion

Al started out as a rookie, but with some wise coaching from Mike, he turned the situation around—even though it took great effort and time. Al thought that he was at the top of the chart. Watch what happens to him when he changes jobs and tries to transfer these skills.

Back to the Case Study:

Five years later, Al had to move to a new town to be near his elderly parents. He was lucky to get work at the Post Manufacturing Company as a first shift production supervisor.

He had a crew of workers: ten men and two women. He was happy to be on first shift and to be near his family. He felt too that he would enjoy a new challenge. He had anticipated that Post was a good, stable company and had a good management team. But after the first month, he started to have doubts. He found that management was disorganized, policies were confusing, and there was a lot of turnover. In fact, the previous supervisor had resigned out of frustration over increased demands for cost savings that had crippled his department—while getting little support from management. At first, this did not bother Al, because he was used to finding opportunities for cost savings. In fact, he felt that he had been an excellent supervisor at Energy Products. Surely, he could overcome these problems.

During his first weeks at Post, Al spent time getting to know each person and developing an understanding of their work, the machines' problems, and who he could rely on to help. So far, so good. But, by the end of the first month, four of his 12 workers had left for jobs in other companies. He was spending most of his time training new recruits, a difficult task because he wasn't familiar with the job himself. By the end of the next month, two more workers had left. At this point, he was not only doing a lot of training, but he was also being criticized for poor quality. To address this, he rolled up his sleeves and started checking and rechecking every step of the process. By the end of the sixth month, the whole 12-person crew had turned over. Al was working long hours again. He was exhausted and his wife was asking him what happened.

Here are some discussion questions

1. What mistakes did Al make as a new supervisor at Energy Products? Have you made any of these mistakes?

2. How did Al learn to become an excellent supervisor? What has helped you to learn to be a better supervisor?

3. What factors caused Al problems at Post Manufacturing? Were these factors outside his control? What impact did this have on his supervision?

Discussion

At Energy Manufacturing, Al was lucky enough to have gotten some good advice. He was able to move from Rookie Level to Moderate Level and enjoyed the better life that that level provides for a supervisor. At Post Manufacturing, the situation was stacked against him. The high turnover was probably a result of actions by company management that caused good employees to leave for better jobs. Training the new recruits and fixing their mistakes forced Al to regress to the Rookie Level, even though he knew very well how to supervise at a higher level.

I hope that this has never happened to you. But, if it has, there is little that you can do. Turnover is the worst enemy of a supervisor and sometimes not in your control. Under good company conditions, though, turnover is a good measure of the effectiveness of a supervisor. My recommendation to you is to learn how to turn people around, not to turn them over. Why? There are many reasons; but, in terms of our present discussion, turnover sends you temporarily back to being a rookie supervisor. Remember the stress?

Why avoid turnover? The Fishing Hole Story

Jesse and Jay loved to fish. Every day that they could, they went to the town fishing hole and enjoyed pulling in three-pound large-mouth bass. What fun. Being year-round fishermen, they knew that the fishing hole was not always the same. In the summer, the water level would go down and fishing would decline. In winter, the fish became dormant. The worst thing was when other fishermen would show up and fish in the same place for days. The other fishermen would throw back the small fry and keep the big, fat ones. After a while, only the bottom feeders and small fry were left—the ones no one wanted. When the weather got cooler and wetter, the fish would replenish, but it would take a while. For now, Jesse and Jay would have to be satisfied with smaller catch. In the winter, Jesse and Jay thought that fewer people would come out to ice fish, but some years people needed to fish even more in the winter. In time, it just wasn't much fun to fish anymore. So, Jesse and Jay sat at home around the wood stove and told stories about the great days of good fishing.

Discussion

Recruiting employees is a lot like fishing. The local labor pool (fishing hole) consists of everyone who wants to work within driving distance of your company. When there are plenty of workers, you can fish all you want and get good employees any day. But if the local economy strengthens and other employers are also fishing in the same labor pool, the best workers will quickly be hired. All you will be able to find are the small fry and bottom feeders. These are the employees who will take a lot of your time to train and may never be a good workers (or at best only average). A tight labor pool will represent a setback for you. So before you decide to fire someone, consider if you will be able to get a better replacement—

and the time it will take to train someone. It would be better to learn how to turn an employee around than to turn one over. Hint: this is a good reason to learn how to motivate your workers, even the difficult ones.

> Joyce, while I was in your class, I wondered about what you said about trying to turn people around. I was skeptical. But in the year since I took the class, I see that some people can be helped. As I look back over my career, I think that there are probably three people that I could have saved. I regret firing those three people, but it won't happen again.

Okay, so you've learned how to function as a Moderate Level Supervisor. Many supervisors spend most of their careers at this level and think that there is not much that they can do to improve. Not so, as you will see at the Advanced Level.

Advanced Supervisor Level

- Does employees work to set an example and to train, not because he has to
- Knows each of his people well—can predict their performance accurately, and has their respect and loyalty
- Spends a lot of time cross-training
- Has developed a group of secondary leaders—develops a replacement
- Has lots of charts and goals so people know how they are doing
- Is selective about who he brings onto his team
- Is aware of and responsive to small changes, such as attitudes, fatigue, temperature, stresses, new work, or changes in processes
- People want to bid into supervisor's department
- Seniority level rises and turnover declines
- Has time to discuss and plan improvements and more difficult goals
- The team runs the department, even if the supervisor is gone—they know the right decisions and make them
- Good use of humor and motivation—employees say they have fun at work
- Rarely has to discipline workers
- Has found skills and abilities in people that they didn't realize they had

- Has frequent discussions with management and pushes for improvements
- Frequently helps and advises newer supervisors
- Has time for family and community activities

Discussion about the Advanced Level Supervisor

An Advanced Level supervisor can be gone for weeks at a time, at training or on vacation, and the department runs as if they were there. In fact, if the supervisor calls in, the workers will relay what problems came up and how they were resolved. And, not surprisingly, it is the same thing that the supervisor would have told them to do if the supervisor had been there. Workers have learned to think as the supervisor thinks—and to make the same decisions. Workers have taken responsibility for their own motivation and performance and do not need the supervisor's constant attention. There is little turnover. If there is, everybody has been cross-trained, so one of the workers could take on the training duties and get the new recruit up to speed. Department performance is consistent, and employee suggestions are constantly evaluated and implemented. All of this serves to improve several well-defined measures of performances—such as safety, quality, on-time delivery, cost reduction, maintenance, and housekeeping.

Sound like a dream job? It is, but it didn't come about because ideal workers were hired. It came about through years of careful communication, training, development, organization, and good old fashioned TLC.

Case Study—Berty at the Rockland Steel Company

Berty worked for the company for eight years. She was promoted to supervisor in the finishing department two years ago when the prior plant manager was fired and the department supervisor quit. A new plant manager was hired, but he had many problems to address and paid little attention to Berty and her department. Before being promoted, Berty was a lead person and ran the forklift, loading products for each workstation. Berty had little education, but a lot of pluck. In addition, she knew each worker and what they needed to make rate. She had always treated each one with respect, despite tattoos, ragged hair, divorces, weekend jail sentences, and swear words. She understood that none of the workers was perfect, but that they all needed each other to make the department work. No matter what their problem, Berty tried to help even though she did not allow for laziness or intentional mistakes. She often told the offender what a dumb idea that was and to not ever do it again. On the other hand, if anyone had a death in the family, the whole department would show up at the funeral. If someone had a financial emergency, they would take up a collection.

Not even knowing how she did it, Berty had forged a rag-tag, de-motivated group of laborers into a working crew and a work family. Her word was law in the department—but it was always fair, honest, and blunt. She hated to leave her department because she loved her job, but she could go on vacation and everyone knew what to do and was motivated to keep their performance high. It meant that everyone's paycheck was consistent and the customers were happy—and it also meant that the team had done what they were capable of doing.

Berty wished that the plant manager would spend more time helping her with problems and teaching her. The manager, though, viewed her department as the best-managed and most reliable one in the plant. Berty had no idea how successful she was at her job or how she had achieved these results. It just came naturally to her. If she thought to get her GED and maybe a year or two of technical school training, she would be highly promotable.

Discussion

This case study brings us to the question, *What do we really mean by motivation?* What does it consist of and how does a supervisor utilize it to get results?

Introduction to the Topic of Motivation

Motivation is a topic that weaves in and out of most supervisory training programs. To most of us, it seems complicated and, in fact, it is. If you are tempted to think that all you have to say is *get with it and get back to work*, or advise someone to get an attitude adjustment, you do not have an effective motivational approach. In this program, we are going to take several different cuts at what motivation means. Each viewpoint will give us some useful insights and tools to use, but none is the definitive approach to the subject.

One way to approach motivation is to think of an old-fashioned weighing scale—one that has two small trays suspended by chains on a bar that tips on a vertical stand. You could put a bag of gunpowder in one tray and a measured weight in the other. When the two trays balance, you have an accurate weight. Think of one tray as the motivator tray and the other tray as the de-motivator. If we put all of our reasons to be motivated in one tray and all of our reasons to be de-motivated in the other, we will easily see if we are motivated or de-motivated. Which way do your scales tip?

When people come to work each day, they weigh all of their reasons to go to work (their motivations) against all of their reasons not to go to work (their de-motivations). If the motivator side is heavy enough, they come to work and work hard. If the de-motivator side is heavier, they think about calling in sick or doing the minimum work required to avoid losing their jobs. If you could get inside their minds, you would be privy to what is on each tray of their mental scale. You would know their motivational status.

You can achieve this insight by talking to workers and discussing what they like and dislike about their jobs. If you listen to what they are saying, they will be listing their motivators and de-motivators. Even when people come to you with complaints, they are at least listing their de-motivators for you. Although it is annoying to listen to complaints, you should actually thank them because they have just told you how you can motivate them to work better. Once you know what is in each person's motivator and de-motivator tray, you can begin to do something about it.

Your options are:

- Remove a de-motivator when possible
- Add a motivator when possible

Case Study—Removing a De-motivator: Rudy's Story

Rudy works in the molding department, where there is a lot of equipment. It is loud, dirty, and smelly. The molds have to be handled with great care and attention to get them set right, and the runs are in the thousands. On one hand, it is a demanding job, but on the other, it is boring. Jason is the supervisor and is glad to have Rudy—he shows up on time every day and works hard. Rudy's performance started out well, but has been slipping lately. Jason has learned to talk to his employees every day, even if only for a few minutes. He wants to find out what he can do to help make their work easier and better. After Rudy has been at work for two weeks, one of the daily conversations reveals the problem.

Over Rudy's workstation is a conveyer belt that runs all day. It drops sand and dirt on Rudy. It falls on his head, goes down his shirt, fills his pockets, and even gets into his shoes and socks. It is annoying. Jason immediately recognizes that this is a big de-motivator and inhibits Rudy from doing a good job—every time he makes a mold, he gets sand dumped on his head. Jason spends some time carefully observing the falling dirt, verifies that it is consistent, and even determines where it is coming from. He calls Keith, the maintenance supervisor, and asks some questions. It turns out that the conveyer belt is supposed to have a collector pan that catches the dirt and recycles it, but it was taken off the last time the belt was replaced. It will take some time, but Keith thinks that he can get it fixed during the weekend shutdown.

Jason goes back to Rudy and explains what he has found out. He is careful not to promise when the fix will take place—experience has taught him that things don't always go smoothly on projects like this. In the meantime, he rigs up a piece of cardboard that deflects the dirt without interfering with the operation. For several days, he asks Rudy if the cardboard is helping. Rudy says yes and thanks him. Rudy's production improves because he can pay more attention to setting the molds. He is not so miserable. Jason makes some notes to himself to follow up with Keith until the collector pan is installed and working well.

Questions:

1. What is the benefit of Jason talking to his workers every day?

2. How do you think Rudy feels about Jason as a supervisor? What is his motivational status?

Discussion about the Case Study of Rudy: Motivators and De-motivators

This is an example of removing a de-motivator. Rudy's natural work ethic is strong but the falling dirt was a de-motivator that caused his performance to decline. Rudy didn't want to complain. But because Jason kept talking to him, Rudy finally told him about the problem. Once he saw that Jason listened to him and did something about it, his expectation that this job was going to work out for him began to increase. He was now looking forward to working for Jason. Rudy had faith that any future problems could also probably be worked out.

Discussion about Adding a Motivator

Now let's talk about adding a motivator. We all know, of course, that money and benefits are universal and powerful motivators. But changing an employee's salary is usually not up to the supervisor. The exception is a job that is on a per-piece rate or an incentive program. Anything that a supervisor can do to help a worker achieve or increase their rate would be a powerful motivator.

Let's look at other motivators that a supervisor can influence:

- Feeling part of a solid team
- Encouragement to offer ideas for improvement
- Listening
- Praise
- Working with preferred equipment
- Working with well-liked team members

Achieving a long, sought-after goal that ensures the company's success—and an employee's job—is a motivator, as is a positive atmosphere of acceptance and joking around. In fact, a positive work environment may be the best part of some people's day. It may be the only time that they are respected or included. In our case study above, having Jason come around and talk to Rudy is a motivator. In Berty's story, inclusion in the departmental work family is a motivator, as is knowing that everyone's success depends on everyone doing their best.

How to Begin to Develop Motivation

Here are some simple things that a supervisor can do to increase motivation:

- Talk to employees frequently about what they like and dislike about their jobs
- Remove as many de-motivators as possible
- Add as many motivators as possible
- Repeat periodically

As simple as this process appears, there are some complicating factors:

Condition:

Other than pay and benefits, everyone has their own set of motivators and de-motivators. For example, we have learned that an Introvert views working quietly, without interruption, as a motivator. An Extrovert would view that as a de-motivator.

Keep in Touch

A person's motivational status changes frequently. For example, if a person has been highly motivated to earn money to buy a new car, the motivation changes once the car is paid off. It is wise to keep in touch with each employee to understand what currently motivates, as the worker's performance may change when the motivational status changes. You need to keep in touch with the worker's thinking.

Seize Opportunities

You may not have the power or time to change all aspects of motivation, but you will have some opportunities. If you can seize these opportunities, it will pay big dividends. Do not ignore them.

Look in the Mirror

The quality of your supervision may also be a motivator or a de-motivator. Always look at yourself and your behavior to see if you are helping or hindering your motivational plan. People like working for an organized, personable, and reasonable supervisor. They dislike working for an ill-tempered, disorganized, and unfair one. Improving your supervisory skills can take you from de-motivator to motivator with the added benefit of making your work life easier.

Case Study--Mildred and the Tootsie Hosiery Mil

Two employees of the Tootsie Hosiery Mills were waiting outside the plant for the bus ride home on a cold, wet afternoon. Mildred is a 30-year-old loom operator and Leon is her coworker.

Mildred: *One more day like this and it's bye-bye Tootsie for me.*

Leon: *What's the problem?*

Mildred: *This job is boring me to death. It's a Mickey Mouse job all day long. I work my fingers raw racking up those yarn spools—two hours straight before the break. Then lunch. Then the afternoon break. That's the same routine four times a day. I handle 800 spools. Toward the end of each period, I can hardly wait until I count the 200th spool.*

Leon: *Wow. I never thought of it that way. It just strikes me that it's an easy way to make a day's pay.*

Mildred: *Easy, nothing. I could show them how to make it easier. All we'd need is some gizmo to let me rack up two spools at a time. But that pumpkin head I work for hasn't listened to a new idea in 30 years.*

Leon: *That could be. But I'm satisfied as long as the supervisor stays off my back. I like the spool job, and I don't like to be hassled.*

Mildred: *If he were to hassle you, you'd know you were something besides a machine. If there were some place closer to home, I'd walk out on Tootsie tomorrow.*

Leon: *I could get a job nearer to my home, but I'd make less pay. The extra money is worth 15 minutes longer on the bus.*

Mildred: *Not for me. I've got kids to feed when I get home. I don't want them out on the streets longer than they have to be. I'd take a pay cut if my job was next door to where I live.*

Leon: (At this point Leon's bus arrived.) *See you tomorrow. That's if you don't decide to quit.*

Mildred: (Speaking to herself) *Fat chance. What other choices do I really have?*

Analyze this Case Study

1. What are the factors that keep these two employees at their jobs? Consider their personal needs.

2. What are the factors that de-motivate these employees?

3. What would happen if other employers improved their employment offers?

4. What could Mildred's supervisor do to improve this situation?

5. Why would the supervisor want to improve the situation?

Discussion about the Case Study on Motivators and De-motivators

Note that Mildred and Leon had different motivators and de-motivators. This will be the case for you on your team. Each person will be different, but all come to work for a common motivator—to earn a living.

	Mildred	**Leon**
Motivators:	Earn a living Close to home Benefits for children	Earn a living On a bus line Boss does not hassle him
De-motivators:	Boss does not talk to her Work is boring Fingers hurt Ideas are ignored	Pay is okay—would leave for better

Mildred, who has more de-motivators, complains the loudest. Leon is somewhat content. At this point, working on Mildred would be a supervisor's best move—removing some de-motivators. He could listen to some of her ideas and make the work less boring and less painful. She would then list *being involved in making improvements* as a motivator and have only three de-motivators. But if he did the same thing to Leon, it would be considered a hassle and become a de-motivator.

Actually, if Mildred's ideas could increase production for no extra labor cost, it would also make the supervisor look good to his boss. And Leon would be able to make a higher rate of pay—he could do more pieces per day. The outcome would be a win-win all around. It would mean that the supervisor would have to have good listening skills, take the time to listen, be able to effectively implement the changes, and be adaptable to change. See how easily you can effect beneficial change if you are aware of opportunities within your reach?

Assignment to Learn More about Motivators and De-motivators:Take the time to talk to one person who works for you or someone else. Ask what they like and dislike about their job. Use probing questions and see if you can identify three or four motivators and de-motivators. Try to determine if one of the de-motivators can be removed or lessened. If you look at the situation closely, perhaps you will find that a removed de-motivator becomes a motivator. Make your notes below.

Your Notes:

Motivators   **De-motivators**

Using Consequences for Motivation

A second way to look at motivation is to consider how actions and decisions have consequences—some good and some bad. We all are aware that we must do some things even if they are undesirable. The consequences of not doing them are worse than the undesirable action. Here are some examples:

Undesirable Action	Negative Consequence
Pay taxes	Go to jail
Fill your gas tank on a cold day	Run out of gas
Pay a high utility bill	Have the utility turned off
Control eating	Get too fat
Weed your garden	Get no crop
Go to work on a nice day	Lose your paycheck

If you look at it another way, these same undesirable actions also have positive consequences. I guess it depends on the glass half-full or half-empty viewpoint.

Undesirable Action	Positive Consequence
Pay taxes	Get good public services
Fill your gas tank on a cold day	Make it home in a warm car
Pay a high utility bill	Always have light, heat, and water
Control your eating	Feel good, look good
Weed your garden	Have fresh vegetables handy
Go to work on a nice day	Have money to enjoy vacations

If you have employees who are not doing their job, you can talk to them about the positive and negative consequences that follow. This may seem obvious to you, but many people choose not to look at or undervalue all of the consequences. This can cause bad habits to form. A conversation on consequences might sound like this:

Case Study Using Consequences

Supervisor: *George, I'd like to talk to you about not doing your cleanup at the end of your shift.*

George: *Yeah, what's it to you?*

Supervisor: *Well, George, if you don't do your own cleanup, then the next shift starts off with a mess and that really annoys them. They have been complaining to me about it.*

George: *They leave me a mess when I get in, so why should I clean up for them?*

Supervisor: *Every shift, including yours, is responsible for its own cleanup. We are a team. When you don't do your part, you are letting others down and they don't want to work with you. Cleanup is just one issue. Your paperwork is sloppy and often late. Don't you want to be a valued member of the team?*

George: *Valued? I value my time at home. I'm tired. I just want to get out of here as fast as I can.*

Supervisor: *George, if you don't get the cleanup done before the end of your shift, you will be written up and that could threaten your job. You sure wouldn't want that, would you?*

George: *Who cares? It's just a job. I can get a job like this anywhere.*

Supervisor: *That may not be true. Other companies in this area are laying off right now. Many of those workers might be happy to take a job like this, and other jobs may not be available. If you lose your paycheck, you might not be able to make your truck payment, your mortgage payment, or meet other obligations. What would you do?*

George: *How do you know that other companies are laying off?*

Supervisor: *You can read about it in the papers. Why don't you take the rest of the day off without pay and make some calls to other companies. See how many are hiring. We'll talk tomorrow.*

George: *Hey, wait a minute. I'm staying till the end of my shift. I'll make sure that the cleanup is done.*

Supervisor: *Good, I'll be by to check on it, so be sure it is complete and is done every day without me having to talk to you again. I expect good cleanup from my crew every day.*

Discussion of Consequences Case Study

Notice that not all of the consequences brought to George's attention actually motivated him. It wasn't until he began to believe that he might not be able to find another job that he began to cooperate. It will be different for each person. Some people will be so unhappy to have you talk to them, they will improve just to avoid the disciplinary talk. Others might be motivated by what their peers think of them or by lost opportunities for advancement. Again, if you talk to your people, you will have a reasonable idea of what might motivate them. Once you discover what motivates a person, you can begin to build a motivational plan that will work for them. Here are some ground rules for using the consequences approach to motivation:

Guidelines for Using Consequences

Stay calm, reasonable, and professional. Don't lose your temper, or the discussion will sound like a threat.

Make sure that the consequences are natural ones that will follow the action or decision. If not, the person will not believe that the consequence will follow and will ignore it. Once you determine what kind of outcomes or consequences will most likely *hit home* with your employee, you can help the employee to avoid the consequence.

You can't overuse this approach—people get clever about resisting rationales. Perhaps the best way to use this approach is to consider it an attention getter that could be combined with other approaches.

This approach can be a positive one as opposed to the example given about George. An example of this is how Berty used consequences in her finishing department. She often would say: *We have to get the baskets staged and ready to go at the beginning of the shift or we might run out of parts, and then we will not make our incentive today.* The beauty of this approach for Berty's team was that they knew that the consequence was true and inescapable, so they were motivated to get it done every day on time. She made sure that it was clearly understood and repeated it when necessary.

Assignment to Learn More about Consequences

Think about an undesirable part of your job and come up with the consequences that motivate you to do it. Look for all important consequences, even the less obvious ones, such as losing face with someone. Make a list below and realize that your workers will also have similar lists of consequences for things that they do not want to do.

Consequences that motivate you:

1.

2.

3.

4.

5.

If you took the time to write your list of consequences, you will have a much better skill level for motivating your workers. Okay, you caught me giving you the consequence talk. See how well it works? You'll have to see yourself using this technique in a calm, reasonable, and professional manner. Congratulations, you have just finished Class Three.

Third *Walkaround* with Cameron

On my third and last visit to Cameron, he had much to report. His conference with Glenn had turned up much more information than anticipated. Glenn revealed that he was having trouble at home with his wife and that they were in marriage counseling. He had been embarrassed to tell anyone for fear that the gossip would be that she was with another man. But since Cameron had been listening and wanting to help, Glenn shared his declining self-confidence. Cameron had wisely asked how he could help. Glenn stated that being on third shift was actually good because he could get to the counseling appointments. Cameron said that he wanted Glenn on third shift—he did a good job and Cameron liked working with him. But Cameron needed Glenn to follow the priorities he assigned each day. Glenn said that he was sorry that he had blown up about that. He was just under pressure and didn't need any more changes in his life. Cameron said that he would assign a few changes each day, so Glenn could get used to them slowly. That seemed to be all that was needed. But Glenn made Cameron promise to keep the talk confidential, which, of course, any professional supervisor would do.

I asked if Glenn's performance was improving, and Cameron said that slowly it was. We agreed to just keep moving the situation in the right direction and to talk to Glenn occasionally to give him some encouragement. At least his job would be going better than his personal life.

The situation with Sal was different. Cameron explained to Sal that the company had to be successful in order to give good pay and benefits to its employees. Then he talked about how important electrical problem solving was to keeping the machines running at peak efficiency. Sal agreed, but didn't immediately respond. Later, in another conversation, Cameron showed Sal the priority list and explained how it was organized to reduce downtime on first shift. Sal just nodded and didn't say much, but he started to discuss the list and make suggestions. Cameron liked some of the suggestions and used the ones that fit. Sal was still complaining, but he was doing the work, didn't quit, and was making a contribution with his suggestions. I commented that Cameron had won some respect from Sal and could use that as a platform to push for more improvement later.

Marlene was taking up a lot of Cameron's time these days. She had tried some of his suggestions and they were working, so she came to him with all of her problems now. This was better than before, but he would have to start asking her what she thought and get her to develop her own improvement plans.

The best thing was that Dusty showed up on third shift one night curious about what Cameron was doing differently. They had a good conversation and possibly a new-found respect for each other. I asked Cameron to summarize what he had learned through these experiences. He said that he was surprised that just talking to people could have such a strong result. I reminded him that each talk was well thought out and even rehearsed. Each talk was individual and built on the motivation of the worker involved. I would have liked to work with Cameron longer, but our time was up. He thought that he could experiment with other problems and see what else he could accomplish.

> *"The hardest thing in life is to learn which bridges to cross and which to burn."*
>
> *Laurence J. Peter*

Class Four

The Second Personality Type Range

Now it is time to change the pace a bit and return to our discussions about personality types. Let's review some basics.

The first range we explored was the Introvert-Extrovert range.

Remember that the two ends of each range are opposites and that everyone fits somewhere on the range. Notice the dotted line at the top of the Personality Trait Range. On the extreme ends are the numbers 6, with 0 in the middle. Use your score from the questionnaire and put an *x* where your number is indicated for S and N. This will give you a rough idea of where you are on the scale.

Neither end of the range is better than the other. Being in the middle is no better or worse than being at the ends. You have to be somewhere. Remember that where you are is neither good nor bad.

The questionnaire that you completed will give you an estimate of where you are on the range. After studying the traits, if you feel that you are really somewhere else, please change your number to match what you think is your true place. Sometimes we answer the questions the way we think that we should be, not the way we really are.

The higher your number, the stronger your traits are likely to be on that half of the range, and the less likely it is that you have traits from the other end. If you are in the middle, you share traits from both ends, but may not be strong in either end. Again, there is no perfect position, just a comfortable place that describes you.

Both ends of the range have strengths and weaknesses. Please notice that a strength at one end is a weakness on the other end. This means that the people at the other end of the range are good at all of the things that you find difficult, and you are good at all of the things that they find difficult.

As we get older, gain experience, and get feedback from others, we begin to develop an appreciation for the people at the other end of the range. We might even learn to use some of those traits ourselves. It may appear that we have traits from both ends of the range, but one end of the range is our true home—the other is always a foreign land that takes effort to understand.

People who learn to use the traits from the other end of the range are usually successful in life because they have compensated for their weaknesses. This could be you. As you learn what your weaknesses are, you can begin to learn the traits at the other end of the range. And your life at home and at work will become far more successful. I'll be talking about this more as we work through the other ranges.

The other thing that you could do to get access to the traits at the other end of the range is to team up with people who are the opposite of you. This teamwork is a joy to experience—and so easy, because you don't have to do things that are either foreign or difficult. The only requirement is to find a good teammate who, like you, appreciates people who are different and has the patience and tolerance to forge a habit of teamwork.

You may already have this teamwork opportunity in your life. You may be married or in a relationship with someone who is the opposite of yourself. From admiration of the traits at the other end of the range, we tend to form relationships with our opposites. This can be a wonderful experience of mutual help and understanding or a source of endless disagreement, conflict, and mutual cancellation. Actually, it greatly depends on our tolerance for differences. Because the outcomes are either very good or very bad, it would be wise to study this whole dynamic closely and see what you could do to make it work at the best level possible. Keep in mind that these relationships are everywhere—both at home and work—so there is no escaping them.

Because we are born with these traits (and they don't change essentially throughout our lives), we can't change who we really are. And we should never try. Also, we should never try to change anybody else. They can't change to please us any more than we can change. Sorry, but it is the truth. We can *moderate* our traits and learn to use the traits from the other end of the range, but it will always be an effort. Others, like our family and workers, can also learn to moderate their traits and develop some traits from the other end of the range. Actually, as a supervisor, you spend quite a lot of time trying to get people to use their strengths and avoid their weaknesses so they can be more successful.

While we are growing up, we naturally think that the way we are is the way everybody else is—or at least should be. It isn't until much later that we realize that other people are much different from ourselves. Maybe you are discovering this right now.

Congratulations. As we discover these differences, we naturally assume that we are right and that others must be wrong, or that the reverse is true: that others are right and we are wrong. The whole right and wrong concept should be discarded. No one is right and no one is wrong. Now that you are starting to look over the edge of your own preconceived ideas, let me take you one more giant leap forward. Not only are the people different than you okay, but they are exactly the people that you most need. They see the world the way you need to in order to have a complete view—the view from both ends of the range. I agree that it is difficult and, thus, patience is required because opposites disagree with us. They want you to slow down or speed up out of your comfort zones. But, the payoff for just a little bit of effort is huge. You could have the pleasure of good teamwork and find completeness in your relationships, as well as be free of your own weaknesses.

Sounds good, you might be thinking, but what if the other person is not trying? You got me there. Both ends of the range have to be willing to understand and accept the other—and not try to change the other. Also, both need to be patient and work at building teamwork. If you are in a relationship where the other is unwilling to adjust, you might try explaining the benefits or getting some professional help. But ultimately, you can't make others try any harder than they are willing.

This bias of being the right or wrong type plays strongly in childhood issues. Your parents may have tried to counsel and discipline you to be just like them. You may have learned that you were not okay because you were different from one or both of your parents. What would this do to any child's self-concept when they realize that they can't really change? Children may try to be the personality type that their parents want them to be, but they miss out on the joy of being themselves. What a sad outcome. Parents were only trying to help their children, but they just didn't understand. As you think about your own children, notice that one may be like you and the other be quite different. Please think about how you can raise your children to be competent in their own traits even though they are different. Remember, there isn't any right and wrong for personality types.

If you grew up in a home where you were not appreciated for who you were, please don't think that your parents were horrible. They were most likely counseling you on your weaknesses to assure you a more successful life. At any rate, permission is hereby granted to forgive all of that, move on to accepting yourself and others as they are, and to developing yourself and others to be successful teammates.

The Second Range: Sensor and Intuitive

Sensor	Intuitive

6-------5------4------3------2-------1------0-------1------2------3-------4-------5-------6

Sensor	Intuitive
Practical minded	Idealistic person
Likes concrete things	Likes ideas and concepts
Realistic	Imaginative
Focused only on today	Focused on tomorrow
Prefers facts	Prefers possibilities
Must verify data	Makes possibilities come true
Steady, methodical worker	Likes beginnings, then bored
Likes detail	Bored with detail. Not accurate
Dislikes change	Requires constant change
Accurate and precise	Insightful, sees the big picture
Like step-by-step routine	Visionary, likes big ideas
Dislikes unclear situations	Bored when everything is known
Poor at long range planning	Good at long- range planning
Slow to make decisions	Makes decisions too fast
Likes things	Likes relationships
Good at data gathering	Good at problem solving
Good at evaluating	Good at brainstorming
Avoids conclusions	Rushes to conclusions
Compares facts to past facts	Thinks of similar situations, trends
Prefers the tried and true	Willing to try new ideas
Avoids taking risks	Likes to takes risks
Knows the lessons of the past	Can forecast the future

Best Case

Reliable, dependable and accurate	Flexible, responsive problem solver
Controls, administers	Leader, designer, visionary

Worst Case

Suspicious, critical, resists change	Inaccurate and over-confident

Weaknesses

Can become obsolete and avoid changes

Head in the sand; doesn't see future

Gets stuck with problems, makes do

Can be unrealistic and underestimate

Can make fast decisions, ignores facts

Sees many solutions, but can't decide

Discussion of Sensor and Intuitive Range

I will start with an explanation of a Sensor person's thinking. But keep in mind that I am describing the extreme 6 level of these traits. Probably no one has all of these traits in this strength, but it helps to understand the differences if I exaggerate a little.

The Sensor Traits

Sensor person is a realistic, down-to-earth individual who is good with facts, numbers, and details. Rather than ideas, a Sensor likes working with concrete things, such as parts, products, numbers, and dollars. Sensors have a good sense of what is real and what is not. In their minds, only things that are concrete or known from the past are real—so they invest a lot of time and attention on these real things. Sensors work with things, talk about them, collect them, fix them, ship them, and buy them, all of the time taking them seriously.

What they do not take seriously are ideas, possibilities, and future events. In their mind, only if these things actually take place and can be verified would they be taken seriously. But as long as these things are only in the realm of possibility, they have little interest in devoting any time or energy to them. Their whole interest is in working with *real* things. In pursuit of this interest, they like to verify by counting and checking—over and over again. They might check on something two or three different ways to be sure that what is in their minds as real is an exact copy of what is fact. Because they hate to be wrong, the time spent verifying things is thought to be well spent. They would be horrified to be caught in error of the facts (or for someone else to be in error), so they consider it their duty to correct other people. There is no intention to embarrass or to be better than others, only a desire to be correct. After all, if you are not correct, you cannot take any action and be right. They think it is better to double check their facts than to take a chance of making a decision and being wrong.

Notice the caution and reluctance to make decisions. Decisions involve risk, which is to be avoided as much as possible. What is the risk? The risk is that not enough is known to be sure of the outcome. The risk is that you might be wrong. This line of thinking guarantees that Sensor people have a high degree of accuracy and precision about their work. This is one of their best traits. These are the people who get things right every day. They usually have good memories and can reproduce a process accurately. They don't get bored with repetition or detailed work. If they are also Introverts, they can work long hours by themselves on detailed work and be happy. If they are Extroverts, they can talk to people for long periods of time and can explain complex and detailed processes at great length and with great precision. They are reliable and predictable workers.

You should be so lucky as to have many of them working for you. These are the people who keep our society running. You will be able to identify them by their painstaking care and passion for correctness. Their hobbies might be collecting things or information about the past. They may enjoy restoring old things, researching, trading, and talking about these activities. If they are interested in sports, they can recite statistics accurately from years past. They may be the keepers of family history and enjoy meeting people who have some connection to them. If they meet another Sensor person, they may have long conversations about where they have lived and the people they know in common. These are wonderful people who take care of everyday concerns and always have a realistic approach to life.

But do not expect them to make many decisions, come up with new ideas, try new things, or be enthusiastic about change. At their worst, they may be skeptical, resistant, unimaginative, and poor problem solvers. They can sometimes be heard saying the famous words, *We've always done it this way. Why change now?* Or, the ever popular, *We tried that years ago and it didn't work, so why repeat past mistakes?*

If you had an organization full of Sensor people, it would reflect the traits of their members. The organization would be focused on getting the current day's work done right every day. It would be slow to change and adapt to competitive challenge, especially through new ideas and innovative approaches. But it would be hard to surpass it in reliability.

The Intuitive Traits

As you might have already guessed, the Intuitive traits are exactly the opposite of the Sensor. Intuitives like the world of thoughts, concepts, and possibilities. They like to think of ways to change and improve things. They like to imagine the project completed and then make it come true. In their minds, they enter the world of the future and wrestle part of it into the real world. These possibilities might be a different way of looking at a challenge, three or four solutions to a problem, lists of things that need to be changed, planning for the future, or creating new and innovative products or experiences for us to enjoy.

These people are generally upbeat, confident, ready to make a decision, and eager to make a leap of faith into the future—or to just try something to see if it works. They don't mind trial and error as a way to solve a problem. It does not bother them to take the risk of being wrong. If they make a mistake, they just try again. It is fun to them. They like a challenge. In fact, the bigger the challenge, the happier they are.

A good example is the job of being a sales person. If you gave a list of companies that are not customers to a Sensor person, he or she would think, *These companies are not customers; why should I spend my time talking to them?* The Intuitive salesperson would look at the list and think, *These companies are not customers, so that's why I need to call on them. I'd like to see if I could make them customers of my company. It will be a challenge, and it will be fun.* Even if the Intuitive salesperson is repeatedly rejected, the Intuitive keeps trying until there is success. *Whatever it takes* is the Intuitive's motto.

In addition to taking risks, they are great problem solvers. If a prospective company says, *We don't want you as a vendor because you can't make our parts at a good enough price*, Intuitives try to solve that problem to get the business. Every objection is just another opportunity to have fun solving a problem. The true prospectors for new customers are the Intuitives. But once the challenge of getting the new customer is over, Intuitives begin to lose interest in the day-to-day fulfillment of orders. So it is wise to turn the new account over to a good Sensor team to give reliable service. Sensor sales people can also do their jobs well, but they sell best to existing customers. Send the Intuitive off on another challenge. The world is full of Intuitives, and you should feel lucky to be able to work with them. They are flexible, adaptable, confident, and great solution thinkers. They never get stuck in the details. They always remember the big picture and point out the direction to go. Whenever the team is bogged down, they can come up with multiple solutions for any problem—and are eager to try them all.

Along with these strengths, Intuitives also have their weaknesses. As I mentioned, they have a tendency to have high interest at the beginning of a project and then lose interest later on—especially when it comes to detail. Their eyes actually glaze over and they stop listening. Their minds are thinking about what is coming next, not what to do in the present. And while we're at it, let's mention that they do not have good memories. They make factual mistakes because they cannot remember what was done before—or maybe they weren't paying enough attention. They can be unrealistic about what it takes to do something and make sweeping statements like, *Sure, we can do that. No problem.* Lastly, they can fall in love with their own ideas and persistently pursue them, despite facts to the contrary.

Conflict and Teamwork between Sensor and Intuitive Traits

The potential for conflict between these two traits in business is high. Details are important when you are trying to satisfy customers and make a profit. Also, the ability to solve problems better than the competition and grow from the addition of new customers is important. It is productive to have Sensors and Intuitives work together successfully. Too often, though, they get into conflict.

For example, let's say that a renovation project has been discussed for the sake of reducing costs and improving safety. The Sensor people will want to study the project in detail before committing to support it. But sometimes studying the details to such a degree takes a long time. And by the time it is completed, the project won't matter much. Intuitives are tempted to think that Sensors are too slow or stupid to get the job done. With the Intuitives being quick to support change and to get off to a good start, they will then want the Sensors around when they are losing interest—when the going gets tough and the details aren't working out right. The Sensors are tempted to think that Intuitives are too rash and uninformed to be trusted with making decisions.

In the end, if the Sensor people are mad because they have been criticized for being too slow and stupid, who will you have to complete the project? If the Intuitives are discouraged from taking any action, who will get the project started and solve problems quickly? You could have a big breakdown and people might not talk to each other at all.

On the other hand, good teamwork would have the Sensor people evaluating the project. They will, of course, have to recognize that timeliness is important, but they can make a good contribution to realistic planning. If the Intuitives have good facts to work with, they can be the leaders for the needed changes. With the project well planned and kicked off with positive enthusiasm, the progress will be fast enough for everyone to stay interested all of the way to completion. Significant time and money can be saved, and everyone can be happy with the results because they liked working together as a team.

Sensor and Intuitive Traits in a Supervisory Situation

Chances are that as a supervisor you will have both Sensor and Intuitive workers on a team. With the right approach, you can get really good teamwork between the two styles. Here is a supervisory story to illustrate this point.

Supervisory Case Study on Teamwork between Sensor and Intuitive

Don was an experienced supervisor who knew his people well. In particular, he thought about how to supervise his two lead people, Bill and Jody.

Bill was a numbers and hands-on kind of guy. He was good at taking measurements, although he was slow because he checked and double-checked the numbers. His reports were always neat, accurate, and on time. Don really appreciated that quality because he had to file a lot of reports. Not having to do them over saved him a lot of time. He could depend on Bill. But the trouble with Bill was that he could not decide what to do if the situation changed or if a problem arose and he had to find a solution. Bill just seemed to get frustrated and go back to the old way that he knew and had perfected. Also, Don had to be very careful about how he introduced change to Bill. Bill resisted change. Don had learned to announce the change in advance and then explain it several times. He would walk Bill through the new procedure several times and check to be sure he did it correctly. Next, he would answer questions to assure Bill that the new procedure was right. Once Bill got it, he was fine and could work independently and efficiently. Don considered the time spent slowly introducing change to Bill to be a small price to pay for such a dependable worker.

Jody was much the opposite. Jody was good at generating new ideas and could solve problems quickly and appropriately. He loved doing several things at one time, adapting quickly to unexpected problems. Don had learned to give Jody the one-time jobs that might not be done again. Jody could figure out a good way to do them and then move on to another one-time job. He seemed to thrive on this type of work and got bored with repetitious jobs. Don just gave him a list of jobs at the beginning of a shift and checked on him throughout the day. But the problem with working with Jody was his inaccuracy. If Don told him to calibrate the pressure gauges, they might not all be done the same way and might have the wrong readings. Don had learned to give Jody job aides, such as a gauge card that listed the correct gauge readings for each workstation. He would then follow-up and check Jody's accuracy frequently.

Bill and Jody did not have to work together often, but Don realized after a while that Jody had pretty-good people skills. He could help Bill solve problems when he was stuck, without getting him upset or angry. Because of his ability to make good decisions, Don left Jody in charge when he had to be away. Don put Bill in charge of auditing the gauge readings, and Jody liked him enough to tolerate the corrections. Don felt that this was good teamwork. Don could leave the department or work on other tasks as long as Bill and Jody were there together. The most important component of the teamwork was that Bill and Jody appreciated each other's abilities and they treated each other well.

1. Identify the Intuitive and Sensor in the case study.

2. How did Don match the personalities to the job assignments?

3. How did Don use strengths to create teamwork?

4. What are the dangers for this teamwork to break down?

5. How could you use these techniques with your team?

Discussion of Sensor-Intuitive Case Study

This case study is useful because it illustrates how important respect, trust, patience, and tolerance are to the success of teamwork. If Bill had made fun of Jody's mistakes, or if Jody had criticized Bill for being too slow to make decisions, it would not have worked out so well. Of course, Don set the tone by insisting that both workers had something to offer and by giving each worker tasks that were well suited to their abilities. Notice that once Don had identified the strengths of each worker and then looked for opportunities to let them each do what they did best. Just as importantly, he avoided putting them in situations where they would be weak. Had he made Bill the supervisor when he left the department, Bill would have been paralyzed with the task of making decisions—and everyone would have lost respect. In addition, Bill's self-confidence could have declined further if he had made what he felt was a mistake. Had Don put Jody in charge of checking detailed work, he would have made mistakes due to boredom and inattention—and everybody would have known it, including him.

I'd like to make the point here that some people who are not performing well might just be placed in positions requiring traits that are their areas of weakness. If they had tasks to perform that utilized their strengths, they might function as model employees. As the supervisor, it is your responsibility to get to know your workers and identify which types of tasks utilize their personality strengths the best—and, which types of tasks intensify their weaknesses. Try to use their strengths and avoid the weaknesses. Even a marginal worker can begin to perform better. Believe me, this is a big insight for any supervisor, but you now have the tools for identifying these strengths and weaknesses.

Assignment for Sensor-Intuitive Case Study

Before we go any farther (and while this insight is clearly in your thoughts), take a minute to write down the strengths and weaknesses of two of your workers. Then analyze how well they are matched to their tasks. Finally, look at the other work that needs to be done. See if you could distribute the work better based upon who had the required strengths. I know that many of you must observe rules of seniority, union agreements, and departmental work instructions. But, even within these constraints, assigning some duties are within your area of discretion. Hopefully, you can experiment with a few of these and see how it works out with the two workers you have chosen for this exercise. Write out your analysis and your plan below so you can check on it later and evaluate how well it worked.

	Strengths and Weaknesses	Current Job Tasks
Worker One:		

Worker Two:		
Plan for matching skills to tasks:		

A Critical Insight for Understanding Sensor-Intuitive Differences

I saved this critical insight until last in our discussion of Sensor-Intuitive differences because I wanted you to get a clear picture of what a Sensor or Intuitive worker looks like. Remember that you are also one or the other of these types. So as I talk about the deepest, hardest to understand parts of your thinking, see if you find yourself in these descriptions.

Sensor people look at the fine detail of the world and thus they can only look at a small part of the world. It is like looking through a microscope. They may only see a square inch of reality, but they see things in that square inch in fine detail—something others never could. While they are looking through this small area, they forget about the rest of the world. Day could turn to night. Rain could turn to snow, and they'd never know it. In other words, Sensors lose sight of the big picture as they focus on one area in depth. I have had Sensors tell me that they often get stuck, forgetting what they are trying to accomplish. Another thing that gets them stuck is their inability to solve problems. They are not good at generating imaginative ideas, they don't like trial and error, and they don't like the risk that making a decision requires. So they just stop and review the facts over and over. This feeling of getting stuck is frustrating. At least now you know who could help them get unstuck or could help them avoid getting stuck in the first place. They could talk to a friendly Intuitive. An Intuitive would remind them of the direction and suggest a solution, maybe even trying it out for them. This is a huge amount of help and support coming from someone so opposite of them

Although we are primarily on one or the other end of the range, none of us is so extreme that we don't have some strengths from the other. In this case, the Sensor could stand up, stretch, and look around. This gets the body out of the microscope mode. Then, the Sensor could think about or talk about the goal—imagining how the performance measures up to the end goal and what else is needed to get there. This amounts to a Sensor trying out Intuitive skills. Try it and see if it works.

The Intuitive's viewpoint is quite different. The Intuitive looks at life in terms of trends, patterns, and open space. It is much like looking through field glasses. If you are an Intuitive, you can see the horizon, the sky, and the movements of animals and objects at a distance. When you identify a trend, you can make predictions about what might happen next. For example, if you see clouds forming you might predict a storm in about an hour. It can even be far more profound than that for Intuitives. They use this ability to understand people's behavior, how business works, how machines work, and how relationships works. They might not completely understand where this ability comes from, but if you are an Intuitive, or work with an Intuitive, you have seen it occur on occasion. It can be spooky at times. If you ask Intuitives, *What do you think will happen next*, they can generally come up with a pretty good idea. Other people admire this trait, and it can be very useful in business and in life. Just don't expect Sensor people to be able to do it—or even to trust it. Also, be aware that although Intuitives can make a fairly accurate prediction, once fact and detail are added, things might turn out quite differently. In other words, the idea was right, but the facts were different by the time it became reality. Your surest method of being right is to have a Sensor check out the details and verify enough of them to be pretty certain that they are correct.

If you are an Intuitive, keep in mind that what you are not seeing is the piece of ground you are standing on. You are susceptible to overlooking small details that make a big difference—such as being so intent on getting somewhere that you do not notice that you are low on gas. You can greatly underestimate how much time or resources it might take to do something, because you don't fully appreciate the detail involved. If you just break through the objections and force the issue, the Sensors in your life get pretty frustrated with you. They know that they will be the ones to have to implement your grand schemes. Your idea may take a lot more hard work and time than you might think, and Sensors are bogged down with the tasks they are already doing. Once again, patience, appreciation, and tolerance of the other personality type are what makes teamwork possible.

A Word about Teamwork in Organizations

Once you get an idea of the complexities of this one range and how differently people think about projects, goals, and decisions, it makes you wonder how any organization can function at all. Teamwork is not easy to achieve. The distance between one end of the range and the other can seem like a million miles. After years of research and practical application, I can assure you that the distance that each has to travel is really only a few inches. **But**—and that is a big *but*—both parties have to be willing to take these short steps and meet in the middle. It just doesn't work if only one person is trying. It is a sad fact of life, but both parties have to be willing to try or neither party can succeed. When I do this training in companies, I appeal to everyone to take responsibility for their own weaknesses and try to meet their teammates on common ground. You will need to employ lots of patience, understanding, tolerance, and professional courtesy.

Not all teams achieve cooperation. Both Sensors and Intuitives have their own secret ways of sabotaging each other when they are in conflict. Sensors can intimidate people by saying, *It will never work. We tried this before. It will be a big mistake.* Also, they can overwhelm people with facts and details until everybody just gives up and forgets the whole project.

Everybody knows that the fatal judgment, *I told you so* could be looming around the corner. Intuitives can overwhelm people with the force of their energy and blind determination. They can completely ignore the facts and just charge ahead by themselves and make it happen. Of course, without a team behind them and a grasp of the facts, they often fail.

I have often been asked to work with a dysfunctional team, something you might be dealing with at your job. I'll share with you what I do. I identify the Intuitives and ask them to appreciate the value of the work of the Sensors. I talk to the Sensors and ask them to appreciate the value of the work of the Intuitives. The motive for each to cooperate is (1) they will then be able to do what they are good at, (2) they will be appreciated, and (3) they will not have to do the things that they find difficult. The truth is that the person who is the opposite of you and is so annoying and difficult for you to understand is exactly the person that you need. They have all that you lack and conversely need all that you have to offer. You really don't have much of an option other than teamwork. A diverse and cooperative team can perform better than any one person, anytime.

Back to our assignment. Have you had time to complete the analysis? Hopefully you have and are now thinking about how you could create better teamwork in your department by properly understanding these traits.

Frequently Repeated Mistakes that Sensors and Intuitives Make in Their Careers

Sensor

- Explain too much detail for the situation.
- Too resistant to change.
- Suspicious of new ideas.
- Expect the negative, not the positive.
- Lose sight of the goal or general direction.
- Fail to solve problems and stall out.
- Get bogged down in detail.
- Overwhelm people with talk, details, or time-consuming tasks.
- Too conservative in thinking.
- Take too long to do something.
- Criticize or build barriers against Intuitives or refuse to work with them.

Intuitive

- Too quick to jump at an untried idea
- Too impatient with detail to see the real facts
- Fall in love with their ideas and ignore all other input

- Not good with numbers, facts, or past events
- Inaccurate memory or miss important facts
- Good at starting a project and then fizzle out when the details emerge
- Always want to change things, even when they don't need changing
- Present too many possibilities
- Tackle too large a project
- Underestimate work, time, or costs
- Tries to work around Sensor people rather than working with them

If you have any doubt about having any of these weaknesses, pull out your evaluations for the last five years. See what your boss has said about your weaknesses. Another way to validate this is to ask your spouse or someone who knows you well. They may even add a few insights that I don't list here. The point of this list is to alert you to exactly what could help you to succeed in your life. Experience has shown that with even a little effort in the right direction people will start talking about how much you have changed and how much easier you are to work with. Many of the conflicts and problems that you have struggled with in the past will just vanish. Guess what? It was **you** all of the time. Even if all you get out of this whole book is this one insight of what to change in your behavior, you will have reaped a huge reward.

Final Thoughts about the Sensor–Intuitive Range

Some people ask me about intelligence and this range. Surely Sensor people are more intelligent than Intuitives or vice versa. Intelligence is a term that is defined by intelligence tests. There are many intelligence tests that require the ability to recall facts and use numbers. So guess who scores well on these tests? Other tests require the taker to use concepts, solve problems, and create plans. Guess who scores high on these tests? Are there tests that require both skills? Yes. But, if a person is strong in only one area, they will only shine on half of the test. The truth is that your intelligence resides in your ability to use your strengths effectively. It is the ability to know and manage yourself that makes you appear intelligent and successful.

Keep this in mind as your children are tested and graded at school. Before you assume that your child is intelligent or low ability, consider the type of test or the subject matter involved. Sensors do better in math and history, and Intuitives do better in language, algebra, and the arts. Also, consider the personality type of the teacher. A Sensor teacher will have a tendency to appreciate Sensor students more than Intuitives, and vice versa. An Intuitive teacher will tend to organize the teaching activities in an Intuitive manner that will mystify the Sensor children—but make good sense to the Intuitives. It is difficult for the school systems to deal with so many different children, and teachers are only human. You, as a parent, need to understand both your child and the school environment.

Work environments are often slanted toward one personality type or the other. Often this is due to the personality type of the boss or the nature of the work. Remember, we all have an inbred bias to our own type. Don't be too quick to judge people. Rather, carefully assess what they truly are, as well as the nature of the task requirements and the work environment. Try to match the people to the job as best you can. Coach people to manage their own strengths and weaknesses, and try to build teams that have appropriate types represented.

How the Sensor-Intuitive Range Affects Home Life

Teamwork within this range is just as difficult to achieve at home as it is at work. The family checkbook is a good example. The Sensor person in the family carefully records each check number, the date, the recipient, and the amount. Balances are recorded in neat and legible handwriting. When the monthly statement arrives, they carefully verify each check and do the math. On occasion, there is a discrepancy between their figures and the bank's. That, of course, is a challenge to the Sensor that must be resolved—even if it amounts to only a few cents. It's not the amount of money that is at stake, but the need to be correct. It is not okay to assume that the bank is correct in all cases. There are many places for an error to occur, and the Sensor is alert to find them all.

How would the Intuitive handle the checkbook? They may or may not record the check. If they did, the handwriting would be more like a straight line than legible words. The amount probably would be recorded, if the checks were not duplicates. When the bank statement comes, the Intuitive would record the balance from the statement, trusting that the bank was correct—and just start over for another month. If you're a really strong intuitive, you might not record anything. You would just go to the ATM and pay for a balance statement, go online, or call the bank. When asked about how much money is in the account, the Intuitive who is not keeping track might say *Whatever*.

Now think for a minute how the Sensor must feel about these slovenly recordkeeping habits—*I can't believe that you don't keep track of your account*—and how the Intuitive must feel about insistent demands to be more precise –*Why are you getting so upset over such a small thing as a few numbers on a piece of paper?* As you might guess, a joint account between a Sensor and an Intuitive is probably not a good idea. This can be a source of real conflict and misery for years and years. On the other hand, it could be an opportunity for teamwork. Intuitives are good about making money. They see opportunities and take the risks to cash in on them. So let the Sensor do the checkbook recording, and let the Intuitive do the investing. Let there be respect and appreciation instead of criticism and demands to change.

Another potential source of conflict at home is decision making. An example: *Where do you want to go tonight for dinner? The Sensor responds, I don't know; what do you want to do? We know that this and this place are good. Let's just go there again.* The Intuitive approach would be, *Oh, let's try something new. It's no fun to go to the same place all of the time.* The Sensor: *Every time we try something new it is horrible. Why can't we go with something we know for sure?* And so on. With a little give and take, you could have some change of menu and some tried and true choices. After all, you didn't know about the good restaurants until you tried them. The same differences will show up on the topic of politics, planning a vacation, and many more. Again, there really isn't any right or wrong, just Sensor and Intuitive points of view. Your home life can become much more enjoyable if you appreciate differences and look for ways to utilize the best of each.

Congratulations

You have now completed Class Four. Rather than go on to the next part right now, I would like you to put the book down. Think about what you have learned, while trying out some of the techniques on the job. In fact, the more you experiment and try these techniques, the more benefit you will get out of this entire effort. Don't be discouraged with a failure. You may only need a few additional changes to be a success. If you do not already have one, find an effective, experienced supervisor as a mentor. Ask this person questions and discuss your experiments. Hopefully you will get feedback on how you are coming across to people and how well your skills are improving. Good luck and see you again in Class Five.

Walkaround for Mary

Mary was the supervisor of the call room of an organization that raised funds for charities. Her crew consisted of both men and women who worked two shifts. When I caught up with her on her *walkaround*, she talked about the people on her crew, starting with Rhonda. Rhonda is a single mother of a disadvantaged five-year-old son. Mary is a sympathetic person and listened to the whole story of the surgeries, the medicines, and the therapies that the son requires. The good thing is that earning good wages and benefits to care for her son is a huge motivator for Rhonda. The bad thing is that all of these medical appointments have created an attendance problem. Mary has tried her best to accommodate all of these appointments. Unfortunately, in the process, she has given the other employees the impression that she is giving preferential treatment to Rhonda. Both Mary and her boss have been getting complaints. Mary has to do something.

I asked Mary what she wanted as an outcome. She thought a long time (which is a sure sign of an Introvert). Finally, she explained that she wanted to give all employees the same access to the company benefits and policies, without preferential treatment. This was an excellent goal. We reviewed the records of all employees to see if there had been any preferential treatment. We did find, in fact, that Rhonda had exceeded her personal and sick day allowance by one half day. I asked her about Rhonda's attitude and how she might react if things changed a bit. Mary said that she would probably go into a long and vocal rendition of her son's needs and her hopes for his future—a sure sign of an Extrovert and possibly an Intuitive.

I wondered if either Mary or Rhonda had been aware of the number of days used before we looked into it. Possibly the Sensor's *get the facts right* approach to life is the solution to this problem. I proposed to Mary that she have a talk to Rhonda and explain the importance of her job to her son's future. Rhonda needed to protect her position at the company. Mary should explain that she did a review everyone's personal and sick days, and it indicated that Rhonda had exceeded her time by one-half day. Show her the dates and let her study them, reviewing in her mind the reason for each one. Then Mary could state clearly the limits of the company policy and suggest that Rhonda keep track for herself of her days off. For the present, she would have to take a half day out of her next paycheck to make up for the half-day overage. She might not be happy, but she will recognize the need to stay in good standing with the company to keep the benefits. As an outcome, Mary will have established a precedent of making the days off a matter of the numbers, not an emotional issue. When the other employees hear the news, they will respect Mary for correcting the favoritism in a fair manner.

Mary thought that she could have this conference if all went well, but what if Rhonda started to cry, as she often did. I suggested that she have some tissues handy. She should wait until she stopped crying and continue in a reasonable, calm, and professional manner, the same as she would do for anyone. In time, Rhonda will learn that tears are not necessary, that the policy is the policy, and she will get no more or less than that. We roleplayed the conference. I volunteered to play an employee, giving an emotional scene to test Mary's resolve. We had to stop and laugh several times, as no employee would behave as badly as I did. But it was good for building confidence. Since Mary wanted to overcome this problem before talking about any others, I left with plans to revisit her in about a week.

"Character is doing the right thing when no one is watching.
J. C. Watts

Class Five

Welcome back. In this class, we will start by working on communication skills. As we mentioned in Classes One and Two, a supervisor accomplishes leadership through a series of conversations. So, we need to study these conversations to be successful. For starters, let me assure you that they will all be **calm**, **reasonable**, and **professional**. If you are calm, your employees will be calm and, when they are calm, they might just listen to you.

> Calm! I have talked and talked to this one worker until I am blue in the face, and I get no response. He is definitely not listening to me.

I will still insist that you be calm, but you might also need to be emphatic. No yelling. No throwing your hat. No bad words. No red face. I know that you might not believe me, so here is an example of what one supervisor did and got really good results.

Tough Supervisory Situation

Sam, the supervisor, had a worker named Alice who was always coming in late. He had talked to her repeatedly. She promised to do better, but still came in late two times a week. Sam even wrote her up. She got better and then relapsed. Sam was getting really mad.

Finally, he decided that he needed to get her attention in a big enough way so that she would take responsibility for the problem and fix it for good. He knew that he needed to remain calm. One day, he came in early, took her time card out of its slot, and put it in his shirt pocket, with her name showing. He then went about his usual duties. When Alice came in late and tried to clock in, she could not find her card. She asked around and learned that Sam had it in his shirt pocket. Alice paused to think and then walked around to find Sam. He ignored her at first. She asked him if they could talk. He said, *Fine. Go to my office and wait.* A half an hour later, he walked into the office, sat down, and said nothing. She squirmed, staring at her time card in his pocket. She finally said, *I guess this is all about me coming in late all of the time. Yup*, said Sam. *Okay*, she said, *will you give me one more chance? What do I have to do? Never, ever, come in late again*, said Sam. *Okay, it's a deal. Can I have my time card back? Are you sure you really want it*, asked Sam, pulling the card out of his pocket. *I'm sure. I really need this job. I've been giving you a hard time. I know you could fire me. You'll never have to talk to me again.* Sam handed the card to her with the advice, *Take good care of this, and it will take care of you.* Alice took the message and her job much more seriously. In addition, she respected Sam more. He managed to calmly get her attention and help her keep her job. Sam used actions rather than words and achieved a good outcome.

What Conversations Supervisors Should Have With Workers

In the past, some of you might have been tempted to be emotional, unreasonable, and unprofessional, but I know that you'd rather not. This type of behavior causes stress and often produces a negative outcome—and you could lose your job over it. So let's talk about the ideal supervisor-employee relationships and how to achieve them through conversation.

What is your relationship with your workers? Are you at odds with them, trying to get them to work, while they do as little as possible to avoid being fired? Many people live through this nightmare relationship for years of their career. It requires constant pushing and constant resisting. If hard feelings develop, it causes a tense, unfriendly, and uncooperative environment. It wears everybody out, even if it is fairly benign.

Another possible relationship is one of *superboss* vs. employee. In this relationship, the boss controls all aspects of the department's functioning, and the employee does what he or she is told to do and nothing else. This is better than the first, but still takes a lot of daily energy to control everything that people do. Actually, the employee gets the best of this deal. If they do everything they are told, they get to collect their paycheck and go home, with little or no responsibility. What could be better?

It can and should be much better. Successful supervisors discover that the best relationship for them to have with a worker is that of a helpful coach—guiding a worker-performer to succeed at achieving a goal. In this relationship, the worker takes an interest in the goal and is motivated to achieve it. The supervisor is like a basketball coach. The coach selects the players, organizes practices and drills, communicates the play schedule, establishes the plays, communicates with the sports organization, enforces the discipline, gives the counseling, gives the pre game talks, and congratulates the winners. All of these activities are required to move a group of people from individual players to a successful team. In this relationship, the worker has to want to be on the team, agrees to come to the practices, submit to the discipline, accept the counseling of the coach, and work cooperatively with others to achieve a win. Remember our list of motivators that bring people to work? If you think of yourself as a coach, you would want players with good motivation and skills—you couldn't tell each player everything to do all of the time or try to coerce them into playing. It's a fact that the coach only succeeds when the players succeed. True cooperation is required. It is, in fact, the only way to win. If you can establish this type of relationship with your workers, you will find that your conversations with them will be geared towards improving their performance and achieving team success. From here on, we will describe how to be that helpful coach supervisor.

The First Helpful Coach Conversation

The first conversation that you have with a worker is the first time you meet. For the sake of this discussion, let's assume that a new worker has been assigned to your department and is reporting to you for work. How could you begin your relationship with this new worker on the terms that you want to establish? How can you get the worker to see you as the helpful coach and him or herself as a motivated performer? Here's one way:

Supervisor: *George, Hello. I'm Sam. I'll be your supervisor. Glad to have you on my team. Where did you work before? Have you lived in this area long? What kind of work are you looking for? What are you good at? I'll do my best to help you. I'll introduce you to Chuck, who will be training you, but I want you to know that you should talk to me about any problem that you have. It is my job to help each member of my team to do the best job that they can. As you get to know the other people in this department, you'll find that they have been here a long time and they earn good pay because we all work together to make sure that we all succeed. After all, we all have bills to pay and kids to feed. We'll start you here, helping Chuck for today. He will explain how the process works. I'll be checking back with you before break, which will be about ten o'clock. Any questions?*

Let's examine this conversation for the critical leadership qualities:

- It was direct. It established Sam's authority right up front.

- It was professional, but friendly. Sam demonstrated his self-confidence.

- Sam took the time to learn a little about George. He now might know something about prior experience or skills that could be useful to the department. He might know a little about George's character, his motivation, and goals.

- Although he used a worker-trainer, Chuck, to train, he emphasized that he is the one to talk to about problems. He has told George that it is his job to resolve problems and to help him over the difficulties that he might encounter.

- He increased the impact of this message by mentioning that the other people on the team have been successful and that George can be successful as well.

- He gave him his assignment for the first day: To learn from and help Chuck. He set an arranged time when he will check back with George to give further direction, ask about problems, and answer questions.

- He mentioned the common goal that all of the team members have—to be a success at this job, earn a paycheck, and support their families. Later, he will introduce the department's goals, how they will be measured, and how the team earns pride as they find ways to surpass their prior performance.

- He has firmly established a good beginning as a helpful coach relationship rather than an adversarial or controlling role.

Discussion of the First Conversation

Please note that none of these words is difficult. They are all plain, everyday words that anybody can say. You don't have to be intimidating, super intelligent, or bossy. Just be yourself and be professional. Each one of you will have your own choice of words and your unique style. Some of you will have a smile. Some of you will not. Some of you will use few words; some of you will use a lot. Find your own way, but keep these leadership elements in the words that you do use.

Assignment

Over the many years that supervisors have attended this program, they repeatedly tell me that finding the right words was one of the most helpful exercises. We practice the words in class, just as I have written out Sam's talk for you. Supervisors listen to each other and see how others say these things. They find words that work for them. Please take a moment to think about first-time conversations that you would feel comfortable with. Think about how you have done it in the past and how, by adding some of the elements we have been discussing, you could do it better. If you know other supervisors who would share with you what they say, try out some of their words. Write down four or five sentences that you could be comfortable using. Once you think it through, you'll find that you will use them over and over again successfully.

1. Your new recruit is Bub who has little experience, but looks like a hard worker. Write down what you would say to him.

2. Your next new recruit is Deb, who is transferring from another department. She knows the work and you know her from years ago. Write down what you would say to her.

Secondary Conversations of the Helpful Coach

Let's say that Sam is talking to George again at 10:00 a.m., after a few hours of observation and instruction with Chuck. What is he going to say that will continue the role successfully?

Supervisor: *Well, George how is it going for you? Do you have any questions at this point?* (Sam patiently answers each question.) *The others have been here a long time so they make it look easy, but each of them had to learn all of the things that go into doing a good job. Things may look confusing and difficult at this point, but you will earn their respect as you work at it each day. We don't expect you to get it all in a short period of time. We will help you. Give your body time to adjust to the pace. You will be sore for about two weeks and then it will get better as you get in condition for this type of work. This is something that we all had to go through, but we all made it. We will help you. Are you willing to work at learning this job and getting into condition? Good. We will help you each step of the way. This afternoon, I want you to observe the quality inspector and see what defects we are trying to avoid. I'll talk with you again before the end of the shift.*

Discussion

What has Sam accomplished here in this second conversation? He demonstrated that he wants to listen to George. He started with questions and answered them carefully so George knows that asking questions is a good thing. He then gave encouragement and offered help so George knows that Sam is serious about solving problems. And then he asked for a commitment from George to learn the job and to work through the conditioning period so George knows that Sam expects honest effort and cooperation. Have you ever asked a worker for a commitment? If not, try it. It builds the mindset of the worker taking responsibility for the job. And then, Sam stated several more times that he and the other workers would help. Finally, he gave him direction for the afternoon.

Additional Benefits of the Helpful Coach Role

If you haven't seen the movie *The Green Mile*, you might do so. It is the story of a prison warden who supervises the death row crew. You will see this supervisor—who obviously has a tough job—deal with some difficult issues in an effective and humane manner. First, he rehearses each execution so that the job is done correctly, and unnecessary suffering is avoided. He assigns roles to each man and makes sure that they can perform them effectively. He has to deal with a young and troublesome officer who he wants off his team, but he makes every effort to get him to change his ways.

Towards the end of the movie, he asks himself a tough question that every supervisor should think about, *When I go to meet my Creator, what am I to tell Him? That I killed His miracle of mercy* (an apparently innocent prisoner) *because it was my job?* He recognized, as all of you do, that doing your job has a huge influence over people's lives. Your influence is not as extreme as the death row situation, but it does involve helping your workers keep their jobs, support their families, work safely, and grow in their skills, knowledge, and abilities. The role of the helpful coach is an inherently beneficial one. You can rest assured that you did your best to help all of those who ever worked for you. You did everything you could to make them a success. If they wind up losing their jobs, it was because they failed themselves, not because you failed them. They ignored all of the help that was offered and willingly took actions that they clearly knew would cost them their jobs. You can let them go with a clear conscience knowing that you were helpful, fair, and professional. That's something that any of us can handle with comfort throughout our careers. In fact, it may turn out that many of the people who worked for you will say that you were a positive influence in their lives and one that they will never forget—even though you required them to work hard and may have even disciplined them. Keep this in mind and take the time to practice these conversations. It is a time-honored way to supervise and will give you satisfaction and peace of mind.

Other Conversations that Supervisors Have: Checking in with People

This conversation is perhaps the most important and most frequently used. If you have around ten people to supervise, you can do this every day with each worker. If you have more, you may do it every second or third day with each person. This is a brief conversation with each person, often done at the workstation or in the work area. It is designed to:

- Keep lines of communication open between you and the workers. Let them know that you are interested in them and what they think. Remember, you want to encourage them to take responsibility for their work and to think about how to do better.

- Keep you informed of the motivational status of each worker. Remember that motivation can change overnight for a person. For example: A person who was motivated to work hard in order to keep up the payments on his beloved red truck unfortunately wrecked that truck last night on his way home from work. As you can imagine, his motivation has stalled out considerably. Will this change his enthusiasm to work hard for you? It very well could.

- Keep you informed of any de-motivators that you could remove.

- Keep you informed of equipment, production, and process changes and problems that the workers might be noticing. This is your early warning system. If you can address these problems before they affect your production, you could avoid a downturn in team performance.

- Give you an opportunity to update them on changes for the day. A change might require each one of them to do something different. Speaking to them in a group is not always a good idea. The group dynamics may work against you, and people may not understand what individual directives apply to them. Speak to each one individually, you can emphasize what you want each one to do differently.

- Give you an opportunity to remind them of a goal, a change, or to retrain them on a mistake that they have made.

- Give you an opportunity for further motivation and direction with a few words of guidance or encouragement.

The Box of Kittens Theory

Have you ever had eight or so kittens and tried to keep them all in a box? As soon as you get one and put it in the box, two others escape. If you go after one escapee, the other gets further and further away. There's only one of you and eight of them. Sometimes supervision feels like dealing with that box of kittens. Any group of people working together has a lot of dynamics going on. Many changes can take place that you might not even be aware of. How are you going to know everything and keep it all in control? The wisdom behind the check-in conversation is that, if you know what is going on in your department—both in the processes and in everyone's mind—you have a chance to keep it all on track to get some work accomplished. In addition, you can carefully explain what you want to each, in their own way of learning, so you can hold each one accountable for staying in the box on their own.

Check-In Conversation Roleplay

What should this conversation be like? What do you say? Here are a couple of samples, but you will have to ad lib for yourself. Each situation and person is different. Note that in each of these roleplays, the supervisor has a small flip over the top notebook that fits into her pocket. This small notebook is one of the most valuable tools a supervisor has. It helps a supervisor organize the day's tasks and ensures that follow-up is done. It also signals to the workers that the supervisor is serious about what is being said. Watch and see how it can be used.

Supervisor: *Good morning Sally. How's it going today?*

Sally: *Okay. Well, I found a big mess from the first shift. Look at this. Who do they think I am, their mother?*

Supervisor: *Yeah, I can see that pile of scrap. I'll get the cleanup crew to help you, and I'll talk to Harry on first. Usually, they only leave a mess when they've had a lot go wrong all day. Anything else?*

Sally: *You know, I only get one more sick day this year. I'm thinking about taking it tomorrow. My mother's got pneumonia and she can't seem to shake it. I want to go with her to the doctor.*

Supervisor: *We can do that. Thanks for letting me know in advance so I can cover your job for you. If it's just a doctor's appointment, would you just need a half day? That way you'd still have some time left, and it would be easier for me to cover for you.*

Sally: *Sure, that'd be fine. I'll let you know for sure by lunch.*

Supervisor: *Okay, have a good day. I'll be back to check on you later*

The supervisor makes a note that Sally needs a half-day off tomorrow and to schedule someone to come in early to cover for her. The supervisor will want to ask Sally how her mother is doing when she gets back. If things don't go well, it will put Sally into a real bind with so little sick leave left this year. Another note reminds the supervisor to call over the cleanup crew and to talk to Harry on first shift, even though Sally is pretty sure that it won't do any good. Nevertheless, it would be good to find out what's going so wrong on first shift these days.

Second Role-Play:

Supervisor: *Morning, Gus. How'd you like the game last night?*

Gus: Didn't get a chance to see it. My sump pump went out and I had a flooded basement when I got home last night. Spent all evening cleaning it up. Luckily, I had bought a spare.

Supervisor: Tough break. Sure has been a lot of rain lately. Say, I want to give you a heads up on a new worker that's coming tomorrow. I want you to take him on as a trainee and show him all of the quality processes, from the press operations to the finishing. I know that you've never done that before, but I think that you would be good at it. What do you think?

Gus: Do you really think that I am good enough? I've only been here a year myself.

Supervisor: I've noticed that, when you learn something, you remember it pretty much perfectly. And you are good at talking to people. I think that you can teach the new worker. If you have any questions, I'll help.

Gus: Well, Okay. How do I start?

Supervisor: I'll introduce you. His name is Kurt. I'll tell him that you will work with him all day. I want you to show him the whole department and explain our process. Then take him step by step through each quality form. The way you train is to tell him once, show him once, and then have him do it. Correct him if he gets it wrong. Same thing that I did for you when you started here last year. Remember?

Gus: Yeah. I remember. It was easy.

Supervisor: Okay then. I'll check in on you before the day is over. I'll see how he is doing and set up a plan for the second day. I'm trying to cross train as many people as I can so we all know everything it takes to run the department. Remember, any problems, just ask.

The supervisor makes a note on his checklist for the next day to check in with Gus and Kurt before the end of the day.

Third Role-Play:

Supervisor: There you are, Alvin. I can see that you are late again. What's up?

Alvin: I know, I know. That's the third time in two weeks. Don't get mad at me. I was out late playing cards and didn't get any sleep.

Supervisor: Alvin, you know that I need you here on time and alert. If you are sleepy, you might get hurt or not get much work done. I'm seeing a trend here of your card playing taking more importance than your job. I'd like you to think about this for a while. After I get the morning duties done, I'll call you. We can sit down in my office and work this out. For now, get your workstation started and see if you can be safe and productive. Okay?

Alvin: *Okay. I guess I'm going to get written up, aren't I?*

Supervisor: *That's how it works. Can you give me a good reason to do otherwise?*

Alvin: *No, guess I have to do better.*

Supervisor: *Good thinking. I'll see you later.*

The supervisor makes a note of the time Alvin arrived and added a disciplinary conference to his checklist for the day. Notice how calmly this was done. Good job.

Fourth Role-Play:

Supervisor: *Erin, come over here for a minute. I know that yesterday I told you to work on number three today, but that line's down for a couple of hours. I'd like you to work with David on two. If the two of you work together, we might be able to speed it up and make up for three being down.*

Erin: *David? You've got to be kidding. He's an idiot. He couldn't find his way out of a wet paper bag. I could do better all by myself.*

Supervisor: *Actually, he's been doing much better since Tom has been helping him. I think he just needs some time to learn. Seems to me that you made quite a few mistakes when you first started on line three. We gave you some help and you got a lot better. Maybe you've forgotten?*

Erin: *Well, I was never that dumb. Did you hear what he did yesterday? It's all over the bathroom wall. I wouldn't be caught dead working with him.*

Supervisor: *I didn't give up on you, and I'm not going to give up on him just yet. I need you to help him, so clean up you attitude and get with it. I'll go over, get him started, and then call you. Around here everybody succeeds or nobody does. That's how I operate. Are you with me on this?*

Erin: *Hey, I didn't say I wouldn't. This is a good job.*

Supervisor: *Now, I mean really help him. Don't set him up for failure or I'll know it was you. Do you understand?*

Erin: *Yeah, yeah.*

The supervisor makes a note to ask the manager to get the bathroom walls scrubbed.

Fifth Roleplay:

Aren't these roleplays interesting? Can you see how much direction, correction, and motivation is accomplished in these brief and focused conversations? This roleplay is for a satellite TV installer crew supervisor.

Supervisor: *Good morning, Peggy. Here's your installation list for today. Please note that two are left over from yesterday that you didn't get done. Did you have some problems when you are out on the road?*

Peggy: *Just because I have an off day, you jump on me and say I'm having problems?*

Supervisor: *Hold on. You know me. I'm here to help. What's got you so wound up?*

Peggy: *I don't know what to do. I am so scared.*

Supervisor: *I can see that you are upset. Maybe I can help. Tell me what's the trouble.*

Peggy: *Promise me that you won't fire me?*

Supervisor: *I doubt that you did anything that bad. Let's just talk it over and see what we can do.*

Peggy: *Well, I went to this one customer location and got all set up with the ladder and all. The customer came out and yelled at me that I was scratching his siding. He just went ballistic. I looked and, sure enough, there was a big scratch. But he just kept yelling. I lost it and just packed up and left. He said that he was going to call the company and get me fired. I was so nervous the rest of the day.*

Supervisor: *You should have reported this to me immediately. The fact that you didn't is a serious infraction of the rules and shows a lack of trust in me. Since you are new, we'll take our time and work this out. Okay, let's analyze what happened. Did you set up the ladder properly?*

Peggy: *Yes I did.*

Supervisor: *Let's check your truck. Let me see the ladder. Wow, this is a wreck. The scratch guards are gone and the edges are all beat up. How did this happen?*

Peggy: *I don't know. This isn't my usual truck. Daniel used this truck last.*

Supervisor: *Well, I'll have to check into this, but you are not fired. Use this other ladder for the day, and I'll get Daniel's ladder repaired and talk to him. Is there anything else wrong with this truck's equipment?*

Peggy: *Yeah. The meter doesn't work right. I can't tell if the signal is getting through.*

Supervisor: *Let me check it. Oh, I can see what's wrong. This battery is dead. Here's a new battery. See, this is how you replace it. Just ask me for a new one when you need it. Anything else?*

Peggy: *No, I guess not. But I don't want to go out today. Can't I work in the shop today?*

Supervisor: *Sorry, not today. We're way behind as it is. I'll call your angry customer and go out to see him. I may have to write up a claim. You were correct in not arguing with the customer, but you were wrong in not reporting the incident immediately and leaving the work site. In addition, you should not have left the shop with a bad ladder. Always check your equipment. You can see how it would have saved you a bad experience and an insurance claim as well, can't you?*

Peggy: *Yeah, but it wasn't my fault. It's Daniel's.*

Supervisor: *Let me be clear. Each employee is responsible for their equipment once they leave the shop. Daniel is responsible for his and you are responsible for yours. I talk to everyone before they leave for that reason. Any problem you have that could keep you from doing a good job and having a good day should be discussed with me before you leave. Is that clear?*

Peggy: *Yeah.*

Supervisor: *Okay. Now, is there anything else that you need?*

Peggy: *Where's my list?*

Supervisor: *Here. Peggy, just relax and get focused on doing a good job at each customer location you have today. I have confidence that you can do this job. I'll let you know how the claim turns out. Every installer we've ever had has had at least one claim in their first year. I'll talk to you later about leaving the work site. You've had your learner mistake, so put it behind you, and try to do a good job every day, with every customer. Can you do that?*

Peggy: *Yeah, thanks.*

The supervisor makes a note to talk to Daniel, have a write-up conference later with Peggy about leaving the work site, and to visit the angry customer. The supervisor is thinking that Peggy can get beyond this incident and be a good installer. If she can't, that problem will need to be addressed. Notice that he was trying to solve the problems that got Peggy into trouble, encourage her to improve, and get his work list completed for the day. If he had more than ten installers, he would have quite a list of things to follow up on in his pocket notebook, but all of them would be the exact things that would help him achieve his goals.

Check in Conversation Assignment

Now that you've heard other experienced supervisors have check-in conversations, it's time for you to try one on your own. Write down the name of one worker that you have and ask the opening question. Then, write what you think that that worker might say and how the conversation might proceed. See if you can get the conversation to uncover some motivators and de-motivators.

Supervisor:

Worker:

Supervisor:

Worker:

Supervisor:

Worker:

Suggestions for Check-In Conversations

Some of you might be thinking that you do not have time to talk to each of your workers each day. You may be right. And there may not be a need to do so each day. But hopefully, you are beginning to understand that the performance of each worker can be influenced by these conversations before the day gets away from you. If you have too many workers to speak to each day, set up an informal rotation schedule so you can get to them often. Some may need it more often than others may, but don't leave anyone out. Just as soon as you think that someone doesn't need to talk to you, that person's performance, motivation, and direction might start to suffer. As soon as you do not talk to a person, they begin to wonder if you care or even notice deficiencies and problems. Things start to go astray. When enough workers feel like this, the box of kittens starts to go wild. And guess who might have taken a step back to the Rookie supervisor level trying to cover a lot of mistakes.

Spending time talking to each worker takes a lot less time than trying to answer for all of the mistakes, find the causes, and come up with the remedies. Keeping on top of things that are going on each day is clearly the better way to use your time.

Also, please notice that each conversation was **calm**, **reasonable**, and **professional**. Two of them involved disciplinary situations that were handled in a calm but serious manner. Both got the worker back to work thinking about what they did wrong, but still motivated to hear what the supervisor had to say about improving.

The calm, reasonable, and professional supervisor knows that he or she has been fair and clear and has not done unnecessary harm to the employee's willingness to listen. If the employee wishes to ignore the message and head down the road to losing a good job, then the supervisor can rest assured that it was not due to his or her doing a poor job of communicating.

Summary of the Benefits of Check-In Conversations:

- Assess motivation daily
- Discover problems that can be solved
- Set daily performance goals
- Train and give corrections
- Get valuable information and suggestions
- Build trust, communication, motivation, and loyalty
- Collect information and tasks to organize your day

Next Personality Range

We have studied some of the kinds of conversations that supervisors have with their employees. Keep in mind that each supervisor reacts in a different manner, as does each employee, depending on their personality type. At this point, we have studied two of the ranges—Introvert-Extrovert and Sensor-Intuitive. A Sensor can be either an Introvert or Extrovert and an Intuitive can be either an Introvert or Extrovert. You may want to turn back to those pages and review what you have learned about people so far. In fact, if you turn to the back of the book, you will find copies of these pages. You may copy and use these handouts for your personal and professional needs. You can lay the range pages side by side and see how the traits intermingle. Please take a minute and do just that. What have you noticed about yourself already? What do you notice about the people that you work with every day? There is much more to be learned. The next range to be studied is the Thinker–Feeler range.

Thinker	**Feeler**

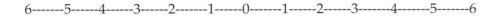

6-------5------4------3------2-------1------0-------1------2------3-------4-------5-------6

Thinker	Feeler
Uses logic to make decisions	Uses relationship issues to decide
Avoids emotional issues	Likes emotional issues
Likes conflict, it generates performance	Avoids conflict, wants harmony
Competitive, wants to win	Values relationships over winning
Sacrifices feelings to get performance	Builds loyalty through feelings
Goal directed	Relationship directed
Wants to excel	Wants to serve
Seeks to control	Seeks to cooperate
Sets standards and gives discipline	Is flexible and accommodating
Reacts objectively	Reacts subjectively
Very persistent, never gives up	Can be a crusader for causes
Highly organized and uses charts	Influences people through relationships
Hash-marks everybody	Green stamps everybody
Respects strength	Understands feelings, has compassion
Performance oriented	People oriented
Driver, sees no need to persuade	Uncritical, very accepting
High tolerance for stress	Suffers from stress, pleasing everybody
Critical thinker	Takes criticism personally

Best Case

Thinker	Feeler
Good manager, gets performance	Good team builder, gets loyalty
Sets goals and achieves them	Good friend, sensitive and giving
Good controller, rule enforcer	Good at customer service, helps people

Worst Case

Thinker	Feeler
Cold, insensitive, negative bully	Weak, easily manipulated, cries
Highly critical, discourages people	Holds grudges, cultivates cliques

Weaknesses

Thinker	Feeler
Can destroy teamwork with over-control	Fails to discipline and loses authority
Too critical, gives no positive feedback	Too subjective and performance falls
Builds resistance and people rebel	Suffers from too much stress
Overlooks people issues and fails control	Keeps everybody happy, but loses

As far as the terms Thinker and Feeler go, don't think for a second that the Thinker doesn't feel and that the Feeler doesn't think. These terms describe the dominant mode of relating to the world. The Thinker thinks first and feels later. The Feeler feels first and thinks later. The dominant mode is the one you first encounter with a person and the mode that is most comfortable and successful for them.

I will carefully explain this range. It can be the source of many misunderstanding and communication breakdowns in the workplace. Because the supervisory style of each is different, if you are a Thinker supervisor, you will not supervise like the Feeler, and vice versa. Finally, this range seems to influence how successful each is with disciplinary problems. So here goes. Pay close attention, thinking of yourself, coworkers, and those you supervise.

Description of the Thinker Type

The Thinker is a goal-directed person. These goals are usually external and therefore objective. These people are always objective and logical. They think about a goal—such as achieving a performance goal at work, winning a game, or getting somewhere in life—and then they think of the logical steps to get there. They love to analyze, organize, and plan in this logical manner. They are sure that if the logic is followed the goal will be achieved. They get a lot of personal satisfaction in winning and achieving goals, but their trust is firmly placed in the power of logic to get them there. This personal satisfaction is so strong that they love to win and hate to lose. They can get angry if things aren't proceeding toward a win. In fact, if they do not believe that the effort is likely to result in victory they do not want to participate at all. However, if they believe that they can win, they will exert all effort necessary to pull it off successfully. Does this sound like you?

In the pursuit of winning, it often becomes necessary to get into conflict. This does not deter Thinkers at all. In fact, they like conflict. This could be a disagreement, an argument, or a confrontation designed to pressure someone else into doing what they see will be necessary to succeed. Here we are getting close to the issue of discipline. In order for a team to be able to achieve a goal, everyone must be disciplined to follow the rules and the plan. Everyone has to endure the hardships of work and effort. Thinkers like all of these requirements and are happy to discipline others to do the same. They admire strength and hate weakness. They might view a good argument as a way to test someone's strength and commitment to the goal. This is what I call *hash marking*. If you are not willing or able to engage in conflict, you might be suspected of being too weak to be of use to them in achieving a goal.

These are tough people. They are relatively insensitive to their own feelings and to those of others. This allows them to endure hardship and to stay focused on the goal. Of course, they expect others to be able to do the same. They are often blunt and insensitive in talking with people. They really don't care if someone's feelings get hurt, or if they are tired, hungry, or cold. They really want people to just keep working towards the goal—just as they do. Remember that I am describing the extremes for the sake of learning the differences. I am also using some humor so you can see your traits in an objective, helpful light. A person might not have all of these traits (or have them in a weaker form) and still be a Thinker.

The best example of a group with Thinker traits that I've ever seen is in the game of football. It has all of the components of Thinker traits. There are clearly defined goals at each end of the field and a big, lighted scoreboard up high so everyone can see who is winning. Remembering how important goals are to Thinkers, you can see why strict rules and referees are desirable to enforce the discipline of the game. Discipline also helps to control conflict. The sport of football gives players an opposing team, permission to tackle each other and come to blows. There is lots of logical strategy and opportunities for demonstrating personal commitment and skill in executing the plays. It is a objective activity. Either you lose or you win. The only emotion is that of *the thrill of victory or the agony of defeat*. Former players are paid large sums of money to provide analytical commentary and conduct interviews, where the players analyze their performance so as to tune themselves up for winning the next game. All of this is great fun for Thinkers.

Whether or not football is your favorite game, you can see how this personality type will perform in the workplace. You should be happy to have some Thinkers working for you—or to be one yourself. They are high achievers. Their motivation is almost entirely tied to achieving goals. If you want to motivate them, just give them a goal and be sure that it is achievable. You could discuss the strategy and analyze the progress through charts and graphs just like the scoreboard on the field. Thinkers are willing to work hard if they think that they can win. And they will even argue with and discipline others to assure success. How wonderful is that! Wouldn't every supervisor want people like this?

I assure you that the military is full of Thinkers. In the military, there's lots of discipline, clear objectives, and a defined enemy to combat. They even give you guns and artillery to use to assure victory. No one wants war, but if we have to go to war, we will want our best Thinkers to be our leaders. In addition, every business needs to have a good supply of them to push the team to success and to keep everything under control.

The Weaknesses of the Thinker Type

All of these traits, properly managed, are wonderful. They are to be admired. But in actual practice, there are some downsides to these traits. The ability to engage in conflict can be exhibited as being argumentative. Some Thinkers relish a good argument and disagree with just about everything. Often there can be head butting between two Thinkers who are sure that they are right and the other is wrong. They see no reason to give in. Giving in would be a sign of weakness, and they would never want that. These arguments can stall out any forward effort. People often get so tired of it that they avoid the argumentative Thinkers at all costs, preferring to work around them. If you have enough of that going on in an organization, no one will work with each other and nothing gets done. Also, the argumentative approach can intimidate some people to the point that they feel pushed around and abused. Remember that Thinkers are not sensitive to feelings. They would have little empathy for someone having their feelings hurt. Left unchecked, you can see how this trait could be pretty pushy and insensitive.

Thinkers are also critical. They can always analyze a situation and find something that is wrong that could jeopardize success. They clearly see what is missing and are not content until full success is achieved. They do not mean any harm and, in fact, are trying to help the effort, but they sure can come across as negative and critical. Have you ever seen this occur? It can be painful to have someone tell you that you are negative and critical. But remember that the positive trait of goal directedness can become a weakness if no positives are ever given and people are over-analyzed and bullied. It is a matter of degree and manner.

While we are at it, let's address the issue of the emotions that the Thinker does exhibit. You can imagine what Thinkers experience when their drive for achievement is being frustrated? Yes, you are correct—anger. That anger can be sudden and intense and show itself as temper. And because Thinkers have no reluctance to conflict, their anger is confrontational to people who aren't performing. Do I hear stories of yelling, bad language, and hard hats being thrown on the ground? Yes, that and more. Do I think that these incidents are signs of being out of control? Yes and no. I know that the Thinker is only trying to ensure good performance. But this type of behavior can easily go past appropriate bounds. These outbursts can get a Thinker into a lot of trouble And they can quickly destroy a lot of communication and motivation that took a long time to develop. These outbursts can get some desirable results in the short term—people are afraid. In the long term, they also tend to reduce a supervisor's authority and ability to communicate. I have seen Thinker supervisors who have so much conflict, temper, and de-motivation, that they lose their jobs or are transferred to jobs that do not require interaction with people. This is a big disappointment and a career setback to be sure.

How can the dedicated Thinker deal with this issue? If you are a Thinker and you encounter frustration, stop and think about it before it gets to the temper stage. One of your strengths is strategy. If you will take a break and walk around a bit to relax and think, you might be able to think of a way to get performance back on track without losing your temper. Your temptation is to drive for the goal like a hammer on a nail. People won't work with you if they feel like that nail. But if they feel like a winning team player being coached by a skilled and committed coach, they are willing to exert greater effort to win. Here we come again to the role of the supervisor as that of the helpful coach. Think of the great sport coaches, leaving out the ones fired for striking players and throwing chairs at referees, and select one as your inspiration. Notice that the coach only succeeds if the players succeed. The coach never goes out on the playing field. He has to use training, motivation, and leadership to achieve success. That is exactly what the Thinker supervisor has to do.

Discussion of the Feeler Traits

What traits do we find at the other end of the range? The Feeler personality is more relationship oriented than goal oriented. In fact, relationships are everything to Feelers. They are deeply invested in their family, friendships, teammates, and organizations. They like to have harmonious and happy relationships and try to please people, including their supervisor. They are accommodating and flexible people. They understand their own feelings and those of others, so they tend to acknowledge feelings and deal with them easily. They would like to avoid conflict because they fear that the relationship could dissolve. Also, they are sensitive and can only tolerate so much stress, but at their best, they try to make the teamwork successful.

They are good at team building because they attend easily to all of the niceties of getting to know people. These are the people who ask about your family and friends to see how they are doing. They know what to say at funerals and at birthday parties. They think to buy an appropriate card on any occasion and genuinely care about their circle of family and friends. At work, they put a lot of energy into building and preserving team relationships.

I like to think of Feeler activities as being much like a spider weaving a web. They talk to each person kindly and build cooperative agreements whereby they can rely on each team member's cooperation. These cooperative agreements are what I call *green stamping*. Those of us who are old enough can remember getting green stamps when we purchased things and trading them in for a toaster or blender. If a Feeler does something for you, she is expecting that she could later trade in that favor for some cooperation from you. After a time, all of these agreements with many people interweave into a strong web of teamwork, loyalty, and mutual caring.

As you might have guessed, these supervisors are naturals for team building and would never think of getting angry or arguing, as that might destroy the trust and collaboration that they have built. This would cut the strands of the spider web. To a Thinker, this all seems invisible and insignificant, but to a good Feeler supervisor this is the only way to gain cooperation and build a team.

The Weaknesses of the Feeler Traits

There is a significant downside to Feeler traits. A Feeler caught in his or her weaknesses tends to focus so much on the relationships that the goal becomes secondary. Less effort is given to driving for the goal. In the interest of avoiding conflict, the Feeler can fail to discipline people enough to get good performance on a consistent basis. Rather than confront someone, the Feeler will put up with poor performance or, worse yet, will try to do it all herself. This demotes the Feeler back down to the Rookie supervisor level. I'd hope to never catch one of you saying, *that's okay; it doesn't matter*, when it does matter and it is not okay. The danger though goes even deeper than that. When Feelers get into a relationship, they can lose their objectivity and make subjective decisions in favor of the people with whom they are closest. This is the possible source of what is commonly known as favoritism.

The last danger is that Feelers have a high level of empathy and compassion for everybody. If Feelers are told a really believable and sad story, they feel that person's pain. Their caring might cause them to act in a way contrary to company policy. Does this mean that a Feeler is not good at discipline? No, but it is quite a challenge for Feelers to remain objective and engage in appropriate conflict with people with whom they have worked so hard to build relationships. The person that a Feeler might have to discipline could be the person who helped them fix their car last weekend. It might be the person who serves with them on a church committee. They might fear that the whole relationship will be lost. Here's where the calm, reasonable, and professional approach comes in. If you can treat people well even when you have to discipline them, you have a chance to salvage the relationship and still keep discipline strong.

Where thinkers are tough people dedicated to an objective goal, Feelers have subjective goals. They suffer from the stress of conflict and failure. They take successes and failures into themselves and carry that stress in their bodies. They can even become ill or depressed.

On the other hand, they experience great joy and excitement at seeing their team succeed. In fact, their self esteem is greatly dependent on whether their thoughts are positive or negative. If they doubt themselves or their relationships, their self confidence can drop like a rock. This is why they do not respond well to criticism. They think to themselves that they are not doing well, they are letting people down, and people are unhappy with them. This all adds up to being down on themselves.

Since they don't have the drive that Thinkers have, they can lose their way easily. This tendency to be positive and excited one day and down with no confidence the next day is often called moodiness. It can be confusing to the Feeler. And it can be difficult for others because they are never sure if the Feeler will be up or down tomorrow. Feelers need to remember the good that will be done when their employee improves a skill or keeps their job—far more valuable than a few niceties. They can get so involved in making people happy that the performance goals are compromised. On the flip side, their loyalty to their people can be high. In fact, they might err by protecting and defending them beyond reason.

Feelers can react strongly to community feeling issues, such as raising money for a sick child, volunteering at church, or adopting causes. Yes, these can be the tree huggers and homeless pet rescuers. While Feelers are prone to such activity, don't leave the Thinkers out of these efforts. I know a tough, blunt Thinker who spends his evenings developing an animal shelter organization in his community. It's not so much that he likes animals. He has none himself. But he knew that it was the right thing to do, and he enjoyed the planning, strategy, and goal achievement of something that would help the community.

How do Thinkers and Feelers Interact Together in a Relationship?

As in the other ranges, opposites do attract. And you may see Thinker-Feeler relationships in friendships, marriages, or between a parent and their child.

In these relationships, Feelers would be the ones sensitive to their own needs and the personal needs of other people involved. Feelers like to take care of people and their personal needs.

The Thinker would be more focused on an external goal, such as making money, achieving success, owning a house, or earning a good living with benefits for the family. This type of relationship could result in wonderful teamwork. All of the family needs could be addressed effectively by the party most suited to its achievement. But on the other hand, it might result in the Thinker being insensitive and the Feeler being too sensitive, with a possible meltdown as a result. Success could be achieved by the Thinker being a little more sensitive and the Feeler being a little less sensitive—and both of them respecting the contribution that the other gives. Most of all, neither party should be working on trying to change the other into their likeness. Not only is this completely impossible, but it would destroy the strength of the teamwork that could result from two people with completely different skills working together cooperatively.

Some of you might be assuming that women are Feelers and that men are Thinkers. Actually, research shows that there are just as many Feeler men as Thinker men and just as many Feeler women as Thinker women. What does a Thinker woman look like? She may enjoy sports and be competitive. She may be committed to her job, taking extra training to qualify for higher positions. She may be strict with her children and create structure for activities and resources at home as well as at work. If she thinks that you are wrong, she will bluntly tell you—and may enjoy a good argument. It is really a delight to see a small and pretty woman with these traits surprise everyone with her honesty, determination, and drive.

On the other hand, what does a Feeler man look like? This man might be a good natured, friendly person who spends time with his family, church, or volunteer activities. He may be too nice to complain vehemently about much, but don't threaten to harm his family or friends. He will defend them to the extreme. He will go off to work every day, thinking of his family and looking forward to spending time with them. If there is a conflict or upset, he is the first to try to make up. If things go wrong, he might get into thinking negatively about himself. People might call this moodiness, but as soon as somebody shows appreciation, the sun comes out again. This is altogether a wonderful type of man who runs Boy Scout troops, coaches little league teams, and collects food for the hungry. The Feelers hold our society together by taking care of everything and everybody.

If these traits are at odds in a relationship, the relationship can deteriorate quickly. It could go something like this: Thinkers objectively points out something that is not right or is illogical. Feelers can get their feelings hurt easily by these comments and possibly draw disastrous conclusions, such as, *you don't care about me*, or *you are insensitive*. Then an argument ensues. Since Thinkers are expert arguers, they usually win the argument, further alienating the Feelers. Having won the argument, Thinkers are at risk of losing their relationships, completely mystified as to how or why this happened. So many relationship issues are tied to these traits that, after studying them for a while, you could write a script just based on these traits. Sadly, much pain and disruption occurs from Thinkers just being Thinkers and Feelers just being Feelers.

All of this could be avoided with just a little effort. The Thinker could be more diplomatic, and the Feeler could be less sensitive. When this is achieved, then, an honest and productive discussion could ensue that would further cement the relationship.

How do these traits show up in a parent-child relationship? If the parent is a Thinker, there may be good discipline and a structured environment. But the weakness may be in a lack of sharing of positive feelings and regard for the child, even though there is much love to be given. There may be high standards set for the child and criticism to be had if the standards are not achieved. If the child is a Thinker, the child will learn not to settle for less than winning and might be just as self critical. If the child is a Feeler, the child may become discouraged and feel that it is impossible to please the parent. If the parent is a Feeler, there will be a lot of attention given to the child, but the child may get away with bad behavior and develop a bad attitude—even taking advantage of the parent. Again, these are extreme definitions. Even modest effort by the Thinker parent to give some positive feedback and encouragement can avoid their child feeling alienated. Even modest effort by a Feeler parent to discipline the child will create a loving, but respectful, family atmosphere.

How to Make Opposite Relationships Work

Those of you who scored in the middle of this or any of the ranges can attest that there is a need to see the point of view of those at both ends of the ranges. It's important not to draw uncomplimentary conclusions as to why people do what they do. This is the logic of the range. After you realize that your traits only represent half of the possible range of human function, you can no longer view the other end of the range as wrong or worthless. After all, people at the opposite end have all of the traits that you do not possess with much strength. Given some thought, this logic elicits a desire to develop all of the traits within oneself. You could set out on the difficult road to develop all of the opposite traits through hard work, discipline, and practice. People who achieve this are usually highly functional and achieve much in their careers. They are also quite rare. It is much easier to form teamwork with another who is at the other end of the range. This can be accomplished through mutual understanding, patience, cooperation, and collaboration. But do not expect your opposite to be like you. Let them be who they are.

For the sake of verifying that this is true, find someone opposite of you who is willing to work toward achieving the goal of teamwork. Then open up some communication, and ask for cooperation in performing the parts of the work that are most appropriate to your opposite's skills. Do not discount the contribution, sabotage the efforts, interrupt, make fun of, give up on the effort, withhold your effort, or overly criticize. It won't take very long to begin to see the benefits. After some time, you will vow that this is the only way to get work accomplished.

True Story of Two People Who Created a Successful Team of Opposites

Eric and Jimmy worked in a high-production environment that generated daily stress. Eric is the department supervisor and a Thinker, and Jimmy is the shift supervisor and a Feeler. Although Eric is younger than Jimmy, he came to his position through hard work and intelligence. He was known for driving his people hard, being a strict but fair disciplinarian, and occasionally showing temper.

Jimmy is an experienced and respected supervisor whom Eric failed to appreciate at first. He tried to step in, offering direction and criticism to Jimmy's people. This made Jimmy quite angry. He had spent years building the confidence and training of his people, and he recognized that Eric was unknowingly on a path to dismantle a good part of it through his insensitive criticism. He sat down and had a talk with Eric. Jimmy explained that he could do anything needed in that department—if Eric would just stay out of his way. They met daily and reviewed the production numbers. Eric had to admit that the department was working smoothly and was steadily improving. As he looked closer, he noticed the high level of loyalty that Jimmy enjoyed from his people. They would do anything that he asked as well as they could. Eric wondered how he did it. As far as he could see, Jimmy just talked to people quietly and briefly. There were never any arguments, and there were few disciplinary situations.

In time, Eric developed a deep appreciation and respect for Jimmy's way of supervising. He even began to copy some of his skills. Eric became less critical and, as his temper declined, people opened up to him and cooperated better with him. They liked his strong approach. As Eric's strong discipline improved performance, their incentives increased as well. The whole department recognized that if Eric set the goals and standards and critiqued performance and Jimmy trained and motivated each of the workers in a way that each could understand and accept, their performance improved and their stress declined. Eric learned not to interfere with Jimmy's style of supervising. Jimmy learned to accept Eric's direction and discipline no matter how unpopular it was. In fact, disciplinary situations became rare because Jimmy anticipated employees' problems and motivated people to work together.

Eric realized that he had a good team working for him. He hoped that it would continue as long as possible—the department was outperforming all others. Jimmy was also satisfied because it made his job easier to have strong leadership and support. And his workers were happy with their high incentives.

Discussion

I hope that each of you reading this book has had an experience of such effective teamwork. Once you have experienced it, you will always hunger for it again. Just keep in mind that such opportunities are all around you in the people who are most different from you. You only have to find a few of them who are willing to try to build understanding.

Story of a Successful Friendship of Opposites

Martha, a Feeler, and Lorraine, a mild Thinker, had met when they were in college. Martha liked Lorraine because of her objective insights, honesty, and high standards. They became best of friends and talked on the phone just about every day.

Martha worked in a series of jobs that she hated because of harsh environments of poor management and neglect of employee concerns. After she was promoted to supervisor, she wanted to make a difference, but felt powerless to change the harsh management style. So she learned to endure these environments, all of the time really caring about the poor treatment of her coworkers—something that seemed to be standard operating procedure. Through all of these experiences, Lorraine gave her helpful suggestions, honest feedback, and provided an example of a disciplined and organized work environment in her own job. Martha learned to tolerate stress and to be organized.

Finally, Martha found a good position in a well-managed company. She saw an opportunity to manage the way that she thought was appropriate. By now, she was a Feeler who had acquired some Thinker traits from years of working in Thinker environments and listening to Lorraine.

She evaluated the people who reported to her and found that most had a good work ethic and were good people who would do anything that she asked. Even though they might have some eccentric traits, she looked at their motivation and set about teaching them to challenge themselves, build their confidence, and to learn new skills. She was known, most certainly, for having high standards for herself, as well as for her people. She was also known for being territorial and for some occasional temper that she always regretted. When something would go wrong, she would carry some heavy feelings of defeat or anger home at night. But a call to Lorraine would help her objectively evaluate the situation and make corrections.

After years of running her plant successfully, Martha had an opportunity for promotion. In preparation, Martha and Lorraine took stock of what kind of a manager she wanted to be and what aspects she wanted to avoid. Through this intense self examination, she blended the traits of the Thinker and the Feeler and emerged as a desirable manufacturing manager candidate. This process of learning to acquire Thinker traits while not giving up the benefits of being a Feeler was not easy. But the results were so successful that Martha enjoyed a six figure income and the pride of a well organized and motivated organization.

Discussion

People who manage to overcome their weaknesses and team up with those who have strengths in the areas of their weakness do very well in life. They are generally successful in their careers as well as in their relationships. Why? Because they are not repeating the same mistake over and over again. They have access to all of the abilities that challenging situations require. They are promotable and easy to work with in a variety of situations. This is your opportunity to learn this simple but complex truth. Are you willing to make the effort? Keep in mind that we are not talking about walking a mile. It may only take a few inches of effort in the right direction to make this possible.

Congratulations, you have completed Class Five. Take a week or so to try to incorporate what you have learned in this important class into your own, real-life situations before you go on to the next Class. So much can be forgotten or not applied if you overload yourself with too much, too fast. I'll see you in Class Six in a week.

Second *Walkaround* with Mary

My second visit with Mary started with a review of her meeting with Rhonda about the attendance problem. Rhonda was indeed unaware of the number of days that she had missed and was concerned that she not jeopardize her job. She offered to work a half day without pay. That decision suited Mary fine, as she had a mountain of paperwork that could be done on Saturday morning that nobody else wanted to do. There were no tears and Rhonda actually thanked her. Mary was happy with the outcome and feeling much more confident of her supervisory skills.

Her next problem that she wanted to work on was with Gertrude, who was within one year of retiring. Gertrude had been a good bookkeeper for the department. But, in the last few months, she was taking long lunches, and it was rumored that she was taking naps in her cubicle. She avoided meetings and often asked people to repeat what they said. Mary wanted to do her homework this time. She and Gertrude had a *peel the layers of the onion* conversation. She had learned that Gertrude's health had been declining since she was diagnosed with diabetes six months ago. She had trouble sleeping at night, which made her sleepy at work. To make matters worse, Gertrude's hearing had diminished. No matter how hard she tried, Gertrude could not seem to overcome the problem. At this point Mary was at a loss. What could she do? I asked about the company policy regarding retirement and disability. Mary said that she didn't know much about it and would have to talk with human resources. The HR manager, Dick, was an irritable, overworked man whom people recommended avoiding. Mary set a goal of finding the best way for Gertrude to either get help or to retire early, whichever she chose. Since there was really no other way to solve the problem other than talking to Dick, we strategized how to get the best response from him.

Mary suggested emailing him first. Maybe he would send her a copy of the policies she needed. I agreed, but knew that we would inevitably have to talk with him personally.

Within a half an hour, we had a return email outlining the policies on retirement and disability. It looked like early retirement was allowed for a good reason, and the company provided six months of disability insurance for those with long-term medical problems. We wanted to offer Gertrude some good options, so we outlined what we thought might work: She could (1) take a disability for six months and then retire, (2) use insurance to seek help with the problem before retirement, and (3) retire early. With these three options, we would need prior approval before offering them to Gertrude, so we would have to talk to Dick.

Our strategy was to make an appointment when he would not be rushed, send an email in advance outlining our thinking, and then be well prepared so the meeting would not run very long. I suggested to Mary that she clearly state the problem and the goal and then ask Dick for approval of a plan for Gertrude. I asked Mary if she wanted to roleplay the meeting. She said that if I did a roleplay like the last one, she wouldn't be able to keep a straight face. I smiled and told her that I would check in with her on my next visit.

> *"Not everything that is faced can be changed, but nothing can be changed until it is faced."*
>
> *James Baldwin*

Class Six

By now, I'm confident that you are beginning to see how you, as a supervisor and partner in relationships, can make a huge difference in your work and personal life by changing how you evaluate others—and by making small adjustments in your own behavior. If you become proficient in using this knowledge to adjust how you interact with others, you will fast become a much more effective supervisor.

Up to this point, we have discussed communication, motivation, and three of the four personality type ranges. This is a start, but your journey has only begun. In this chapter, we will be talking about setting goals, measuring performance, and organizing for performance improvement. Don't think for a moment that your prior lessons on communication and motivation are not central to your goal achievement. No amount of goal setting or organizing will have any effect if you do not have motivated and attentive workers. I have presented the topics of motivation early in this course because they are most often overlooked and underrated in supervisory training. In this chapter, I will attempt to demonstrate how these soft skills of talking to people, properly combined with goal setting and organization, translate into higher performance.

I know that those of you who are Thinkers are glad to finally be studying about goals and performance improvement. In fact, you probably need little help with this. This is an area where you are proficient. For the rest of the participants—and to recognize your contribution to the highly competitive American economy—we will dedicate this chapter to you, our thinking-type leaders.

Why Goals Are Important

The moment that a person or a team sets a goal is an exciting occasion. At that moment, a group organizes to work together to achieve a goal outside of themselves as individuals. In order for the whole team to be motivated to achieve a goal, they must fully understand the goal and its benefits. They must have some stake in its fulfillment, and they must believe that it is attainable, without their own demise.

Returning to the example of a football game, a group of individual players, each with a different skill and level of expertise, get together, put aside their own individual activities, and focus on winning a game. If it is just a neighborhood game, the only compensation may be the fun of playing and winning. But in professional football, players are compensated in proportion to their ability to win the game. The goalposts are big and easy to see. The scoreboard is visible and well lighted. There are lines on the field to show progress toward the goal. There are rules, ratings, commentators, opponents, and referees to settle disputes.

Comparison of Football to Work:

Football	Work
Game	Business or service
Goalposts	Mission or vision
Scoreboard	Reports, charts, graphs, P&L
Coach	Managers and supervisors
Rules	Company policies
Referee	Supervisor's discipline
Opponent	Competitors
Players	Workers
Training Camp	Job Training
Plays	Supervisors planning the work
Winning	Getting paid by happy customers
Rewards	Pay, benefits, security, teamwork

All of these elements of football are essential to team play at work. And you can use them to supervise your team to achieve the goal. In business, goals consist of a desire to address a particular need in the marketplace in order to create a profit. In the service sector, the goal is to provide a service in a beneficial and economical manner in order to improve our society and to make a profit. Our goals must come from the greater good and then descend throughout the organization into sub-goals, standards, and rules. Your departmental goals should directly support the mission of the whole organization.

Those of us who live our professional lives lower in the organization sometimes lose sight of how we contribute to the organization's success. If we, the supervisors, lose sight of the larger goals of the organization, guess what the people who work for us must be thinking. Our subordinates depend on us to describe for them just why this difficult work needs to be done. If we lose sight, they come to work merely for a paycheck, go home and think of how to spend the money they make. The next day they come back looking forward to the next paycheck. If you want a motivated team that is committed to doing whatever it takes to achieve organizational goals, it is essential that they know that they are contributing to a higher good. There are some workers who do not care and never will. But there are many who look for more reasons than a paycheck to roll out of bed in the morning. It is to these individuals that you must speak about goals.

To be effective, a goal must be well defined and clear, usually in numbers, just like the goalposts on that football field. Your production goals might be in the number of parts, processes, customer orders, or services completed per hour or day. Keep clearly in mind that good performance comes from motivated workers—so you can't just throw numbers to any group of people and get good performance. On the other hand, if you have motivated people and don't give them numerical goals, you won't get good performance either. You absolutely need to be investing energy into both motivation and goal setting. How well you develop both of these greatly determines the team's performance—and your own in the eyes of your superiors.

Now, let's say that you have motivated your team and told them how many parts, services, or deliveries they are to make. But just giving them numbers does not explain to them what good these parts, processes, or customer orders or services are doing. For instance, if these parts, products, and services are making a profit, then they are also providing workers with jobs and benefits for themselves and their families. If there is no profit, there are no jobs. If a customer is lost to a competitor, then jobs are lost. If they don't perform a service well, then the service will go lacking, customers will leave, and they won't have a job.

Let's say that when having these conversations with your team, you emphasize the daily production goals. The team reaches that goal, but the company still didn't make a profit. Suppose we did achieve our goal to produce parts worth $3,000 per hour, but the competition produced parts worth $3,500 per hour, and they sell them a bit cheaper than we do. We then find ourselves losing orders and may not be able to stay in business with the higher costs—even if we lower our sale price. In this situation, we could run out of motivational fuel for our team because we didn't get commitment to the larger benefit of the goal (profitable success of the company), not just the daily performance goal itself.

As a supervisor, you are the immediate, local, everyday caretaker of the goals. You have a huge influence on the success of the whole organization. Actually, you have more influence than the highest-paid top manager. You see to it that the actual work that directly contributes to the larger goals gets done every day. Without you coming to work every day, trying hard to get everyone motivated to achieve the goals, the organization fails to achieve its mission.

How Should You Talk About Goals?

Talk about them every day, all of the time, to everyone. Thinker workers get satisfaction in achieving goals. Feeler workers care about goals. Because you are authorized to act by grace of the goals, you gain authority by talking, organizing, directing, correcting, and training to achieve them. Here is a look at how the hierarchy of goals may function in your organization.

Mission: The company's overall goal. Example: To provide our customers with products and services that allow us to earn a profit.

Objective: The specific set of achievements that the company must obtain in order to arrive at the Mission. Example: To be a consistent high quality delivery supplier at a reasonable cost.

Specific Goals: The specific performance levels that the company must achieve in order to meet the objective, as determined by what the competition is able to provide. The strategy is to outperform the competition in the eyes of the customer in order to retain their business. Example: To perform at the current quality, delivery, and cost expectations and be able to improve when change is required.

Your Departmental Goals: Since achieving these performance goals requires that each department do its work at a pace and level that allows the other departments to achieve their goals, these goals can get complicated. But this is where your supervision makes the difference. Example: Your general manager sets goals for you, expressed in specific terms, such as product or service per hour, defects, or errors per thousand, downtime, on-time shipments, etc.

Employee Goals: It is your job to translate departmental goals into worker goals in order for the department (and the whole organization) to achieve its goal. You will need to analyze what each person is capable of doing by workstation or work process. Your correct assessment and management of each person's performance is critical. If you go back to our earlier discussions about motivation and check-in conversations, you will see how it is useful for you to know the level of motivation and performance possible for each worker. Also, recall our discussions about attendance and turnover. If you suffer turnover, you do not have a known level of performance to predict how your department is going to perform. You must take the best that you can get and begin the lengthy training process—including all of the mistakes that a trainee makes. It is a day-to-day challenge to keep your workers productively working on a consistent and high-quality basis.

Your boss has the right to hold you accountable for the performance of your department or crew. And you have the right to hold your workers responsible for their individual employee goals that you have set for them. You will find yourself carefully explaining these goals over and over again and training each person to achieve these goals. When you succeed in this effort, other departments can meet their goals, the company meets its objective, and the customers continue to send business to the company. As a result of all of this, you and your workers get a paycheck and benefits. And you, your family, and the community prosper.

Bottom-Line Message

The paycheck is not the goal. Customer satisfaction is the goal. The paycheck is the byproduct of customer satisfaction. Expressing the goals in this perspective is motivationally important. It raises the workers' thoughts and expectations to a level that realistically reflects the business environment. It allows you the latitude to require much more from them in terms of cooperation. It gets employees out of the dead-end thought process of *I'll just do exactly what I'm paid to do and no more. I work for a paycheck, so my goal is to do as little as is necessary to keep it coming.*

On an even more positive side, stating the goal in this manner allows you to train, discipline, and request involvement in order to achieve on-going improvements. This may actually increase the commitment required, but ensures the success of the whole organization. Although you will talk about the goal, you will still need to post the goals in a specific numerical format. You might post charts and graphs in your area. You might try giving copies to workers to show them their performance in relation to the goal.

The Motivational Impact of High Expectations

If you have never heard of the wisdom *perception is reality*, I would like to take a minute to think this through with you. Consider one supervisor's experience. He was planning to build a deck on his house. It was the first time he had attempted it. The instructions looked complicated. He had heard horror stories from others about problems. He perceived that it was going to be a difficult project—and so it was for him. The project got off to a bad start and went downhill from there. Then a fellow supervisor stopped by to talk to him. The fellow told him how easy it was and how many decks he had done. He showed him a few shortcuts and said that what he had started was good. From then on, the project went easily and the result was beautiful. Notice how the change in expectations of how difficult the project was going to be changed how well he performed and what results he got. If you expect the worst, you will get the worst. If you expect the best, you will get the best.

Consider the example of your children. If you told your children that they were lazy, stupid, messy, and disobedient, guess how they would act. If you told them that they were bright, energetic, organized, and a joy to have around, guess what you'd get. If you are thinking that you would be telling them a lie, you might miss a big opportunity. Telling them the worst that they are is also a lie. It is an after-the-fact statement as well. Stating expectations is announcing what is going to happen—not what has happened.

The point of all of this is that expecting the positive works with everyone, including your workers. As a supervisor, if you set appropriately high goals and positive expectations, you stand a good chance of getting those achieved—just because you stated them. If you state low goals, you will probably get low performance—just because you stated it that way. A rather well-known study in work performance found that a group of workers was told that they could be expected to do 50 units per day. Another group of similar workers was told that they could be expected to do 3,000 units a day. Both groups used the same work process and easily met the expectations, with no argument, stress, or discipline. Think about this for a minute. How could you raise the expectations of your crew and help them to be better performers? In the roleplays and discussions in this class, we will see many opportunities to set high expectations, but you will probably find many more in your work situation. Use this often, but use it appropriately.

Motivational Supervisory Conversation Using Goal Expectations

Supervisor: *Your goal is 350 quality parts per hour. On this graph, it shows a gradual trend downward from 350 to 300 over the last month. Today your performance was 300. No less than 350 parts is acceptable everyday because if we don't perform at that rate, the next department cannot perform any better and the customers will be disappointed and start to look for another vendor. Let's see what you have to do to achieve the other 50 parts per hour. I'll help you to strategize what you need to do. I will train you and will help you solve problems that come up. I know that you can do it because you were doing it before.*

How Not to Have This Conversation

Just for fun, the class sometimes discusses the wrong way to say these things. Here are some examples:

- What's wrong with you? You are way behind. Get your numbers up or you're fired.
- You lazy, no good dummy. Get these numbers up or you are history.

Critique of How Not to Motivate

List five reasons why these two *not to* conversations would work against your performance:

1. _____

2. _____

3. _____

4. _____

5. _____

This time, I am not going to give you the answers, but think about what we've discussed about discovering performance problems and addressing them, the role of the helpful coach, and assuming the negative, rather than the positive.

Goal Setting Roleplay

Supervisor at a normal daily crew meeting: *Hi, Sally, Hi Bart and Barry, come on in, we will only need a few minutes to go over our schedule for the day. As you know, we've been running 450 units of part 6097 per hour. Since the economy is in a recession, sales for our customer, Top Frost, have been declining, and we only have orders for ten hours per week. Fortunately, our other customer, Tip Top Co. is ramping up for a good Christmas. Last year our best production on their part 7292 was 431 per hour. To compete with the offshore vendors, we would have to do 500 or more per hour. That is a big goal, but I would like you as a team to look at it and give me some ideas about how we could achieve it. If we could figure out how to work smarter, not harder, and make the goal, we'd stay busy throughout the season and make up for the lost Top Frost production. That would make us all happier. I'll be around to talk to each of you and get some of your ideas. Thanks, and have a safe day.*

Supervisor talking with Sally: *Sally, how are you doing today?*

Sally: *OK, I guess. Did you really mean that we might have layoffs due to orders being down? I've got kids to feed. What about Christmas?*

Supervisor: *Sorry to bring up bad news, but the reality is that the country is in a recession. We can't do much about that except to do a better job to keep our customers. Do you have any ideas that might help?*

Sally: *Well, 7292 is an easy part to run, but we waste a lot of the material and just throw it away. I couldn't do that at home. I make my kids eat everything on their plates.*

Supervisor: *Sally, you have a good point. The material that we throw away is worth a lot of money. I'll run some numbers and see how much we can save. (Supervisor makes a note in his notebook). Any ideas of how to better use the materials?*

Sally: *Sure. Design the pattern better. Put twenty parts on each cut, rather than 15. It's like making cookies from cookie dough. I'll draw up an idea of what I mean.*

Supervisor: *Great. I'll be interested in seeing it.*

Supervisor talking to Bart: *Good morning Bart, how's your kid doing in basketball?*

Bart: *Lost the game Sunday, but they will have two practices this week and maybe he'll get the plays better. What were you talking to Sally about?*

Supervisor: *I was asking her for ideas on how to run 7292 better. Do you have any ideas that could help?*

Bart: *Well, you could upgrade this machine a bit. I've been noticing that it runs dry of oil often and that makes it run slow and make poor cuts. It might need an oil pressure gauge so I could watch it and change the oil more often.*

Supervisor: *Good suggestion, Bart. Show me how you think it should be mounted. I'll make a note to bring maintenance over and get their opinion.*

Supervisor talking to Barry: *Hi Barry, how's your production going today?*

Barry: *Well, I was thinking of slowing down after your talk this morning. Maybe if we stretch out the Top Frost orders, we will have a longer work week. That means more in my paycheck.*

Supervisor: *I can see how that would make some sense, but actually, that would increase the labor cost of our parts and raise the cost of the end product. Then our customers might not buy as many freezers from Top Frost, which will only make the situation worse. On the other hand, if we reduced the labor costs, then customers might buy more freezers and we'd have more orders. And the recession might get better. Understand?*

Barry: *I thought that was what you might say.*

Supervisor: *Do you have any ideas on how to improve our production of either the Top Frost part or the Tip Top Co. part?*

Barry: *Nope, I just do my job and take my paycheck home.*

Supervisor: *I notice that you spend a lot of time with the school sports teams, and I know that you like to see them win. I'd like you to think about us as a team and help us to win as well. Let me know if you have any suggestions that might help.*

Barry: *Okay.*

Roleplay Discussion

Notice how different the responses were to the same general announcement. If the supervisor had not talked to each worker, he would have not known what each of them was thinking—and would have missed two great improvement ideas. In addition, his production might have slowed down due to Barry's thought process. As it stands, the team has a good shot at actually improving the profit without much effort or expense. The involvement in ideas will insure that they will be supportive of the changes. They now understand the higher good, as well as their own good and how working together will assure the success of both.

Manufacturing Case Study for Goal Setting

In this case study, we will show how to do goal setting from start to finish. It will take figuring of numbers and motivation of people, so it will draw on all of your skills.

Daily Departmental Goal: 3,000 good units per ten-hour shift.

Work Constraints:

- Five work stations. One worker per workstation.
- One lead worker who can cover rest breaks and you, the supervisor.
- Each unit requires three sub-assemblies to make one unit.
- The schedule calls for a ten-hour shift with two half-hour lunch breaks and two fifteen-minute rest breaks. That means ten meal breaks and ten rest breaks.

Standards: An experienced worker can do 90 per hour but not every hour. They get tired and the production declines to 80 by the end of the shift. A new employee can only do 50 per hour until they become proficient, which takes about three months.
Equipment downtime is typically 3%.
Scrap is historically 2%.

Individual Workers:

- Albert: Experienced, but often grumpy and hates Sam.: Productivity: 85 to 90 units per hour.
- Sam: Experienced, but diagnosed with sleep apnea: Productivity: 75 to 80 units per hour.
- Carrie: Experienced, but often tardy: 75 to 80 per hour.
- Becky: Newly trained by Carrie. Has been late once. So far, only 50 per hour.

- Billy: Experienced, but is the shop steward and is out for union business at least four hours per week: Productivity: 85 to 90 per hour.

Assignment: Calculate the numbers required by each worker for the whole team to meet the goal of 3000 units per shift.

	Hours Worked	Units per hour	Total
Albert			
Sam			
Carrie			
Becky			
Billy			
	Total:	Average:	Total

The answers:

If you know that scrap will be 2%, you already know that your goal is not really 3000 units per shift. It has to be 3060.

If you deduct from each worker's hours the breaks, equipment downtime, and time away, no one really works the full ten hours. Here's how it breaks down:

	Hours Worked	Units per hour	Total
Albert	8.5	85	723
Sam	8.5	78	663
Carrie	7.5	78	585
Becky	8.5	50	425
Billy	8.0	85	680
	Average: 8.2	Average: 75	Total: 3,076 Average: 615 per hour

Notes

- You can count on Albert, Sam, and Billy to get to work on time each day. But Carrie loses about a half-hour per day between being tardy a few minutes at the start of the shift and being slow to come back from lunch breaks. You would like to get Carrie to improve because she is otherwise a good worker. Becky is starting to show signs of the same behavior, but she is still new and can hopefully be motivated to avoid bad habits.

- Billy is the shop steward and is away from his work area four hours per week. That translates into losing about a half-hour per shift.

- The lead worker can cover the rest breaks, but the lunch breaks represent downtime for your workstations. These account for an hour per worker.

- Some days you might get lucky and not have any equipment downtime, but other days you might have a lot. Better to figure the average of one half-hour per day for each workstation.

The People Skills Part of this Supervisory Plan

Now that you have figured the numbers, what are the people-performance issues that you would need to address to maintain this performance plan? This is where you look at each person as an individual. If you are doing the recommended check-in conversations everyday with each worker, you are very much aware of what is going on in each person's motivational mindset. You are now in a position to work out a plan to improve your situation. Here are some possible suggestions:

Working with Sam would be a de-motivator for Albert, so give them workstations far apart from each other. Make sure that they don't go on breaks together. Even though Albert is grumpy, keep talking to him and be good-natured with him. He is actually your highest performer and doesn't give you any trouble otherwise.

When you are talking to Sam, encourage him to seek treatment for his sleep apnea—he may be subject to accidents or slowed performance. Watch for signs of drowsiness since he works with machinery all day. Having Sam injured and on the disabled list would get you another trainee, and your hourly average would suffer severely.

Carrie needs serious counseling and a disciplinary plan. Although your goal should be a positive one because she is a good performer, you will have to figure out how to get her to her workstation on time. (We'll talk later about discipline and will ask you to recall this situation.) Make a note to do a counseling discussion with her soon.

Becky is being trained by Carrie, which is both good and bad. Carrie is teaching her how to be fast and accurate, but Becky is getting the idea that she can be tardy like Carrie. Here is another opportunity for counseling and a disciplinary plan. If you can avoid letting her get into a bad habit from the start, your job will be easier later. You might let Sam or the lead worker train her for a while.

You should be happy to have Billy on your team. He is an experienced high performer. Because he is a shop steward, you have to conform to company policies regarding his union duties. Be sure that your supervisory skills are professional at all times. He would be obligated to file a grievance if he saw a breach of the agreement.

You can use your lead worker to give rest breaks and to check on the sub-assembly supplies. Have him alert you long before supplies get low, or your work stations will come to a standstill. Have him alert you immediately if there is an equipment problem so you can get things running again quickly and not jeopardize your performance plan.

Notice that you are not accounting for lost production time due to other unforeseen reasons. But if things went drastically wrong, you could step in and assist any workstation or the lead worker. Most of your time outside of your daily check-in conversations, should be spent solving departmental problems, communicating between management and the workers, doing employee counseling, discipline, and evaluations, reports, and planning improvements. Our next section will to elaborate further on how to get performance improvements.

Summary

Congratulations, now you have the major pieces of a performance plan, using both a numerical and a motivational approach. You are light years ahead of most rookie supervisors who think that being a supervisor is issuing orders and making decisions. Remember through all of this that you are the helpful coach—all conversations are calm, reasonable, and professional.

Performance Improvement

Once you have begun a performance plan, you will want to find ways to continually improve it before a competitor finds a way to do what you do cheaper or better. Keep in mind that the more profitable your company is, the better able it is to provide jobs, good wages, and benefits. Also, performance improvements will surely get you noticed if there are bonuses and promotions available. For these reasons, you will want to work on performance improvements constantly. As you succeed, you will be getting more production for the same labor costs. That's good for everybody and no harm to you because performance improvements usually involve less work and effort. Think of it as working smarter, not harder.

Performance improvements come from finding ways to remove mistakes, time, material, and waste from your plan. In our first example, if you could remove 1% scrap from your work process, you would have to make 30 fewer units to reach your goal. If you could make the work easier for the workers to do and they could do even 1% more with the same effort, you would produce 30 more units per shift, with no additional cost beyond the cost of the sub assemblies. Together, that would be 60 units to the good. The profit on 60 extra units every shift, every day, would soon add up to a good profit figure. You would feel good having that discussion with your boss, wouldn't you?

Where to Find Performance Improvement Opportunities

Start with simple organizing. Look for ways to reduce the amount of steps a person must take to do their job. This may include moving things by means of a forklift truck In some plants, walking out on the plant floor is as dangerous as walking across a six-lane super highway—forklift trucks are racing around trying to get material and parts to and from work stations. If you look, you may be able to eliminate some of that by better stocking levels or by positioning commodities in a better location. In addition, make sure that things are labeled and well stocked so people don't have to waste time searching. Things that are not needed should be removed to avoid confusion and to save space. I'm sure that you will be a big fan of keeping the place clean and orderly, so you have open space to use and accidents are reduced.

Next, look to better communication and training. If workers are unsure what to do or are doing the wrong thing the wrong way, a lot of rework will be required. These simple misunderstandings are rampant in any organization and provide workers with de-motivators for doing the right thing right now. In our examples, I said that you, the supervisor, are not directly involved in doing the work on most days, but should focus on training and communication. I hope that you can see here why this is so important. If you are so busy and stressed that you can't even see these opportunities or do anything effective about them, then they go on causing wasted time and money. And your workers have to produce more to overcome the cost of this waste.

The next area for performance improvement is process flow and work procedures. The best place to get ideas for improvements is from the workers themselves. They stand there and work hour after hour, thinking that there must be a better way. The plant engineers will look at a workstation in one way, but the workers will look at it in a unique and possibly more valuable way. Most of their ideas come from a motive of making the work easier or safer—and are often practical and low cost. If you evaluated all of their ideas and picked the best ones to discuss with management, you would have a rich supply of ways to improve performance. And your workers would be supportive because the ideas came from them.

Keeping management informed is important. There may be unforeseen consequences from even a small change that might not look like it has a downside, but does. As discussion with employees and management progresses, there might be an even better idea. At any rate, you are including employee input with management input and generating improvements that make the workers' jobs easier, company's profit better, and your job easier. That's a lot of benefit to be had by just listening to workers' ideas.

The best time to ask for this input is in your check-in conversations at the workstation. Employees will often show you what they are thinking right there so you can see it clearly. You can thank them individually. Be sure to write it down on your pad so you can follow up later. Let them know how you are evaluating their idea. Never promise them a change until it has been fully approved. In some companies, a new work instruction might involve a formal review. It might be some time before a change is implemented. But you, in the meantime, are talking to others and evaluating ideas for further improvements.

An additional place to find improvements is by working with other mid-level management and professional staff, such as engineering, customer service, purchasing, quality, and safety. These professionals do their jobs every day, thinking to themselves, *There's got to be a better way*. Here is another rich source for performance improvements.

Performance Improvement Case Study

A good example of a performance improvement involves a complaint that a customer service agent took about scratches on the surface of the product. It led to a discussion of how the scratches were made. The root cause was determined to be too many moves from location to location within the plant on a forklift truck. The safety officer was interested in the problem because there was a rise in injuries due to truck accidents. The quality department was interested because a surface scratch is a significant defect that costs the company scrap and returns. The supervisor was interested because moving parts around costs his workers time that he would rather devote to filling out the paperwork better. The workers were interested because the constant movement of parts increased fumes in the plant and caused them to run out of parts while the truck was somewhere else moving something else. The question became, *Why do we have to move the parts so often?*

The supervisor went to talk to the workers. They said it was because they had no space to put the parts in their proper place the first time they moved them. One problem was an older machine that was only used once a month was taking up storage space. The machine was moved to an area where it could be used, but not take up storage space. There was an immediate production improvement. Because the parts were only being moved once, they were not scratched, the truck driver had more time to get other things done, shipments were faster, costs were down, and the workers supported the idea—it made their job easier, safer, and caused less hassle. The area was more orderly and accidents were reduced. All around, this was an excellent improvement. And the supervisor who made the improvement was viewed as a positive leader in the department. Secretly, though, she was happier than anybody was—her productivity went up, the hassles went down, the motivation improved, and it would be easier to get future improvements. Good job!

Some Guidelines for Employee Involvement

- Ask everyone to get involved. Don't leave others out even if they do not immediately contribute.

- Let everyone know how the ideas will be evaluated. For example: Safety, Quality, Productivity, Cost Savings, etc.

- Keep people informed as to the progress of the ideas. They may be able to improve on the original idea when they hear objections. They also have a sense of ownership of the idea and want the satisfaction of making it successful.

- Always give credit and acknowledgement to everyone who was involved. Publicly state what each person contributed—no matter how small. You might post the team names on a bulletin board or report, or you might discuss it at a meeting. And when you go back to personally thank each person in your check-in conversations, you might get another good idea. If nothing else, you will build a good motivator for people to work for you and your department. People like to get recognition.

- Always get management involved and get approval before you talk to the workers. It would look bad if you said that something could be done, and later management had to say no.

- Keep employee involvement an ongoing effort. Don't stop at one success or failure.

- Don't let it go sour once you get it started. If you get feedback from workers who feel that a performance improvement causes them more work for the same pay, remind them that the work is easier, safer, and improved—from their own ideas. Also, if the company is more successful, their jobs are more secure. Finally, just tell them how much you, the other workers, and management appreciate their help. Keep it positive.

You have now completed Class Six and are equipped with some powerful motivational skills. You understand motivators and de-motivators. You understand how Introverts and Extroverts, Sensors and Intuitives, and Thinkers and Feelers see the world and what they need to be motivated and effective workers. Finally, you understand how a good use of goal setting and employee involvement can focus your team on performance goals to constantly improve their output by working smarter, not harder. I recommend (as I have at the end of other chapters) that you take a week or two to think about these approaches and to try these skills in your real world. Hopefully, you will have some successes and failures to recount at our next class. Keep trying. Don't let these skills go untested and untried. You want to get as much benefit from the classes as possible, considering all of the effort that you have put into them. See you in a week or so.

Third *Walkaround* with Mary

On our third and last visit, we reviewed Mary's meeting with Dick, the HR manager. Mary reported that he was not as difficult as others had predicted. He was just busy. He appreciated Mary's email and prepared approach. He reviewed Gertrude's work history, evaluations, and Mary's notes, and asked a lot of questions. He said that he would handle the situation personally because it involved a management decision as well as possibly an application for disability or retirement. Mary was glad for his interest, but felt that Gertrude might not yet be ready to make such a big decision. She asked Dick to wait—she wanted to talk to her a couple more times and prepare her for the decision that she would have to make.

I asked Mary how she was going to handle these talks with Gertrude.

Mary: *I guess I'll just get her to talk it over with me and tell her that options are available when she is ready and see what she says.*

Me: *But what if she does nothing and you still have the problem of her declining performance.*

Mary: *I guess I will have to make it clear to her that napping and long lunches are unacceptable. Worst case, I would have to write her up.*

This could be a difficult conversation to have with someone with a good work record and only one year before retirement—and with a legitimate health problem. I suggested we could all (including Gertrude) set a goal to avoid that conversation. Mary should ask Gertrude to select a solution within a reasonable period of time and keep Mary informed. Mary felt that was the best that she could do. She'd also invite Dick to talk to Gertrude about how the company could help.

As I usually do, I asked Mary to evaluate what she had learned as a result of her supervisory classes and *walkarounds*. She was surprised at how well problems worked out when a good goal and plan were thoughtfully analyzed. She also realized that she had a lot of responsibility and power as a supervisor. Being thoughtful and skilled made a big difference in the lives of her crew. Finally, she had never before realized how much help human resources could be and how easy it was to communicate with them.

For many reasons, it is rare to find seamless teamwork between supervisors and human resources. I urge all of you to make it a priority to establish a good working relationship with your human resources department. Since you must work within their policies, you can get a lot of guidance from that department as to what you can and cannot do in sensitive situations. In addition, some problems must be turned over to human resources to resolve. So talking to them in advance will prevent problems that would be embarrassing, costly, and de-motivating. These days, there are so many legal aspects to human resources, and all supervisors need the support and guidance of their human resource professional.

I congratulated her and thanked her for sharing a little bit of her supervisory life with me. I assured her that there were many people just like her out there who took their job seriously and felt much the same as she did about being a supervisor.

> *"You might be disappointed if you fail, but you are doomed if you don't try."*
>
> *Beverly Sills.*

Class Seven

In this class, I will share some experiences that other supervisors have talked about in the classes and encourage you to reflect on what progress you have made for yourself. Also, in this class, we will address the issues of employee counseling, discipline, and evaluations. Finally, we will learn the last of the four personality ranges. Here is a case study of a supervisor who made a great deal of progress.

Supervisory Case Study:

Every employee evaluation that Curtis ever had mentioned him being argumentative and stubborn. In fact, people tried to avoid working with him because it was such a hassle to gain his cooperation. But he did have everyone's respect for his technical knowledge and his commitment to doing things correctly and completely. People knew that he had the company's best interests at heart. When he attended this class, he was working in the engineering department where he did not have to supervise anyone. In class, he listened but wanted to argue each point. About six months later, he had an opportunity to take an important supervisory position. The people he would be supervising were discouraged, poorly disciplined, and lacked organization and direction. It was a tough challenge to take on, but he dove in determined to make it a success.

In the beginning, he pointed out to the crew all of the mistakes they were making. The result was a host of complaints, threats to quit, and general rebellion. These people had had enough negative. Fortunately, he saw a crew that he respected and cared about. He remembered some of the lessons from the class and began to talk to each crewmember individually. Slowly, they understood that he was trying to help them and began to give their cooperation and loyalty.

As people started to open up to Curtis, they began to share their personal problems with him. He wondered why they thought of him as a source of advice and help. After all, he was generally thought of as being difficult. He had never been in this situation before, and he was sure that he was the last person to give advice on personal problems. He had plenty of his own. The more he got involved with their problems, the more he saw why they were having trouble. He made sure that they were properly trained to do what he asked of them. He was careful to be clear about what he wanted and disciplined several people who were creating confusion and stress. He upgraded their tools and simplified their paperwork. They began to see that they could be a success and that he was helping them.

But that was only half of the problem. Curtis worked for a boss who was even more critical and negative than he had ever been. On one occasion, his boss criticized his crew for doing something wrong. Curtis stepped forward and protected his crew from the criticism, telling his boss that it was his fault, not that of his crew. He stated that he would personally take responsibility for any problems. His boss respected that and began to talk to Curtis more clearly and frequently about the company's expectations. They walked around the department daily, discussing together what needed to be done. Slowly, things settled down. Curtis could count on his crew, and his crew could count on him. Although his boss began to give some good reports and better evaluations on his performance, Curtis knew that he would have to learn to live with his boss's frequent complaints and criticisms about mistakes and failures because that was just his nature.

These improvements were not easy for Curtis. He had to work hard to prevent getting into arguments and losing his temper. He had to work hard to listen to his crew and not to judge their behavior—before he heard their problems. He hated his boss bringing up problems because he wanted so much to be right. But he listened and slowly solved each problem. Despite some occasional outbursts, Curtis was well on his way to being considered for future promotions. He would just need to continue to work on his personality traits by utilizing his positive traits rather than suffer from his weaknesses.

Discussion of Case Study:

Curtis is a Thinker, as you might have guessed. This was both his strength and his weakness. His drive to achieve high standards and goals was admired. But his stubbornness and argumentative habits were viewed as disruptive. Actually, though, they represented the same traits—just used inappropriately. The prior job in engineering did not require him to supervise a crew, so he had not perfected the required traits of listening, motivating, and directing people. In fact, the engineering job encouraged him to be argumentative because of the need to avoid technical mistakes and unnecessary costs on projects.

In the supervisory position, he had to dig deep into his people skills in order to change how he interacted with his crew and his boss. It was hard for him to suppress the urge to argue—he had done it for so long—and arguing and getting angry at least let off some steam for him. But as that urge began to decline, the positive results of the listening, coaching, and directing began to appear.

So it will be with you too. All of you have some traits that are comfortable to you. You have used them for a long time successfully, but in certain situations, you must now learn to suppress them. There will be other traits that have been underutilized that will have to be brought into play. All of this takes a real understanding of yourself and a dedication to making a positive change. You might not be like Curtis. You may be a Feeler and be too weak with discipline. You will have to suppress the urge to give in and ignore a problem behavior, bringing your ability to confront people out of the closet. Do you doubt that you even have these opposite traits? You might not have used them very much or for very long, but whatever you do possess, be prepared to brush it up and begin to exercise it. It is like being left handed in a right-handed world. You would really like to use your left hand, but the situation calls for a right-handed approach. Your right hand does not do a good job and is slow and difficult. But if you persist, you will be ambidextrous and able to use both hands well. That makes you a much more effective person than you were before, easier to work with and better able to understand people who are different from you.

How will you know what your strong traits are—the ones that sometimes work well for you, but in other times work against you? How will you know what your weaker traits are –the ones you will have to work on developing? At the end of this book, I have an extra copy of the personality ranges with some of the strengths and weaknesses of each. Feel free to go to a copier and make several copies. On one of these copies, go down the list of traits and check which ones you think apply to you. Take another copy and let your boss or trusted co-workers do the same. Finally, ask your spouse or a trusted family member to check your traits. Put all of these pages together, and look for the ones that all agree belong to you. Recopy these traits on the *Self Guidance Worksheet.* See what traits you could be working on that would really help you to be a better supervisor, parent, spouse, and person. I promise you that the people around you will be pleased to see these subtle changes, as you become easier and more effective to work with. As you become more effective, others will find their jobs easier as well.

Eventually, you will probably find yourself trying to explain these traits to other people in an effort to encourage them to work on their traits. After all, you count on their performance too. You can do the same thing with the handouts. Give coworkers the handouts, explain the range, and ask them to check off what they think applies to them. You should complete a check page yourself. As the two of you discuss the common traits that you see, you can help that person see what direction to go towards to gain improvement. This type of counseling can be enjoyable and can get good results. This process addresses the root cause of multiple problems, and places the responsibility for change on the individual—where it belongs.

Employee Evaluations

Most companies require a supervisor to do annual employee evaluations. There is usually a form to use that outlines key performance areas. Your job will be to rate and compare—from year to year—what progress is being made, with an action plan for improvement. Here is a sample of what one might be like:

Employee Evaluation Form

Name of Employee_____ Date of Hire_____ Date of Evaluation_____

Directions: This evaluation is required to be completed on or before the annual date of hire of the employee. The Supervisor is to complete this form privately, then meet with the employee, and explain the ratings and comments. The supervisor and employee are to develop an action plan to address any deficiencies or to further the development of the employee's skills, abilities, and performance. Both are to sign the bottom of the form and submit copies to Human Resources. The employee is to receive a copy and the supervisor is required to keep a copy on file for reference throughout the year. This form becomes a permanent part of the employee's personnel file.

Rate the employee's attendance, punctuality, and readiness for work:

Low   Medium Low   Average   High Average   High

Explain the rating: _____

_____

Recommendation: _____

Rate the employee's productivity:

Low   Medium Low   Average   High Average   High

Explain the rating: _____

_____

Recommendation: _____

Other categories for you to evaluate might include: personal appearance, knowledge of work skills, willingness to learn, safety compliance, computer skills, writing skills, cooperation with others, initiative to take responsibility, quality of work, etc. You must use your company's form and follow all policies and directions given to you by your human resources department.

How Should a Supervisor Do An Employee Evaluation?

A performance evaluation is an area that is usually important to an employee, both from the aspect of how they might personally react, but how the evaluation might affect their job and thus their income. For this reason, the situation can be negatively charged. Another dynamic that makes the situation difficult is that the employee might evaluate his or her own performance higher than the supervisor does. This reality check has all of the makings of a de-motivator, rather than a motivator.

Case Study of an Employee Evaluation

Norma Jean has worked three years as a buyer in the purchasing department of the Barnwell Company. Her supervisor, Mr. Morgan whom she liked very much, consistently rated her performance as *very good*, with a point total of 85 out of a possible 100. Typically, Norma Jean got top rating for her knowledge of the job and the quality and dependability of her work. The only reason that her aggregate score did not move her into the excellent range was that her rating for *Quantity of Work Produced* was never better than fair. Six months ago, Mr. Morgan left the company and was replaced by Mike Hale. When the semi-annual evaluations were filed, Mike judged Norma Jean's overall performance as only fair, with a score of 60 points. Yesterday, Mike called Norma Jean into his office for the employee evaluation interview.

The news that her present rating was only fair upset Norma Jean.

How can that be? she asked. *I'm working as hard as I always have. My previous supervisor was more than satisfied with my work.* Tears were forming in the corners of her eyes.

I'm sorry, Norma, said Mike. *That's the way I see it. The amount of work you turn out is deplorably low. If you can't pick up speed, I'm going to have to put you on notice. As it is, I certainly won't be recommending you for a raise when that time comes around.*

That's not fair, said Norma Jean, now angry and scared. *I work on purchases that need very precise specifications and quotations. You can look at my record and see that I make hardly any mistakes. No one else in the department is as reliable as I am.*

You're placing emphasis on the wrong thing, said Mike. *You slow everything down with your nit picking on every requisition. There is no need for precision on 90% of what you do; yet you triple check every five-cent item as if it were worth millions. Either you learn to pick up speed, or you'll be looking for work elsewhere.*

Questions on Case Study

1. Mr. Morgan felt that he was being objective, fair, and truthful with Norma. Mike did too. How could such a discrepancy of perceptions happen?

2. Why was Norma angry and scared?

3. Mike wants Norma to shift the focus from accuracy to quantity. Suggest the best way for him to achieve this and improve Norma's motivation, attitude, and loyalty.

Discussion of Employee Evaluation Case Study

Any two people rating any one person are likely to see the performance differently and disagree on the exact rating to give. By reviewing her past evaluations with Mr. Morgan, Mike could have realized the difference in perceptions between the prior evaluations and his own. He then could have worked out a plan to explain to Norma how he wanted her to change and still maintain her motivation and loyalty. Perhaps he could have put the two evaluations side by side and shown her how they were so different. He could have explained that this big gap was going to be hard to bridge, but that he would help her. She was probably a Sensor person and would always have a tendency to spend too much time on accuracy. He might set several small quantity goals for her to work on each week, give her praise for her improvement, and then set higher goals. A plan like this would avoid her being so afraid of losing her job that her performance would crash. If he did this right, he could have both quantity and quantity--a good outcome. If Norma trusted that Mike was being fair, truthful, and helpful, he would be able to establish a cooperative working relationship.

Guidelines for Doing Employee Evaluations

- Think through your evaluations carefully before you ever talk to the employee.

- Collect any documentation that would show examples of points you want to make.

- Review past evaluations to determine how much gap the employee will be looking at when you present your findings.

- Develop a plan to present the gap in a manner that increases motivation.

- Be prepared for an emotional reaction. Do not be intimidated, but be considerate.

- Be prepared to offer help. Have a plan in mind that will really work for the employee.

- If the plan requires frequent follow-up and additional feedback, be prepared to do so. You could reap great rewards from a performance improvement.

- Ask the employee to sign the form. Give them a copy so they can think it over in private. Often a person will come to agree with you later.

- If there is severe disagreement, offer the review process that most company policy provides.

If you have been talking to the employee all along about your expectations and giving them feedback, the annual evaluation should only be a recap of what you say to them every day. The best evaluations are ones that reflect the on-going mutual effort between a worker and supervisor to meet the company's goals and to make the employee a success at his or her job.

Employee Evaluation Exercise

Take out your own employee evaluations that you may have saved from other jobs and look at the different ways that your supervisors viewed your performance. If you can, identify which supervisor did the best job of the interview. Who motivated you to do your best? Make some notes here for you to remember to use as you move into being an outstanding supervisor yourself.

Notes on Your Evaluations

Evaluation One:

Evaluation Two:

Evaluation Three:

Employee Counseling

Now we are ready to look at how to do an employee counseling session. In this type of discussion, your goal is to try to find what problems an employee might be having that cause his or her performance to suffer. So let's start with the performance issue first. It might be a tardiness problem, continuous errors, a bad attitude, accidents, or any of many other problems that are common in the workplace. Many of our case studies are examples of situations that a supervisor may encounter. Please notice that a counseling session is essentially a problem investigation action. It might end with a solution or might not. It might be conducted before a disciplinary action is required or after one has been done. At the beginning, you won't know exactly what will be discussed. You won't know how or if it will be resolved. It depends on what you uncover.

The first rule of an employee counseling session is to keep your options open. If you find out that the employee has a drinking problem and is coming in under the influence, you will have to follow company policy on substance abuse. If you find out that the employee was up all night with a sick child, you may decide to do nothing at all. You may go into a counseling session and find any situation, so start the session with an open mind. Ask questions that will help the person identify the root cause of the performance problem. Remember here the listening skills that we have learned in prior classes, specifically *peeling the layers of the onion*. These skills are the cornerstone of a good counseling session. Here is a sample of a supervisor doing a good job of such a conversation. This conversation is held in a private office, without interruption. It will take about 20 minutes.

Case Study of Employee Counseling No. 1

Supervisor: *Come on in Aaron. Have a seat. I wanted to take a few minutes to talk. We have had many good conversations in the past.*

Aaron: *Okay.*

Supervisor: *Since you came to my shift, I've always been able to depend on you to be here on time. In fact, I gave you the start-up duties because you are always energetic and ready to work on time. I really like that about you. That helps me a lot. Lately, I've noticed that you are coming in later and later and that worries me that something might be wrong. Could you tell me a little about why this is happening?*

Aaron: *Well, I'm not going to get written up am I?*

Supervisor: *If the situation caused you to be late more than once, the policy calls for a write up, but I hope that by talking we can work it out before it gets to that point.*

Aaron: *Yeah, I suppose that I've been cutting it pretty close lately. I'll watch it. Can I go now?*

Supervisor: *Great, that's what it takes. Just keep focused on the importance of being on time because that means that you will have a good day and won't get written up. Is there anything that I can do to help?*

Aaron: *Now that you mention it, there is one small problem. It's Gordy.*

Supervisor: *What's going on with Gordy?*

Aaron: *Well, last week I borrowed his bass boat. I returned it, but it got scratched up some. I'm sure that it was scratched up already when I got it. Well, he's mad and says that he's going to scratch up my truck unless I pay to get his boat painted. He's being a real pain about this.*

Supervisor: *How does this cause you to be late?*

Aaron: *I have to stay by my truck until he gets into the building so he can't scratch it up, of course.*

Supervisor: *I see. So you are really here on time in the parking lot, but you wait around until you see him go in, right?*

Aaron: *Yeah, wouldn't you?*

Supervisor: *Well, that's one way to solve the problem, but maybe you should work out a solution on the boat.*

Aaron: *Like what? I ain't paying for a whole new paint job when I only used it once.*

Supervisor: *Maybe you could work out a deal that you could use it several times and then paint it. That way you would get the use of it, and he would get a new paint job.*

Aaron: *Hey, that's not a bad idea. I'd like to try it out for a while before I decide to buy one myself.*

Supervisor: *How about you two talk it out and let me know if you have settled it, so you can get back to being on time. My advice is to be positive about it. Remember that if you buy a boat of your own, you wouldn't want someone to mess it up any more than he would. Do we have an agreement?*

Aaron: *Yeah, I'll talk to him at lunch and let you know.*

Discussion of Employee Counseling Case Study No. 1

Notice that this supervisor got to the root cause of the problem without prying too much into the employee's personal life. He opened the door and let Aaron talk if he wanted to. If Aaron had said that he didn't want to talk about it, the supervisor would have left the conversation with an agreement that Aaron would be more careful about when he clocked in. But since they discussed the cause, the supervisor was able to offer some help. The boat problem may seem like a small problem in life, but much less than that has lead to fights, injuries, and disruption. Some of the people who will work for you do not think deeply about their problems. They just go on with their life, and things often go sour on their own momentum. You may be the most positive leader, counselor, and adviser that they have in their lives. You should watch for opportunities to show them how to avoid trouble and resolve problems. As they learn, they will be easier for you to supervise.

Many people ask me just how far they should go in helping workers with their personal problems. The answer is it depends on the employee and the situation. But a rule of thumb is to get involved just enough to ensure that their performance is dependable. For example, if Aaron comes back and the compromise did not work, suggest that he think of another compromise, and to keep trying until it works. You have put him on the right track in thinking about a compromise, so let him work on it. It's time for you to back out. On the other hand, I know a supervisor who talked with a worker repeatedly as his aged mother went through her last year and died. The worker had to go to many doctor appointments and had only a few days of family leave near the end. The supervisor helped to arrange his work schedule to accommodate these needs. He even stopped in at the funeral home for the viewing on his way home from work. The worker appreciated this help and support and returned to work even more motivated because he felt that the company cared about him.

Employee Counseling Case Study No. 2

As I said before, you never know where a counseling session might lead. Here is one that turned into a much more complex issue:

Supervisor: *Walt, come in and have a seat. I'd like to talk to you about some things.*

Walt: *Things, what things? All I got these days is trouble.*

Supervisor: *That's what I'm trying to help you to avoid—trouble. I've noticed that your attitude has changed. Workers are complaining that you are often too ready to get into a fight. You seem so angry. What's going on?*

Walt: *It's nobody's business, but mine. I can take care of my wife just fine by myself. I don't need anybody else telling me what to do.*

Supervisor: *The fighting at work is not like you, and I really can't let it continue or somebody might get hurt and you could lose your job. I know that you can handle your problems by yourself, but why is it coming to work with you?*

Walt: *She's driving me crazy, that's why! She says that she's leaving. But I know that if I knock her around some more, she'll shut up and get back to cooking and cleaning. I'm sure you know what I'm saying.*

Supervisor: *Sounds like things are pretty upset. I can see why you come in angry.*

Walt: *What am I supposed to do? I can't figure out what her problem is.*

Supervisor: *Well, just between you and me, it would be a good idea if you got some help with this. I know that you would want her to stay and be happy, wouldn't you?*

Walt: *Yeah, I guess.*

Supervisor: *You might not know it, but as part of your company-paid benefits, you can get professional counseling with a low deductible. I've recommended it to several other workers and they got good results with it.*

Walt: *Who's that?*

Supervisor: *Well, I'm not going to give names. I won't tell anyone about what you've said either. The counseling center is just west of town on the right. Just stop in and they will get you started.*

Walt: *I don't know if I want to be talking to no shrink.*

Supervisor: *I think that you should do this. Just like at work, hitting anyone is a crime and the police could arrest you for it. If you go to counseling and work out your problems, it could help you avoid being arrested and may help you both to be happier. It will also help you to handle your anger at work. I think that you had better do this.*

Walt: *Well, I'll think about it. You won't turn me in to the police will you?*

Supervisor: *All somebody has to do is to call the police, Walt, and you could be in jail. Fighting with people is not going to make them get along with you better. Go get some help. You'll be a better man for it.*

Walt: *I guess you're right.*

Supervisor: *I'll check back with you in a week to see if you have set up your first appointment. If you continue arguing and starting fights at work, I will have to give you your first written warning. Are we clear about this?*

Walt: *Yeah, yeah. Thanks, but no thanks.*

Supervisor: *Walt, if you really try to work on this, I will have a lot of respect for you. I'd like to see you succeed with this. I'll try to help you as much as I can, but you will have to make up your mind to put a positive effort into it.*

Discussion of Employee Counseling Case Study No. 2

This counseling session was a much more serious issue. Of all of the things that a supervisor hears about, domestic disputes are the most common—and the most dangerous. Be careful not to take sides or to make specific suggestions. Your goal is to get the parties into professional off-site counseling, where a counselor can spend the time it takes to deal with a situation like this. You can only advise him to seek help, and you can only deal with the discipline at work. This is all that this supervisor did, but he may have helped to open the door for these people to get some help. In addition, he has laid the foundation for coming back again and talking about the work issue as a disciplinary action. Notice that the supervisor was honest and straightforward, but also calm, reasonable, and professional. Some of these situations may be offensive and intimidating to you personally, but rely on your faithful trio: Calm, reasonable, and professional. Additional note: If you have certain knowledge of child abuse, check with your human resources department. Many states recognize that, because children are defenseless, it is society's responsibility to be proactive. You may be required to report it.

Employee Counseling Case Study No. 3

Supervisor: *Timmy, come in. I'd like to talk to you. Have a seat.*

Timmy: *What for? I didn't do anything wrong? You should talk to Shorty. He's the one to watch. Not me.*

Supervisor: *Really, I just wanted to talk to you about your attitude. It seems that you are so de-motivated lately that you are not paying enough attention to your work. Where's your mind been wandering lately?*

Timmy: *What do you mean? I'm here on time every day.*

Supervisor: *Well, actually, that's what I mean. You seem to be able to get yourself here every day, but the rest is of little interest to you. You haven't always been like that. What's changed in the last two months?*

Timmy: *Nothing's changed. I'm just fine. Can I go back to work now?*

Supervisor: *Not just yet. I've noticed that you make a lot of cell phone calls and you and Shorty trade lunch boxes a lot. I don't have any evidence yet, but I'm interested in getting you both focused on work, not outside of work issues. Anything that you want to talk to me about?*

Timmy: *No.*

Supervisor: *Well, I hope that that means that you are taking this to heart, because our company random drug-screening program has been in force for six months, and some people have decided to come forward and ask for help. Others take their chances that they won't get screened and fired if they test positive. I just want to make sure that you know that you can come to me at any time and ask for help if you have a problem. That may save you your job, if you had a problem, which I sincerely hope that you don't.*

Timmy: *I don't.*

Supervisor: *Well, good. Say here's today's list of drug counseling programs. The company is serious about stopping the spread of drug abuse. In time, I'd guess that drug dealing will be a thing of the past in this company as people either get help or get fired. Again, if you want to talk to me, I can get you some help. Other than that, I don't want anyone using cell phones at work. Leave it in your locker. If I see cell phones used, I will have to start disciplining people. Do you understand?*

Timmy: *Yeah. Say, are you serious about people asking for help? You know that people can get shot or beat up if they narc on somebody.*

Supervisor: *Yes, I'm serious. The help is for the individual to kick the habit and stay sober. Is someone threatening you?*

Timmy: *Is this really confidential?*

Supervisor: *To some degree yes, but I have to follow the law and company policy.*

Timmy: *I'll just tell you to keep an eye on Shorty. Check for a gun in his locker. That's all that I can say. Can I leave now?*

Supervisor: *Yes, but keep in mind that I will have to discuss this gun issue with human resources. I'll do my best to keep you out of it.*

Employee Counseling Case Study No. 3 Discussion

This session contained serious issues. The supervisor determined that Timmy might very well want to get some help with a drug problem, but was afraid of Shorty. At this point, the supervisor must immediately turn the situation over to the human resources professionals or upper management. They will probably have to call in the police. The worst thing would be to have a shooting at work. I've read reports about violence in the workplace and have wondered how the supervisor either helped or hindered the problem long before an event like a shooting took place. At any rate, the supervisor and the employee might both be in danger themselves. The worst thing is to do nothing. Talk to management or human resources—or both—and work out a plan. Be sure to emphasize that Timmy might be in danger of retaliation.

Employee Counseling Case Study No. 4

Supervisor: *Thanks for coming, Cindy. Have a seat. I want to talk to you.*

Cindy: *Whew, it's good to get to sit down for a while. What's up?*

Supervisor: *How do you like your job?*

Cindy: *What did you say? I didn't hear you so clear.*

Supervisor: *I never noticed that you had trouble hearing. Is this something new?*

Cindy: *Trouble hearing? Not me. What makes you think so?*

Supervisor: *I notice that I have to say things twice. Often, you say huh.*

Cindy: *Oh, everybody does that. That doesn't mean that I have a hearing problem, does it?*

Supervisor: *Well, I don't know for sure, but hearing problems can be caused by noise at work. Do you wear your earplugs every day, all day?*

Cindy: *Oh, those things make my ears itch. I hate them, don't you?*

Supervisor: *Preserving your hearing is important to me and to the company. That's why it is company policy. If you don't like the plug, we can investigate a head set. But I don't want this to go any farther without a hearing test and an assessment of what we can do to help your hearing.*

Cindy: *Well, if you think all that it is necessary. What should we do?*

Supervisor: *First, I'll call the safety director to see if we have past records of your hearing tests. We'll schedule another one to see if there is a problem. In the meantime, I want you to wear either the earplugs or a headset. Which would you prefer?*

Cindy: *I'll try the headset and see if it bothers me.*

Supervisor: *Fine, I'll get one from the stock room right now, and I'll check back with you later today to see how it is working for you.*

Cindy: *Thanks, I didn't realize that my hearing would be such a big deal.*

Supervisor: *All employees are important to the company. You are the team that makes this place run. Cindy, we all need to take care of ourselves and our health. I'm glad that you understand this now.*

Employee Counseling Case Study No. 4 Discussion

In this case, the supervisor was not sure what was wrong with an otherwise good employee, so she just asked a general question, *How do you like your job?* The result was she uncovered a problem that she had only suspected. Since the supervisor had a good working relationship with Cindy, she was able to address the problem in a brief, effective conversation. If you do all of the basics right, you can have many of these types of conversations. If you do your daily check-in conversations, you will see if workers are correctly using their safety equipment. In fact, the check-in conversation is an excellent way to do a safety check each day. These conversations will alert you to any changes that represent a safety problem.

Employee Discipline

I have saved a situation requiring discipline to the last of the supervisory conversations because if you do the other well, you may not have many disciplinary sessions. As always, the disciplinary session is much like the other talks: calm, reasonable, professional, and helpful. These sessions focus on a specific behavior and follow company disciplinary policy. If you have done your usual outstanding job of checking in with employees every day, you will have prevented problems that could lead to discipline. In addition, you will have built a level of trust between you and your worker—and the two of you could have worked out small misunderstandings that could lead to discipline. Hopefully, you have the employees so focused and dedicated to improving performance that they would never think of doing anything that would cause performance to decline. But, in the real world, you will find people who just get crossways of the rules and need discipline.

Employee Discipline Guidelines

Be sure that the forbidden action did occur. Investigate and confirm exactly what did and did not happen, so you do not have to argue the facts.

Be clear about the reasons why the action is forbidden. You can then clearly outline all of the consequences of the action or failure to act.

Review your records for past disciplinary actions, evaluations, and notes so you know if you are talking about the first time this has happened, the second, or the third. Most companies have a progressive policy that requires different penalties for each of the three steps. Some actions require a write-up, but others require immediate termination. If necessary, talk to human resources to confirm the policy related to the offense and the response expected of you. If a layoff or termination is required, be sure that you know how to process the paperwork so the consequence is prompt and clear to the employee.

Have a plan—know what you are going to say, when and where you are going to have the meeting, and what you need to do after the meeting. I have found that if you get the first minute or two of a meeting clearly worked out, the rest will follow. Write down exactly what you are going to say. Your plan should sound calm, reasonable, and professional and should offer a way for the employee to resolve the problem and to improve. If this works out well, you may be able to improve motivation. If the situation is hopeless, you may have to adjust your plans to accommodate a new employee.

Follow your plan, take notes of the conversation, and follow-up with required actions. If you feel the need, have another supervisor sit in on the session as a witness. The witness should also make notes of the meeting. If you need to escort the employee out, take them to human resources first. There are often termination forms that need to be completed and benefits discussed.

Do not discuss disciplinary sessions with other employees. Keep it confidential, and try to preserve the motivation of the rest of the crew.

Case Study #1 of Employee Disciplinary Conference

In this case study, the supervisor is Melissa who runs the accounting department. An employee, Dewey, appears to have made some major mistakes that have cost the company thousands of dollars. Melissa reviews Dewey's file and finds that both she and the prior supervisor, Sam, have previously talked to Dewey about mistakes—but none as big as this one. Dewey seems to be able to correct a mistake if it is pointed out, but there is always another one to be found. Melissa even suspects that Dewey might be pocketing some of the petty cash and leaving false receipts. She pulls out the petty cash receipts for the last two years and finds suspicious receipts for hundreds of dollars with dates changed.

She stops in to talk to Jeff, the human resources director, and discusses what she has found. They agree that Dewey must be terminated. In order to avoid a wrongful discharge suit against the company, Jeff asks Melissa to run copies of the changed receipts and summarize the mistakes that Dewey has been making. Finally, he needs copies of the big mistake that Dewey made today, and the consequences to the company that it generated. Now they are ready to proceed with the conference.

Melissa: *Dewey, come in and close the door. I need to talk to you.*

Dewey: *Sure, Melissa, what's the problem? You sure look nice today.*

Melissa: *Dewey, this is not a social visit. I need to show you the account entry mistakes that you have been making and explain their consequences. You remember that we've discussed mistakes on several occasions. Here are your last three evaluations.*

Dewey: *Hey what is this? All of that happened a long time ago, and I corrected those mistakes, didn't I?*

Melissa: *Some of them you did correct, but you still have more. In fact, the mistakes have become more serious. Today, I found this mistake. Look at the entries to this account.*

Dewey: *What's wrong with them?*

Melissa: *Look at the correct list and the total at the bottom. Do you see how the company lost over $5,000 in billings?*

Dewey: *I will fix that. Give it to me.*

Melissa: *Dewey, there is another issue that is even more serious. I reviewed the receipts in the petty cash box that you keep. I have found the same receipt for postage over and over, with the date changed in pencil. I can only conclude that you have been keeping the cash and submitting a false receipt. This is unacceptable to company policy and requires termination at once.*

Dewey: *Not true. Someone else must have put those receipts in there. Not me!*

Melissa: *I checked that out, and no one has the key except you. And the box is your responsibility. I have the unhappy duty to ask you to leave now. Your employment is hereby terminated. Please gather your personal items and we'll go to Jeff's office to sign the papers.*

Discussion of Disciplinary Conference

Notice that most of Melissa's work was done before the conference itself, which only lasted seven minutes. Because she was so well prepared, there was little doubt as to the outcome. Notice too that she was unhappy to have to terminate an employee, but she was calm and professional, due to the preparation. Finally, the human resources department will be pleased—the likelihood of a wrongful discharge is reduced because she was so well prepared. Do you think that you could conduct this conference? Here's another one that is different, but is handled in much the same way.

Case Study #2 of Employee Disciplinary Conference

Check back in the last chapter under the topic of *performance planning*. Notice on page 137 that Chuck, the supervisor, wanted to have a conference with Carrie. She was frequently tardy, despite his discussions with her. He plans a disciplinary conference to hopefully correct this problem. Before you read the case study, take a minute and write out the plan that you would use to have this conference.

Your notes for planning this conference

Case Study for Improving Attendance

Supervisor: *Come in Carrie. I need to talk to you.*

Carrie: *Sure, what is it?*

Supervisor: *Carrie, I really need your skill and experience in this department. I hope that you know that and understand that this conversation is an effort to improve your promptness in getting into work on time each day.*

Carrie: *Oh sure, you've mentioned that several times. I can do that.*

Supervisor: *Good, I'm glad because we need you here for several reasons. First, you are experienced and can produce parts at the level that we need and at the quality that the customers require. And you have been training Becky. She hopes to learn the skills to have a good job here. Unfortunately, she is getting the idea that she can be tardy once in a while because she sees you being tardy.*

Carrie: *Oh, I hadn't noticed that.*

Supervisor: *Yes, here are your attendance records for the last three months. Take a look at them and see what you think.*

Carrie: *Wow, I didn't realize that I was the only one who had some tardies, and you say that Becky started having some too last month. I can see what you mean.*

Supervisor: *Yes, this is a significant problem, and we have talked about it several times. I'm hoping that we can work it out in this meeting and never have a problem again. Are you willing to work with me on this?*

Carrie: *Sure.*

Supervisor: *Okay. The first thing is the company policy. It says that an employee can be late up to ten minutes on three occasions before being written up. How does that fit into your record?*

Carrie: *Looks like I just slid under the wire. What does that mean?*

Supervisor: *It means that one more occasion of even a minute and I have to write you up.*

Carrie: *I've never been written up before for anything.*

Supervisor: *Of course not. You are a good employee and you want your job. I want the same thing for you. That's why I'm talking to you now before we have to have a write up meeting.*

Carrie: *Would you really write me up?*

Supervisor: *If I want to do a good job as a supervisor, I have to follow the policy and make sure that everybody gets fair treatment. I would have to write you up if you were late one more time. Is there a way that we could prevent this? What do you think it would take to get you here every day on time from here on out?*

Carrie: *Well, I get up and get out of the house at the same time every day. Then I stop at the convenience store and get my coffee. I can't get going in the morning without it. Sometimes the store is busy, and I get behind.*

Supervisor: *I'd never ask anyone to pass up coffee in the morning. You know, I keep a pot going here in my office. You're welcome to have your coffee here. Some of the other workers do that, and we talk about the work for the day. All I ask is that you come in ten minutes early so we start on time. And you'll need to bring in a can of coffee once in a while. Would that work for you?*

Carrie: *Yeah, but I'll bring in some good coffee, not that sludge you guys drink.*

Supervisor: *Sounds good to me. I'm sure we could use a cook's touch. Now one other thing. While you are talking to Becky, would you emphasize to her, as I will be doing as well, that getting here on time is essential. I think that we could get her off to a better start here if we nipped this thing in the bud.*

Carrie: *Yeah, that would be good. Can she come in for coffee too?*

Supervisor: *Of course. We work together all day, so we may as well have coffee together. I'll make a note in your file of how well this policy violation warning meeting has gone. I'll see you early tomorrow morning for coffee. Thanks, Carrie.*

Discussion of Disciplinary Conference Case Study #2

Notice that the supervisor was prepared and had the attendance records ready to show Carrie. This provided impact, got Carrie's attention, and showed her the importance of the problem. Also, he did not stop when Carrie said she would improve. He went on to show her exactly how bad the problem was, why she needed to improve, and inquired about the problem. Not all of these conferences turn out so well, but I would encourage you to understand that often workers just don't understand the urgency of a problem. Once the problem is a given, the discussion for a solution should be an easy one.

In this case, the supervisor had dealt with this problem before with other employees. He had initiated the morning coffee meeting as a voluntary option to ensure that the crew was ready to start on time. He just didn't realize that Carrie and Becky had a low opinion of his coffee-making skills. Actually, this small social interaction over coffee can be useful. During this informal time, the supervisor can make announcements, listen to concerns, and joke around to lighten the mood for the day. Finally, the supervisor said that he would be writing up the warning as a good meeting and, hopefully, he won't have to have another with Carrie or Becky.

> That doesn't sound so difficult. You don't have to get all mad and all of that, do you? I keep thinking of Harry, an old boss of mine, who was a terror. He demeaned the people who worked for him. We hated having any meeting with him at all. I vowed that I would never behave like him if I ever got to be a supervisor

Employee Discipline Case Study No. 3

Sometimes things do not go as well as in No. 2. This case study demonstrates how to handle a much more emotional situation.

Supervisor: *Shirley, come in I need to talk to you.*

Shirley: *What is it this time. You are always bugging me about something.*

Supervisor: *Calm down, Shirley. This is a time to talk and to listen, not to fight.*

Shirley: *Fight? Is that what this is all about? That fight on the floor this morning was not my fault. I was just defending myself.*

Supervisor: *Have a seat and take a deep breath. First I'll tell you that fighting is not allowed—no matter whose fault it is. I have to write you up, but then how about you reflect on the situation and tell me what was really going on.*

Shirley: *What was going on was Shelia, that fat slob, she's sleeping with my husband, and I hate her.*

Supervisor: *That sounds pretty miserable, to have her and your husband together and have to see her at work every day. Sorry, Shirley.*

Shirley: *Well, he's not much of a husband—or a father either. This isn't the first time. I've had to raise my son all by myself.*

Supervisor: *Are you getting any help with this situation, Shirley? It must be hard on you all around.*

Shirley: (Cries big tears). *Help? That's a laugh. My father left us when I was only three, and we had to fend for ourselves. All men are jerks.*

(Is this your worst nightmare conversation yet? Hang in there and see what the supervisor does next.)

Supervisor: (Hands her a box of tissues.) *I can see why you might say that, but you will be making your situation worse by getting into fights at work. Shirley, if you seek help, you can turn this situation around. I would really like to see you do that. You are part of our team, and you have a good job here. Why don't you calm down. I'll get the names and phone numbers of some counseling centers that are covered by our insurance plan. I'll help you with this—if you're willing to try too. Are you willing?*

Shirley: *Does that mean that I won't get written up? I already have a write up for fighting from last year.*

Supervisor: *I have to write you up, just like I'd write up anyone who picked a fight with you. This ensures that we have a safe and comfortable workplace. This will be the second write up on the same offense. The next step is termination, so if you want to keep your job, you will have to keep a clean record from now on. So much more the reason to get some help, don't you think?*

Shirley: *Yeah, I've got to keep this job. I guess I'll try. But what about Shelia?*

Supervisor: *Same thing goes for her. Don't worry about her or your husband. You can't change them. They'll do whatever they are going to do. Just think about you, your job, and your son. Remember that I'll help you with this. I'll check and make sure that you get the names of some good counselors and that you get to the appointments. Now, stay here for a few minutes until you are calm and then get back to work. I'm going to assign Shelia to the backroom for the rest of the week, so you two get a break from each other. I'll call you in with the write-up papers and the counseling names after lunch. Are you okay with this?*

Shirley: *Okay.* (Shirley wipes her eyes, blows her nose, and takes a deep, miserable breath).

Discussion of Disciplinary Case Study No 3

I'd be proud of you if you were this supervisor. Shows of emotion are common in disciplinary situations. As we have mentioned before, let the emotion flow for a while until the person gets calm. Then continue on with your plan. Always keep a box of tissues around. If it gets too bad, you can send the person home and reconvene the conference when the situation is calm and reasonable. If the supervisor had been a man, the insult of all men being jerks would have been offensive, but the supervisor merely ignored it. If the supervisor had been a woman, she would have ignored the temptation to agree with that negative assertion. In both cases, the supervisor would continue on with completing the write-up and referring her to counseling. Using his best motivator of helping her to save her job, the supervisor remained the helpful coach. The supervisor also had an interest in Shirley getting help because he or she didn't want to see a good worker fired and have to train a new one.

This issue is far from being resolved. Shirley and Shelia might meet somewhere outside of work and decide to have it out, resulting in one or both spending some time in jail, or worse. But the supervisor cannot control that. The supervisor made a good contribution by getting a positive goal established. If the supervisor does eventually have to fire Shirley, it can be said that he represented the company well—and did everything possible to help Shirley save her job, while protecting the safe working environment in the plant.

Additional steps that must be taken are (1) to complete the write-up papers and to have Shirley sign them, (2) conduct a similar disciplinary session with Shelia, and (3) to follow-up with the counseling referrals. When talking with Shelia, do not get into marriage counseling issues and do not condemn her personal life, or take sides. It would take a professional counselor months to determine who is telling the truth and how to resolve this situation. You don't have those skills or the time, and it is not part of your job. Discipline her for fighting and offer to get her counseling assistance, just as you did for Shirley. I hope that you are seeing that this is actually a rather simple plan and can be accomplished in a calm and reasonable manner. It's a situation that you can handle and still maintain motivation for productive work.

Summary

Take a moment and fill in the following questions:

1. What is your worst disciplinary situation that you might be dreading? Reread the case studies and write out an approach that you think might work. If you can imagine a good plan, when it happens to you on the job, you will be ready to handle it.

2. List five things that you have learned about having these conferences with employees:

The Last of the Personality Ranges

Go back to your questionnaire and take note of your score for P or J. Put an X on the dotted line where your scores fall.

Perceiver	Judger

6-------5------4------3------2-------1------0-------1------2------3-------4-------5------6

Perceiver	Judger
Takes time to gain perfection	Wraps things up ASAP
Quality thinking	Production thinking
Avoids decisions	Pre-empts decisions, avoids input
Flexible, adaptable, experiments	Inflexible, gives orders, controls
Open for changes	Limits change and flexibility
Bends rules	Enforces rules
Thinks the unconventional thought	Conventional thinker
Has time for everything	Prioritizes and ignores the secondary
Often doesn't finish projects in process	Makes lists and gets things done
Has multiple projects	Likes one project at a time
Wants to lighten things up	Wants to tie things down
Does not manage time well	Manages time very well

Asks important, but unpopular questions	Makes good time on wrong road
Very patient	Very impatient
Is scarce in manufacturing	Dominates manufacturing
Likes to challenge with alternatives	Hates alternatives, wants to control
Values disorder and chaos	Values order and structure
Capable of being brilliant at something	Prefers to conform to standard
Interested in having fun	Workaholic
Seems irresponsible and uncontrollable	Overly responsible and controlling
Works well without structure	Always creates structure
Frequently tardy, but works overtime	Fiercely punctual
Resists schedules	Makes and enforces schedules
Does not manage money well	Manages money through budgets
Free spirit, likable	Hard worker, reliable, humorless
Doesn't like to be boxed in— needs options	Likes to box people in and limit options

Best Case

Takes on difficult, time-consuming jobs	Good scheduler and production mgr
Argues for better quality	Gets goods out the door

Worst Case

Sloppy, unorganized, unproductive	Humorless, controlling taskmaster

Weaknesses

Can destroy teamwork with perfectionism	Fails to get enough input, teams suffers
Takes too much time or money, unrealistic	Doesn't allow enough time for quality
Too late and disorganized to function.	Works too long and hard. Dies in boots
So rebellious and disruptive that people avoid	Overcontrols until people rebel

Description of the Judger Personality Type

Note: Do not be too concerned with the names Judger and Perceiver. These terms came into use when they were popular psychology terms. For our purposes, we can refer to them as J and P.

Judgers are people who are concerned with getting things completed on time. Their idea of being productive is to set timelines and lists in their minds and work hard at getting as much completed within the timeframe as possible. They have strong organization skills and can prioritize well, based on time. In pursuit of this goal, they guard their own time closely, while trying to hurry everything and everyone along—even at the risk of having quality suffer. For this reason, they give the impression of being impatient.

This approach, often called production thinking, gives the impression that Judgers don't have time for anything other than their own agenda. You may find these individuals hard to locate when you need to talk, as they are always on the phone or in a meeting. Yet, you know that they get an enormous amount of work done. Even if you catch up with them, they may want you to be brief and get to the point quickly. They will probably have a pad to make note of what you want and then get back to you later. Note that completing that list is central to the success of their day. If you can get on that list, you are pretty sure to have your concern handled. Conversely, if you want to get them to work on something for you, give them a list. Judgers feel compelled to go down that list until all is completed.

Another characteristic of Judgers is their ability to control. They seem to have an internal agenda, and they set out to get all of us to do what they want. This is not to say that this control is for selfish ends. Rather, it is for the sake of completing the schedule or list in a timely manner. If we want to talk about it or try something else, we create frustration for them. The Js would really rather we just do it their way. This can seem bossy, and people can take exception to the tone of their direction. Again, this is all done to accomplish a goal.

Judgers are actually conventional thinkers who follow the traditional and prescribed methods of thought and action. These traditional methods are predictable and thereby efficient. They can be trusted to yield predictable results in a predictable period of time. These are not *think outside of the box* people. This tendency to control through conventional methods often comes across as being inflexible and rigid, since additional input or creative ideas are avoided. A Judger wants you to *just do it the right way right now*.

These traits are essential in our society. Judger thought process ensures that all banks do transactions the same way, telephone calls go as routed, computers function as expected, airplanes fly as scheduled, etc. A Judger is a good disciplinarian, controller, and production-oriented force in any organization. They are responsible, prompt, and generally productive. In fact, one of their faults is that they work too hard. They can be guilty of being workaholics in pursuit of standards and schedules. When it comes to time off and relaxation, they are sometimes at a loss, preferring to work when they are at home. In fact, if you Judgers would tell the truth, you are making mental lists of tasks to be done as you drive into work. And be honest, you make lists for work at home too.

What a wonderful worker this person is. Are there any faults that you could find with such an approach to life? As with all of the traits, the greatest strengths can become weaknesses through overindulgence, without consideration of people or circumstances. Imagine a Judger who over controls a group of people by not accepting their input. In time, it would become de-motivating, and the workers would feel like they were order takers and not really teammates. If the Judger was extreme enough, it is possible that the team would rebel and refuse to follow the Judger's leadership. The production mentality might demand that we ship a product regardless of the quality and thereby jeopardize customer relations.

There would also be personal consequences to the Judger. Over controlling and over working could lead to fatigue, illness, and disability. As in all of the ranges, traits need to be used in an appropriate manner that furthers teamwork and productivity.

An additional factor to consider here is the combination of the Thinker traits with those of the Judger. The T-J combination has a multiplying effect in regards to controlling and driving people past their limits. If you recall from our previous classes, the Thinker is a high control set of traits focused on achievement of goals. If you combine the T with the J, you have a person who is dedicated to the goal. They control time, money, resources, and people to achieve that goal. What a good definition of a high achiever. If you add the trait of being an Extrovert, you will find that this high achiever is also persuasive and possibly aggressive. Experience has shown that there many T-J's in the business world—they are so good at getting work done. Done properly, these traits make a super worker or boss. Overdone, these traits can make a humorless taskmaster who unwittingly undermines teamwork. If you find yourself in this category, welcome to the key insight that will cause you to be even more effective in whatever career you pursue. In order to further this insight, I will proceed to explain what is at the other end of the range.

Description of the Perceiver Personality Type

Perceivers are people who do not like to control or be controlled. This personality always likes to have options and choices. They do not work with a list. They see possibilities that are constantly changing, requiring adaptation, flexibility, and spontaneity. They are usually unconventional thinkers who do not follow the prescribed methods, rules, or procedures. They are creative and adaptive and often develop new methods of doing things each time they do something.

There is nothing predictable about a Perceiver. They see the world as a constant surprise and opportunity to respond in a unique manner. While the Judger's thought process is as straight as an arrow, the Perceiver's thought is circular, looking all around, and considering all aspects of a question. It would be common to be talking to a Perceiver and have the conversation *change channels* frequently. The Perceiver discusses all that is known about a topic. It might seem laborious, but such a process includes many people into the discussion—and all of the information that is available. Although it is hard to make too many mistakes with this approach, it will take a lot of time.

Here's the downside. Perceivers do not look forward to completing a project or task. They are having so much fun doing the work that they don't particularly want it to end. For that reason, they are not good with schedules and deadlines.

They are such good multi-taskers that they are perfectly comfortable starting several projects at a time. Their method is to work on one task for a while, then another for a while and so forth. Consequently, they usually have several uncompleted tasks underway at all times. If you look at their workspace, it will look like piles, each pile representing a project. Before you ridicule the seeming mess, remember that all of those projects could be completed at a given time. A lot of work could be represented in what looks like an unorganized pile.

On the other hand, Judgers have neat and tidy workspaces, and like to work on one thing at a time until completed. Then they will take on another.

If you think that the sharing of workspaces or home spaces is difficult between the two, you are correct. The J wants to clean up, organize, and throw away unnecessary items. The P wants to collect anything that might be pertinent, keep it around, handy at all times, and use any materials to create a new project for no particular reason, other than to have fun.

At home, the battleground is often the garage or workshop. The potential for conflict is enormous unless each realizes the value of the other's approach. With better organization and scheduling, the Perceiver would do better, and with more flexibility, patience, and creativity, the Judger would do better. Patience, tolerance, and respect are key.

While the Judger likes to control and limit choices, the Perceiver wants freedom, choices, and input. The Perceiver is the one who argues to protect our freedoms, objects to limitations, and is willing to go way out on a limb to be different. Perceivers may have their own non-conforming style of clothes, car, home, or lifestyle. They may not be effective in production environments, but on projects and unique situations that require research, perfectionism, and innovation, they cannot be matched.

An example comes to mind of a car mechanic that the team called Gizmo. His hair was a mess, his clothes were from Goodwill, and his truck was a collage of bumper stickers. He knew a little bit about everything and was skilled in all aspects of maintenance, but was not time efficient. His teammates had learned over the years that, if there was a difficult problem that would take a long time to figure out or needed custom parts fabricated, they should assign it to Gizmo. After everyone else had given up on a problem, Gizmo would take hours studying the problem, trying different approaches, and fine-tuning ranges of parts until he got it to work. In the meantime, the rest of the team worked on all of the other cars in the shop and did all of the routine maintenance work. They would all look forward to seeing what he came up with—they learned so much from his *out of the box* thinking. Although he looked a little strange, they respected the quality of thought and work that he contributed to the shop. And he appreciated that they gave him the challenge and freedom to do what he was good at doing.

Perceivers have a tendency to be perfectionists and to lose track of time. But they are usually patient people who take the time to do things, even if they miss their other assignments. An example would be a Perceiver parent who has chores to do, like mowing the lawn, changing the oil in the car, paying bills, or doing laundry, but the Perceiver's child comes home with a school project—making a bird feeder. The Perceiver parent will let all of the other chores go unattended and get all of the best equipment, glues, and paints. The parent will patiently teach the child how to build the bird feeder. This parent provides quality time with the child, while teaching skills that might launch a future career. But, of course, the rest of the chores are undone.

On the other hand, the Judger parent would work the bird feeder project into the schedule later. The Judger parent would put minimal time into the project, but make sure that everything was done on time. Neither approach is right or wrong, and most of us are a blend of the two. There are times and situations where one or the other is better, but also times when a blend of the two works well, such as when Perceivers do projects and Judgers do schedules. Since the Judger finds projects difficult and the Perceiver finds schedules too confining, both will be better off investing respect, patience, and tolerance into achieving true teamwork.

How Perceiver-Judger Traits Interact at Home

How these personality differences affect home life is both obvious and important. It is easy to spot the Perceiver children. They are likely to be disorganized, messy, late, happy, brilliant at some things, and sometimes lost in thought or work. They may not get along well in school because they are nonconformists. They will excel on projects, art, music, writing, shop, or science. They are not purposely disobedient or difficult, but have their own ideas about what they want to work on, how to dress, and are oblivious of time. They can function well without structure and rarely create it themselves. These children have the potential for greatness, but it will probably not be in highly regimented environments.

Judger children are neat, tidy, organized, prompt, and motivated to get good grades and to seek approval. They happily conform to rules and procedures and are comfortable with boundaries and limitations. In school, they do well in math, history, science, sports, and test taking. Teachers like these children because they are so organized, respond well to direction, and follow the rules. They are capable of greatness in situations that require organization, control, discipline, and timeliness.

In families, there is a tendency to favor the child who is most like the dominate parent. If both of these types of children show up in one family, the one who is most like the dominant parent will be preferred. Can you imagine (or perhaps you can remember) the question, *Why can't you be like your brother? He keeps his room neat and gets good report cards. What's wrong with you?* This is probably a Judger parent comparing a Perceiver child to a Judger child with this completely irrational question.

As we discussed early in this book, children exhibit their dominant traits by age five, and those traits do not change substantially for the rest of their lives. Comparing one type against another is assuming that one is better than the other—and that a child could change just to please a parent. The best advice for parents is to recognize the different strengths and weaknesses of your children and to help them to be their best—within their own type. Unfavorable comparisons only serve to destroy self esteem. In addition, try to guide your children into courses, activities, and careers where they will be well suited and able to excel. Urging a Perceiver child to become an accountant is setting them up for failure, just as urging a Judger child to become an artist has a low likelihood of success.

How a Supervisor Can Use the P-J Traits to Improve Performance

Keep in mind that a supervisor can be either a Perceiver or a Judger. A Perceiver supervisor tends to be good at reacting to situations on the spur of the moment and able to multi task, but poor at organizing, enforcing rules, and discipline.

A Judger supervisor tends to be structured, organized, good with standards and rules, and a good disciplinarian. The Judger supervisor, though, is poor at communicating, listening, motivating, and employee involvement.

All of the workers who report to you will be either Perceivers or Judgers, and the work environment that you manage will have either Perceiver or Judger aspects. It would be wise to put Perceiver workers in any position that requires multiple concurrent activities or interactions with people that require spontaneous reactions. Situations where there is a lot of change, batch work, or project work would be appropriate for Perceivers. Judgers would be effective in situations where there is a lot of structure, rules, deadlines, procedures, and discipline. They don't mind work that is repetitive because they delight in being able to perfect the pace and timing of work.

When you see these traits in people, you can now understand how best to utilize these strengths and avoid putting people in situations where they are likely to fail. The other aspect is that when you see a worker underperforming or even misbehaving, look at how good a match the work situation is to the worker's traits. You'd be surprised at how many work problems can be resolved by personality matching.

I've been giving you case studies that relate to your supervisory situations, but just for curiosity sake, let's look at how the Perceiver-Judger traits play out on a larger scale. This case study is about two people who build a successful company from the ground up. You might see some parallels within the management structure of your own company or organization.

Case Study: Perceiver and Judger

Ten years ago, Steve, the founder of Pro Motion Industries, was tinkering in his garage with his motorcycle. After months of painstaking work, he perfected a type of throttle that improved the performance of the bike and made it easier and safer for the rider to control the bike's speed. Deciding to develop a business to promote his invention, he applied for patent protection and began to promote the product. He started by making each part by hand, but soon bought some automated machines. The first three months, he shipped six parts and lost $10,000. Ignoring the loss, he was happy doing what he loved and was proud of his work. All of this so absorbed his time and attention that his wife and kids had to look to see if the lights were on in the garage just to know where he was. His wife got a part-time job and took over paying the household bills.

The second year of business, he could not keep up with the orders and was forced to hire a machinist, Dan, against his better judgment. This turned out to be a disaster because even though Dan had a great deal of machining experience, he could never do it well enough to suit Steve. Dan tried to get along with Steve and to please him, but they were not shipping enough parts to make payroll, so Dan quit.

Several more machinists followed Dan, until Steve met Bill. Bill understood the need to get parts made, shipped, and paid for. Instead of making parts, he took over the management of the orders, and Steve got back to making parts. After learning to trust each other, Bill eventually convinced Steve to hire another machinist, and Steve trained the new recruit in all of his ways of making parts. Bill made prints, schedules, standards, invoicing, and did bookkeeping for the business, and good parts were soon being shipped on time. Money began to flow in, so they bought more machines and improved their advertising. The business grew and grew until Bill started talking about having part ownership. Steve felt that Bill had been a big help, but he had been the inventor and would be the only person able to see the company's future. Bill reasoned that managing the business so that it was profitable was what was important. Eventually Steve saw the wisdom of giving Bill some ownership. Bill took over the business management and production, and Steve managed the sales. It turned out that Steve talked with customers so enthusiastically about the product that orders increased. The company continued to prosper, but Steve was always looking at new ideas.

At one point, Steve thought that it was time to improve the product again and began experimenting in his garage. Bill pointed out that improvements would mean re-tooling, and the results would not be substantial enough to warrant the costs. They would, in fact, be in competition with themselves. He was in favor of just making as much money as possible with the current product. Bill would not give in. Because he was part owner, Bill created a major obstacle to Steve's vision. Eventually, Steve felt so limited and boxed in by Bill that he sold out his share and patent to Bill and left the company. He then returned to his garage and began his beloved experimentation. He came up with several more good ideas, but none of them ever got off the ground. Bill continued to build Pro Motion Industries on the existing products, fearfully watching as better products severely cut into his market share. Eventually, the company declined due to lack of innovation. The result was that neither was successful on their own. Steve and Bill actually remained cordial, but secretly were happy not to work together. Unfortunately, they bailed out on the challenge and success of putting all of their traits together into a long term successful business.

1. Discuss how Steve's Perceiver qualities were both a strength and weakness.

2. Discuss how Bill's Judger qualities were both a help and a hindrance to him.

3. How could better teamwork have made this story turn out differently?

Discussion of Perceiver-Judger Case Study

Take note of Steve's strong Perceiver traits—innovation, wide spectrum of skills, losing track of time, perfectionism, enjoyment of the work, lack of concern for the many aspects of a business that need to be controlled to generate profit, patience, resisting limitations, sales ability, and desire to return to the original work of innovation. Despite the potential for conflict, it was a great day when Bill, thinking from the other end of the range, started to build the teamwork. His ability to schedule, price, invoice, standardize, and discipline placed limitations on Steve, but the trade off was beneficial. The efficiencies created by the control and structure generated the profit needed to fund the growth and to assure reliable products on time. Every business has a need for both traits, and it requires good teamwork from the P-J range to become productive.

Steve needed to learn to tolerate some limitations, and Bill needed to learn to let Steve do some of his activities unimpeded. In the end, the teamwork broke down, as Steve's desire to further innovate could not be supported by the rigid structure that Bill had built. The stress and difficulty of two extremes working so closely together had also taken its toll on a personal level. After the break up, they may have felt some relief from the stress, but neither of them was as successful as they would have been together.

Summary of Class Seven

In this class, we looked at some of the many meetings that a supervisor will need to have with his or her workers. Take a minute and review the roleplays that you have studied, and list what you have learned about these critical motivation opportunities.

Notes

As you learn about your own traits, you will naturally see how you can improve on your weaknesses and thereby become a supervisor with all of your strengths and few, if any, weaknesses. This is exactly what we hope to accomplish through this program. In the last class, we will be more specific about individual combination of traits and how to utilize them to your benefit.

As we have done in past classes, take a break and tryout some of the approaches that you think will work for you. Try adapting them to fit your work situation. If necessary, reread the roleplays and try again. As you have some successes, you will become more and more comfortable with finding the right words and approaches that work for you. Look at your team. Identify who might be a Perceiver and who might be a Judger. Question how well matched each is to their job situation. If the answer is not favorable, look for a way to adjust duties so that the people who work for you are able to work at their best potential.

> *"Be who you are and say what you feel, because those who mind don't matter and those who matter don't mind."*
>
> Dr. Seuss

Class Eight

In this class, we will discuss one additional conversation that you might have to conduct—Employment Interviews. Even if this is not typically something that you do, it is a professional skill that you will someday need to have. And it is always interesting to see the process from the other side of the desk.

Second, we will take all that we have learned and put it together into the career of one person so that you can see how the sequence occurs in real life.

Third, we will take all that you have learned about the personality traits and see how much you now know about what makes people behave the way that they do.

Last, we will have a graduation exercise that will acknowledge your study, experimentation, and application of the material that we have presented.

Interviewing Skills for Supervisors:

How many times have you sat in front of someone's desk interviewing for a prospective job? We have all been successful and unsuccessful. Now that you are the one hiring, your purpose for interviewing is to get an accurate and complete view of the applicant's appropriateness for the position.

Most people's resume is useful for pre-screening an applicant before the interview. Let's say that you have 20 resumes in front of you for a job that requires a high school diploma, at least three years experience in the career field, and basic computer skills. Before you even consider talking to a candidate, go through every resume and discard any that does not meet your three criteria. Your pile is now a bit smaller.

Next, you need to evaluate those you might talk to on the phone and possibly schedule a face-to-face interview. Sort the remaining resumes into three piles according to how well they match your job description: *best*, *good*, and *least*. Now go through the best, call them up on the phone to find out if they are still available and interested in the job, hours, and pay range. If so, pick the top five and schedule five interviews. At this point, you have already achieved a lot with only a small time commitment. Since the interview is the time when you can best assess the candidate, be sure that you are only talking to people who can meet the job criteria and are interested—and you are interested in them.

How to Conduct an Interview:

Your first goal is to get both the candidates and yourself relaxed. This is the best way to get a true picture of the candidate, not a carefully constructed persona that disappears as soon as you hire them. Be friendly and cordial and talk about something of common interest—the weather, the local community, or the company's products or services. People will give you a non-verbal sign when they relax, such as sitting back in a chair, smiling, crossing their legs, or visibly relaxing their posture. Be sure that you are relaxed. No candidate will relax if the interviewer is tense. If you begin the interview before the candidate is relaxed, the rest of the talk may be an inaccurate presentation of the candidate.

Next, you can start with the resume. As you know, it is hard to put your life story on one sheet of paper. I ask candidates to tell their work history from the start to the finish. Start with the town where they grew up and maybe what kind of work their parents did. I've seen candidates who are third generation masters of their craft. Stories from childhood and school often can also reveal a lot about a person's character and personality. I remember one candidate who was the oldest boy of a large family and took over the operation of their small farm, while his father worked in the city. The work ethic, responsibility, initiative, self reliance, and problem solving skills that he learned from this difficult childhood was evident throughout his career. It was a strong trait that I was looking for in the opening that I was trying to fill.

Proceed onto the first full-time work experience. Ask why they started work in that position. What did they like about the job? What did they not like? What kind of a supervisor did they have? What did they learn? Why did they leave? Go through each job listed on the resume looking for any gaps of employment, evidence of being fired or obvious setbacks.

If you are sincerely interested in a candidate, you can then construct some hypothetical situations and ask them to respond. An example would be: *Suppose that you receive customer complaints about your work. What would be your response?* Or, *Suppose that the work instructions that you were given were obviously not working and your supervisor is nowhere to be found. What would you do?* Or, *Suppose you were working on an AC1200 and it would not start.*

What would you do? This is assuming that you know what a non-starting AC1200 would be like and could determine if the candidate was accurate in their answers.

As you listen to the interviewee, evaluate what personality type you might be hiring. The test that I have supplied for you is not appropriate for pre-employment testing, but once you learn the ranges, it is relatively easy to spot the main personality types without a test. If you are pretty sure, for example, that you are interviewing an Extrovert, you will know what their weaknesses might be. You might observe how well they have listened to you. This might give you an idea of how well the candidate has overcome the Extrovert's main weakness: failure to listen. Do the same with the other ranges, and you will soon have the ability to predict how the person might perform. Remember to look for a good match to the job situation. You might enjoy talking with the Extrovert, but if the job is a lonely one in an isolated area, the candidate will not be happy and won't perform well. You'd be wiser to find a good Introvert. In addition, consider the other people the new hire will need to interact with. If they are all pretty well introverted, a mild Extrovert might improve the communication to a better level. Consider also the person that the candidate will report to. If that is you, think about how happy you will be to see that person show up day after day for years and years.

Finally, remember that all of us have a little intuitive voice within us that sends completely irrational hunches. You might have no particular reason, but you might suspect that the candidate is lying about one job. Never . . . I repeat, . . .never ignore these hunches. People communicate with much more than words, and your subconscious can pick up on more information than your conscious mind can. At some point in the interview, you should ask an off-the-wall question. Examples are: *Why didn't you stay at such a good job?, What else was going on with you at that time?, Why do you want this job?, What was the worst day you've had at work?, What was the best?* The answers to these unusual questions can sometimes tell the real story about a person's motivation, work history, and character.

After you have asked questions to your satisfaction, thank the candidate, tell them that you have other candidates to interview, and that a decision is still a while off. Leave yourself the option of interviewing further candidates and taking more time to consider the hire. Don't ever offer the job on the spot, unless you are desperate. The next candidate that you see might be the best that walks the earth, and you might have to retract your offer made to the first. Also, comparing one candidate against another can help you to decide which qualities are really going to be the best match. It is always an option to call the finalists back to talk on the phone or interview again before you decide. A good match can reap rewards for you for years to come. A bad match will be problems, misery, and setbacks for years to come.

Guidelines for Interviewing

- Try to put the candidate at ease. Start with small talk. Smile. Discuss something of mutual interest.

- Try to get the candidate to do most of the talking. Avoid saying too much yourself.

- Ask the candidate to explain job history from start to present.

- Ask questions about why the candidate chose jobs, why the candidate left, and gaps in between.

- Rephrase important questions several times and compare the responses.

- Observe body language, changes in speech, facial expressions, etc.

- Ask what the candidate liked about previous jobs and what was disliked or difficult.

- Ask what the candidate wants out of this prospective job.

- Ask about the type of supervision the candidate had at other jobs, the work environment, etc.

- Remember that candidates try to sell themselves , so will put their best foot forward. Look for weaknesses and strengths.

- Try to identify the personality type. Ask questions to determine how strong the candidate might be in particular traits. Think about how the characteristics would match the prospective job.

- Let the candidate ask questions. Observe what questions are asked.

- Observe dress and manners, but don't be deceived by appearances. Look at consistency of appearances to attitudes and values.

- Ask questions that will allow you to check references.

- Thank the candidate for the time and explain the next step in the process. Don't promise anything. The next candidate may change the picture significantly.

DO NOT ASK ABOUT

It is illegal—and most likely against your company policy—to ask the following:

- Age. Graduation dates are OK.

- Religious or social affiliations.

- Marital status.

- Ethnic status, race, or national origin. You can ask if they are a U. S. citizen and you can require immigration papers.

- Health history or disability history. You can ask if they are physically able to do the job.

- Criminal history other than a felony.
- Credit history.

Any testing that you want to do must have been approved for pre-employment testing purposes. Check with your human resources department.

Interviewing Roleplay

Interviewer: *Welcome, Roger. Have a seat. Did you have any trouble with the snow?*

Candidate: *Oh no. I used to live in Wisconsin, and I'm used to heavy snow. This is just enough for skiing.*

Interviewer: *Sounds like you enjoy the snow. How long did you live in Wisconsin?*

Candidate: (Relaxing in his chair) *Actually, I grew up there. We had a big family and lived in a small town. There weren't many jobs, so we all left and moved to bigger cities.*

Interviewer: *Raising a big family is a challenge. What did your father do for a living?*

Candidate: *Dad was a welder and he was a perfectionist about it. People came from far and wide to get him to do work, but for a while he traveled with an oil company doing welding on oil rigs. I was the second oldest, so me and my brother did all of the chores at home, and Dad taught us how to weld early on so we did some of the local jobs when Dad was away.*

Interviewer: *Sounds like you got an early start on your career. How did you find your first job at Jenkins Metalworking?*

Candidate: *Mr. Jenkins knew my Dad and hired me the day after I finished high school.*

Interviewer: *What did you like about that job?*

Candidate: *The money. I made more money than any of my friends. The work was repetitive and not much of a challenge. I worked there for two years and started looking around for something more interesting.*

Interviewer: *What makes a job interesting for you?*

Candidate: *I like to have a different weld each day—something that I have to try to figure out and perfect. Once I perfect something, I want something new to try. That's why I went to Wilson's Custom Fab Shop. I liked it there a lot, and I worked there for ten years until the owner died and the family sold the business. It was never the same after that. Old man Wilson always made work fun.*

Interviewer: *So, that brings us to this job. What are you looking for in this position of production welder?*

Candidate: *I heard that you paid really well and that the work wasn't hard. I have a family, and I need good benefits. Do you give two weeks of vacation the first year?*

Interviewer: *No. Just one week the first year. I want you to understand that this job requires doing the same weld over and over again, day after day. There's not much that is new in terms of welding. Do you think that it would suit you?*

Candidate: *Sure. I need the work. When can I start?*

Interviewer: *I can't offer the job today. I have a number of other candidates to interview. The next step in the process is to finish all of the interviews and then select the best candidates. It may take several weeks. Thanks for your time. It's been nice talking to you. Is this the best number to reach you if we need to?*

Candidate: *Yeah, that's my cell phone. You can get me anytime. I hope that I get the job.*

Discussion of Interviewing Roleplay

What do you think of the candidate? The interviewee is probably a talented welder with a good work ethic, but definitely not suited for repetitive production work. Although you could hire him—and he would come to work—he would not be happy long, and would start looking for a more custom welding work environment.

What do you think of the interviewer's skills? The interviewer got to the conclusion rather quickly in a relaxed and friendly manner. There was no need to go further, since he was sure that this candidate would not be a good match. Had the position required a talented and versatile welder, the interview might have gone longer so that the interviewer could satisfy himself about the work history and the skills. A request to do a welding skill test with the supervisor observing would be appropriate, as the skill level could only be demonstrated with actual conditions. Also, notice that the interviewer was using an easy and comfortable line of questioning that got the candidate to talk. Does this sound like something that you could do?

Interviewing Skills Notes

1. List some of the questions that you liked and think that you might use while interviewing.

2. List three guidelines that you learned about interviewing that you did not already know.

3. List one or two personality traits that you know this candidate has. How would these traits affect his work performance?

Putting it all together: Supervising John

In this exercise, we will assume that you are the supervisor and John is a candidate to work for you. Let's roleplay to see how you would interview, train, counsel, direct, discipline, and evaluate him over a period of several years. This exercise will require you to assess his personality, skills and experience, learn how to motivate him, and translate all of this into excellent performance. You will have to use all of the skills that we discussed. I'll put some comments in brackets to guide you. This is part of your graduation exercise. It will give you insight into how to take all of the skills we have been discussing and blend them into a successful supervisory experience.

Interviewing John

Notes regarding John's interview: He is in the early twenties, big and strong, but has minimal work experience. During high school, he worked in fast food, mowed lawns, and helped his Dad as a car mechanic. In school, he took industrial arts and did well in machine trades, but did poorly in social studies and English. He is applying for the position of general factory worker and will report to you.

You: *Welcome, John. Have a seat. Nice day today isn't it?* (Get him to relax)
John: *All week has been good. My car club did a rally last Saturday and it was beautiful.*

You: *You like cars?* (Get him to tell stories that might reveal his motivation)

John: *Yeah, my dad taught me how to work on cars, and I saved up my money and bought a 'Cuda' and fixed it up. It's pretty hot. Do you want to see a picture of it?*

You: *Sure, let's see what you did.* (You can see that he did a great job on his car.) *It must have taken a lot of work to restore this.*

John: *Work nothing. I spent a year and every penny I made on it, but all of the guys in my car club say that it is the best that they've ever seen.*

You: *Good. There are several people here who are into restoring cars. Tell me, John, about your work experiences other than cars.* (Get him to discuss his job history.)

John: *Well, I worked a fast food job for two years. I started doing stocking and cleanup and then moved up to the drive-up window. I liked talking to customers.*

You: *What did you like about that job?* (Get him to talk about his successes.)

John: *I like to be busy all day. I liked the stocking job because I work out and lifting builds body. I noticed that they were wasting space in the cooler, so I suggested a way to keep large boxes on the bottom and small on the top. The manager liked that. Working the window was a lot of sitting, but I liked talking to the customers. A lot of my friends would come by and talk to me.* (His good idea might indicate that he is an Intuitive.)

You: (You are getting the impression that John is an Extrovert.) *What did you dislike at that job?* (Get him to talk about his weaknesses.)

John: *It didn't pay well and the hours changed every week. I wanted better pay, regular hours, you know, a real job. My Dad says that it's time for me to grow up.*

You: (You can see that John's motivation in life right now is to hold a good job with good pay in order to support his car interests. And he is willing to do physical labor. He doesn't have any factory skills, but he seems intelligent and can get along with people. He is a good candidate for your entry-level position. You are thinking about how he will work with you.) *John, how did you get along with your manager at the fast food store?*

John: *Sid? He was a pretty good manager, I guess. He was friendly, but not well organized. Like I said, I don't like standing around doing nothing. I like to be busy. Just tell me what to do and I'll get it done.*

You: (You are thinking that if he needs to be busy and likes organization; he is probably a Judger.) *If you get this position, you would report to me. I have a lot of work to be done, but I am organized, and I need the work done exactly by the work instructions. No changes without approval.*

John: *I am always getting new ideas that can improve things. Do you want me to make suggestions?*

You: (This is an indication of an Intuitive and may be the one area where you will have to watch John. He will have to be trained on the necessity of following instructions.) *Yes, I always ask for suggestions, but we have a process for reviewing changes, and we don't make any changes until it has been approved. Can you live with that?*

John: *Sure, boss.*

You: *Thanks for coming in. The next step in the process is for me to interview all of the other candidates, finish the screening, and then make a selection. It will be a week or so.* (Don't make any promises at this time.)

John: *Thanks, I'd really like to have this job.*

John's New Employee Orientation

John has been screened, hired, and has completed the standard company orientation video. He is reporting to you for work today.

You: *Welcome, John, to the assembly department. I am your supervisor. I will give you your work assignments and, if you have any problems, you will come to me. We will work it out together.* (Establish your authority early.) *In fact, I like to talk to everyone everyday at the beginning of the shift, so that is a good time for you to bring up any question that you have. But don't hesitate to talk to me anytime.* (Establish good communication early.)
We're going to start with a plant tour, and then I will assign you to work with Harry, my trainer, who will show you the products and how the department works. After Harry has worked with you for a while, I will assign you to this stock room. As you can see, it needs a lot of work. I'll show you how we need it organized, but I'll be glad to hear your ideas as well. (If he is an Intuitive, don't miss out on any good ideas that he can give you.) *Any questions?*

John: *Great. When do I get started?*

You: *Harry, I'd like to introduce you to John. He will be our new stock service man. Would you give him a plant tour and explain how our plant produces our products?*

While Harry shows John around, you have talked to all of the other workers, set up the schedule for the day, and checked the quality report from yesterday. You've also attended the morning production meeting. There you were told that, since orders are down, reductions in operating costs are required. You leave the meeting trying to think of some ideas for reducing costs, but know that your best suggestions will come from discussing ideas with each worker tomorrow as you make your daily rounds of check-in conversations.

When John returns, you ask him for any questions and then take him to the stock room.

You: *Well, John, this will be your project. As Harry explained, some of the smaller parts and supplies needed for assembly are kept in this room. You are responsible for making sure that no assembler ever runs out of essential stock. We've kept records and know how much you have to keep at each workstation each hour. Don't over stock because we don't have much room at the workstation. Each assembler makes a bonus based on how many units they produce, so if you let them run out, it costs them money in their paycheck. Don't ever let that happen. There is a big paperwork part to this job as well. We need to keep track of every part and supply so we can contain costs and keep our quality high so our customers keep buying from us.* (Explain the goals in terms of the customer needs.) *Glenn will be working this job until we get you trained, so he will show you how to stock the workstations and fill out the paperwork. Also you will have to take the company forklift training and get certified to operate the lift. We'll do that tomorrow. For today, help Glenn and ask a lot of questions.*

John: *Wow, I didn't know that I'd get to drive a forklift. This is going to be fun.*

You: *Now don't be thinking that it is anything like your 'Cuda,' John.* (You both laugh.) *By the way, Glenn restored a '67 Mustang. You two will probably get along just great.*

You leave John with Glenn and finish out your day. You have notes in your notebook to greet John in the morning and answer any of his questions. You will also discuss cost savings with your crew as you make your rounds. And you have to arrange for John's forklift training the next day.

The next day, as you make your check-in conversations, the workers have already sized up John. They say that he struts around as if he has a lot of self confidence, but really, he has no idea of what he is doing. The older, experienced employees immediately give him the friendly nickname *The Pup*. They can see that they will have to help him while he is learning to do the stocking job. You come away from your rounds with three good suggestions for cost savings. You take a minute to write them up and evaluate how well they might succeed. You email them to the plant manager, who is impressed with how quickly you got back to him and what good ideas you have. Your notebook helped you to impress your boss with little time or effort. You chuckle to yourself that all good ideas come from the workers, and you plan to give them all of the credit when credit is due. Praise is a positive motivator for getting future suggestions.

You also have a note that one worker will need to leave early next Tuesday, so you talk to Harry about covering for her. Following up with her communicates that your care about even a small employee concern. You review the production reports and notice that another worker is improving, so you make a note to ask her tomorrow why she is doing better. A short conversation may help you to capitalize on an improvement opportunity. She may have learned a better way to do part of the job. You make sure that John gets to the truck training. You check in with Glenn, who thinks that John will do well at this job. Glenn says that he learns fast, is strong, and works hard. Glenn thinks that he could turn over the job to

John within one week. You make a note and thank Glenn for helping John as a positive motivator for Glenn.

John's Employee Involvement Conversation

When John has been working for about a month, during one of your daily check-in conversations, you ask him if he has any ideas for improving the stock room. In particular, you are looking for something that would save some operating costs. At this point, you are glad that John is an Intuitive rather than a Sensor.

You: *Hi, John, how's it going today?* (Good open-ended question.)

John: *Pretty good. I think that I'm getting the hang of this. There haven't been any complaints about being out of stock have there?*

You: *Nope, not a one. That's a pretty good record for having only been here for a month.* (Mentioning that you have high expectations for him encourages high performance.) *Good job. I've got something that I need some help with, John. The company is trying to reduce costs so that we can stay competitive while keeping our workforce intact. You are a new set of eyes around here and maybe you can see ways to improve that the rest of us have overlooked. Would you think about it and bring me some suggestions?* (Use his natural Intuitive traits to improve performance.)

John: *Sure can. In fact here's one to start. See all of those lights overhead? If I store the least used items in back, we can leave the lights off most of the time and only turn them on when we need to get to the back. I don't know if that counts as much of a cost reduction, though.* (Note that John seems confident in his ideas, but really he is not.)

You: *Good place to start. I can research the electric usage for our department and see what the costs are. We might be able to estimate what a 50% reduction might come to. Thanks, John and keep thinking. We'll keep talking about it until we get some good results.* (Encourage his idea, but don't make any promises until you find out more.)

John's First Disciplinary Conference

John has been coming to work regularly and doing a better and better job each week. In the second month, he got into a yelling match with Harry, who says that John told him to buzz off when he came over to show him a mistake on his quality form. Harry usually tells the truth, so you figure that you will need to talk to John. Your goal is to get him to be more respectful of Harry, who is the most experienced worker and can teach John a great deal about the job. Without your talk, Harry has said that he won't talk to John anymore. He doesn't need the hassle of the arrogant and inexperienced *Pup*. Not only do you need to correct John's behavior, but also to further motivate him into being a good worker.

You: *John come in and sit down. I need to talk to you about Harry.*

John: *Tell him to stop calling me 'The Pup'. He thinks that he knows it all and can boss anybody around.*

You: (Don't jump to conclusions, *peel the layers.*) *Tell me exactly what happened, John. We need to work this out because I can't allow workers to yell at each other.* (Set the expectation clearly up front.)

John: *Well, he came into the stockroom when I was really behind and trying to get caught up and said that I screwed up the paperwork again and threw it on my desk. I told him to get out of my way.*

You: (Peel another layer.) *You sound pretty hot. Was there something else that got this whole thing going?*

John: *Yeah, he goes around the break room calling me 'The Pup', and how he's going to break me in. I'm a lot smarter than he is. I could break him in two.*

You: *Sounds like you two are both putting each other down.* (Peel another layer.) *How did that get started?*

John: *Well, one night he came into the bar where me and my car friends hang out and started bragging to them that he was my boss and I was 'The Pup'. It embarrassed me in front of my friends. Now they're all calling me 'The Pup'. I hate Harry.*

You: (You are now convinced that John is a Feeler since he is taking this personally.) *Maybe Harry didn't mean to be such a pain to you. He probably didn't realize how much it would bother you. I'll speak to him. He is our most experienced worker, and he can teach you a lot, so I need you two to talk to each other. In the meantime, I need to give you a verbal warning about yelling. Our policy is that no one gets mistreated in this company—and especially not in my department.* (State the policy and consequences clearly.) *I don't ever expect to have to talk to you about this again, understood?*

John: *Well, you'll have to get him off my case or out of my face.*

You: *John, I hope that Harry apologizes and never again embarrasses you, but to tell the truth, that's just part of working together. You could have handled it better with humor.* (Address the real problem, John's oversensitivity and immaturity. This is a sure sign of a Feeler.) *Don't take these kinds of things too seriously or people will just ride you all the harder. I'll suggest that you talk to Glenn. He's worked with Harry for years and knows how to handle his rude comments. John, you are doing a good job in the stock room and everybody likes you here, even Harry.* (Keep it positive.) *See if you can get past this. I'd like to see our great teamwork return to normal. Are you willing to give it a try?*

When you talk to Harry about the situation, you find that he does not realize why John is mad at him and offers to apologize. You counsel him to be more considerate in what he says to people. Things settle down, and Harry learns to be more respectful of John. And John once again starts to listen to Harry.

John's Employee Counseling Session

John has been working for you for six months now. His paycheck has attracted a pretty girl named Sandra, a woman he met in a bar. She has been borrowing money from him and getting him to buy her expensive gifts. For the last three months, he has been proud to have her living with him. But last weekend, they had a big fight over her flirting with other men at the bar, and she moved out. He got to work late on Monday and had signs of a hangover. You decide to have a counseling conference with him. Your goal is to correct his behavior, counsel him about how to manage himself better. You want to further develop him as a motivated, good employee.

You: *Come in John, and have a seat. How are you feeling today?* (This is an open-ended question.)

John: *Not so great, as a matter of fact.*

You: *It's not like you to be late and you look pretty rough. Would you want to talk about what's going on?* (Another open-ended question to *peel a layer*.)

John: *Women, I hate them. They take your money and leave. Who needs them?*
You: *How did this happen?*

John: *Well, I met this girl Sandra at the car club bar, and we hit it off real good. I took her to the car shows and rallies, and she moved in. I even loaned her $2,000 to pay off her credit card and fixed her car for her. Then Saturday, I saw her flirting with another guy at the bar because he was flashing a big roll of bills. We had a fight and she left. She's probably seeing Mr. Moneybags right now.*

You: *That's a pretty raw deal. I can see why you are down. But I hate to see you come in late and hung over. Your job here is a pretty good deal for you. You make good money and you are a valued part of our team. You get treated well here, John.*

John: *Yeah, I feel like such a fool.*

You: *Well, what did you learn from the experience?* (Get him to state the consequences of his actions himself so he takes responsibility.)

John: *Don't give any women in bars any money.*

You: *That's a good start, but don't be sour on all women. Try to find a good person who really cares about you, not just your paycheck. You have a good future here, and you could support a family if you wanted. If you want some advice, I'd say to look for women who are good people in places other than a bar. What do you think?* (Give him some common sense counsel based on his own statement of the consequences.)

John: *That's what Glenn said.*

You: *See, you have friends who want to see you succeed and not be taken advantage of. Listen to them and try to do better the next time. Since this is your first time, I'm not going to write you up, but I am going to send you home for a sick day. I don't want you driving the truck in your condition.* (Consequence of his being hung over.) *Come in tomorrow with a better attitude and a clear head. Okay?*

John: *Okay, don't tell anyone else, will you?*

You: *I won't, but you know how news gets around the plant.* (Another consequence. Sorry, John.) *There are lots of people here who have gone through the same thing, so if they say something, just ask them what they did when it happened to them. You're needed here, John.* (A positive.) *Go get your head together and I'll see you tomorrow.*

You make a note to turn in a sick day for John. (Keep yourself organized.) You reflect on how often people's personal problems get in the way of work performance. It is a good investment in John to try to get him to see that he needs to grow up. He will probably take your advice and be able to build a good life for himself. (This is the helpful coach role.) If he could be a long term, reliable worker for you, it would save you a lot of hassle in trying to get another worker. (That's a good consequence for you.)

John's Employee Evaluation

It is time for John's first-year evaluation. Upon reflection of his performance, you have noticed that he is a fast learner, a good communicator, has good ideas, has good attendance, and works hard. He is young and sometimes overconfident and definitely too sensitive to criticism, but shows promise by listening to your guidance. You would like him to be more mature about his teamwork, more accurate on his paperwork and drive his truck a bit slower. In addition, you would like to expand his duties to include more paper work and cleanup. Your goal is to develop him into an even better-motivated employee and move him from the trainee category to a better than average experienced worker. You remember that you have to be positive with him and that, when asked, he shares good ideas.

You: *John, come on in and have a seat. We're going to do your annual employee evaluation today.*

John: *What's that? I'm not in trouble again am I?* (There you go being negative, John.)

You: *Oh no, I would have told you if you were. An employee evaluation is a time that is devoted to looking at the strengths and weaknesses of each employee and finding ways to improve our departmental performance.* (Communicate what you want John to get out of this experience.) *Everyone gets one each year.*

John: *I never had one before. What's it like?*

You: *Let's get started. I've done these for years and I haven't lost anyone yet,* (a little humor) *so I think you will find it interesting and helpful. First of all, here is the company form. I have to fill in all of these ratings and make comments. Keep in mind that I have to rate a person's performance against the standard—which includes what others can do who have been here many years. Take a minute and look it over, and then we'll go over each one step by step.*

John: *What do you mean by average? I thought that I was above average.* (This is a Feeler being sensitive to criticism. You anticipated this, right?)

You: *First of all, everyone here is an exceptional person. We are just comparing the work generated on a scale from beginner to a pro.* (Encourage John to look at this in an objective manner, not a subjective one.) *Remember that no matter how experienced we get, there is always room for improvement because we get better and better at improving all of the time. Let's start with the category of attendance and discuss each category separately. Here's your attendance record. As you can see, other than that time when you had the difficulty with your girlfriend, your attendance is very good.*

John: *Yeah, that was really embarrassing. It took me a long time to live that down, but Glenn introduced me to his sister-in-law's girlfriend and she's been real nice to date.*

You: *Good. I'd like to encourage you to listen to the good advice of your friends. You can build a fine life here. I hope that any concerns that come up in this evaluation will fall in the category of good advice too. We all want to see you do well.* (Pile on the encouragement for him to manage his life well.) *The next category is safety. I've make some notes in my notebook that you are generally safe, but that you drive the truck too fast. Someday it might cause an accident. Do you remember that*

I've spoken to you several times about this? (These conversations would have taken place during check-in conversations or maybe even a disciplinary conference.)

John: *Yeah, I remember. More than once, in fact. I just want to get a lot of stock moved and, besides, it's fun. Sort of like my car.*

You: *Can you think of something that will remind you to go slower, especially around the corners? Research shows that speed at the corners causes the most accident, because you can't always see around well.*

John: *Well, I remember once when I rolled a car by going too fast around a corner. That cost me a week in the hospital and totaled the car. I keep a picture of that wreck at home.*

You: *What if you made a copy of that picture and tape it up at the corner of the stock room door? Would that help to remind you?* (Make the consequences real to John.)

John: *It just might. I'll give it a try.*

You: *I'll stop by and look for it. I'd like to see it anyway. The next category is teamwork and cooperation. I have a few notes about you and Harry not getting along. If you remember, Harry made an effort to watch what he said, but you had to work at taking his comments less personally.*

John: *Glenn told me that Harry doesn't mean anything, he's just got a big mouth and doesn't think about what he says. I guess I just got used to it.*

You: *That's right, John. There are lots of people in life who are like that, and you can learn to deal with them more effectively by the experience that you have had with Harry. I'd also like to point out that there are people like you who are much more sensitive to words. It doesn't mean that one or the other is right or wrong, just different. The way that teamwork develops is when people realize that and take these differences into consideration. For example, when Harry talks to you, he has to think about if his words will be insulting to you. On the other hand, when you listen to Harry, you have to remember that he doesn't mean to be insulting. In the middle, between the two people trying to understand, teamwork happens. Do you see what I'm talking about?* (You are starting to teach him about personality differences.)

John: *I think so. I never thought about people being different like that. I always assumed that everybody was pretty much the same, but some were just mean.*

You: *Yes, most people assume the same thing, but I'm trying to teach you some important insights that will help you to be a better team player. Are you willing to work on this?*

John: *I'll have to think about it.*

You: *Good. Here's a way to practice. Take notice of Glenn. He is more sensitive like you, but Allen is blunt like Harry.*

John: *You're right. What about everybody else?*

You: *That's what I'd like you to figure out on your own. When I come around to talk to you, why don't you tell me what you've noticed about other people on our team. We'll be learning a lot about people that will help you in all aspects of your life.*

You continue with the evaluation, going through each category. You outline how his performance rates, but you always emphasize high goals and point out skills that he will need to excel. Over the years, you hope he will mature and advance in the company. That would be a good thing—for both of you.

Congratulations, you have successfully taken an employee from the first interview to the first year evaluation. You have effectively utilized the motivation techniques in a way that was appropriate to the personality type. In all cases, you have been calm, reasonable, and professional. In all cases, you have had a plan and used your notebook to organize—so, you were never harried, upset, or pressed for time to think things through. Your department constantly improved, and you had little turnover. Your boss has been happy with your work, and he views you as an advanced, professional supervisor. That wasn't so difficult was it? The test is to do it well and do it consistently. Let's hear some comments from other participants about how they changed due to this course.

Participant Comments—How Did You Improve as a Supervisor because of this Class?

I don't jump to conclusions as much anymore. I try to get input from the employee before I decide what to do.

I'm more patient, more helpful to others, and more aware of what's going on in the workers' minds.

I have more confidence. I'm not afraid to tell people clearly what I want them to do and take the time to be sure they understand me.

I have learned to recognize traits in coworkers that will allow me to interact respectfully in a teamwork environment. I am aware of traits in my personality, and I know exactly what to work on to begin to improve them.

Knowing to communicate with everybody everyday has made a big difference. People are starting to do what I want.

I'm starting to develop a good team of workers in a good and positive way because I understand each one of them.

I'm calmer and more open minded now, and I take the time to listen more. Things are going better so I have less to get upset about.

Personality Type and Supervision

You are now at a powerful moment in time when you can make commitments to try some of the approaches described in this program. It is a good time to review all that we have learned about the personality types. There is a great deal of wisdom to be gained from this small amount of information about people. Many supervisors tell me years after the training is over that this is the one area where they have gained the most. I've been studying and applying these simple basic truths about people for 20 years, and I am still finding fascinating new ways to improve performance and teamwork. The following section is devoted to reviewing and summarizing. It would be good for you to pull out the pages devoted to the personality ranges, run some copies, and lay them out across your desk. I'd like you to see the whole spectrum of human behavior in one glance.

Introvert–Extrovert   Sensor-Intuitive   Thinker-Feeler   Perceiver-Judger

In addition, make note of the Xs that you placed on the questionnaire you took in the second class. Fold the range pages in half vertically, so only one range shows, and lay your type side by side.

Example: Introvert   Sensor   Feeler   Judger

Now you can see all of your traits combined and blended into the personality that is you. Take a few minutes and study how these traits combine. If you have someone who knows you well and is helpful, ask for examples of when you have exhibited these traits. Keep in mind that you will not have all of these traits in equal strength, so some of them will be apparent and others will seem faint. Also, keep in mind that some of your traits may be suppressed. For a variety of reasons, you may not allow yourself to exhibit these traits, but you secretly know that they are there. A common example is the Feeler man who knows that he is sensitive and kind, but because others consider these traits unmanly, he will pretend to be tough and demanding. The opposite sometimes occurs. The Thinker woman often pretends to be soft, compliant, and agreeable because these are considered feminine traits. But deep inside, she is as competitive, controlling, and demanding as any Thinker man. For the sake of this study, allow yourself to be who you really are. And remember that when you try to be something that you are not, your natural strengths are being underutilized. And this could be costing you stress and loss of energy.

Since you have now figured out that there is benefit to all characteristics in the personality ranges, it doesn't really matter where you are on the range. What matters is that you know where you are and can use your strengths to your best—and learn to avoid the weaknesses. This can be a freeing experience for some of you as you begin to settle into your unique supervisory style. You will find it is much easier to work within your strengths. Remember that you are okay no matter what traits you have. You just have to learn how to use your traits well.

The next section is devoted to more detail about each of these combinations of traits. I will suggest what strengths the types usually have, but you might be a bit different. Trust your knowledge of yourself, or if you have someone helping you, ask them to verify what you are seeing.

Combinations of Traits: Personality Traits

In the following section, I will describe the different combinations of the four traits that combine to make a Personality Type. Each Type has strengths and weaknesses. I have given you a short case study to see how these traits appear in different job situations. Keep in mind that the case study is only one version of the particular type and may not closely resemble you or others with the same type. You will, of course, want to find your individual strengths and weaknesses, but also consider those of your coworkers, family, and friends.

Finally, think of people who you supervise and look for insights into how to help them succeed, as well as how to blend your team's abilities into perfect teamwork.

ISTJ

Strengths

- Works independently, thinks deeply, and in great detail about things
- Can remember and use large amounts of information effectively
- Is neat, tidy, and organized so information or items are available
- Can control vast quantities of things and information with ease
- Verifies information to be sure that things are correct
- Can meet deadlines and high standards
- Is a good disciplinarian
- Prevents too much variation, thus assuring consistent performance

Weaknesses

- Can get bogged down in detail and forget the end result that is expected

- Can be out of touch with others and fail to communicate enough

- Can be seen as aloof, using information as a defense against communication

- Can get upset if others do not appreciate the importance of accurate information

- Can get upset if others do not follow the rules

- Can be too blunt and factual, ignoring the need for diplomacy and motivation

- Can be closed minded and stubborn, always ready to argue what is right

- Can be so resistant to change that opportunities to improve are avoided

- May not be able to prioritize well

ISTJ Case Study

Richard had been the general manager of a small manufacturing company in Canada. He started as a line worker, was promoted to supervisor, then to plant superintendent, and eventually became general manager. His promotions were based on his ability to know and control every detail of what was going on in the plant. He knew every person's name, their family, their history with the company, and what they did right and wrong at work. He judged people as trustworthy if they also knew every detail accurately. If he found the smallest error, he became suspicious and spent considerable time tracking down the discrepancy. If things went wrong despite his best efforts, he would occasionally lose his temper.

He managed the plant by studying performance charts and resolving each problem that could cause performance to stall. He was frugal by nature. He knew what the plant needed to run efficiently and controlled expenditures tightly. He was loyal to his employees—he had been there and understood the hardships that could come to an employee's life through thoughtless management decisions. His strength was that he kept things under control and attended to all of the many details required to make a plant run. At the time that he took over management of the plant, things were disordered. He expertly calmed anxious thoughts and put things on an even keel. People respected and appreciated him, and the plant ran fairly well.

His shortcoming was that he did not have a strong direction for the future of the company. He sometimes avoided decisions that could have prevented problems if he'd taken a longer-term view.

In retirement, he took up the hobby of animal recordings in the wild, carefully cataloguing various animals and their behavior and calls. He enjoyed having people from the plant come and visit, but he was glad to have the relief from the endless hours and responsibilities of running the plant.

Questions and Comments

List the items from the case study that indicate Richard's strong Sensor traits.

The Sensor traits worked well for the situation, with one exception: the ability to forecast and plan for the future –an Intuitive trait. With Sensor traits being so strong and successful, it is unlikely that Richard would be able to develop the ability to forecast so late in his career. His best strategy would have been to find a manager who was an Intuitive and work together to do strategic planning.

ESTJ

Strengths

- Works well in groups, speaks in front of others, sociable
- Can impressively remember and use large amounts of information effectively
- Is neat, tidy, and organized, so information or items are available
- Can control vast quantities of things and information with ease
- Verifies information to be sure that things are correct
- Can meet deadlines and high standards
- Is a good disciplinarian
- Prevents too much variation, thus assuring consistent performance
- Can discuss past history to the benefit of the team not repeating mistakes
- Can be very convincing because of ability to discuss facts

Weaknesses

- Can get bogged down in detail and forget the end result that is expected
- Can be so talkative that it disrupts others—does not listen well

- Can be seen as aggressive, using information as a defense against communication
- Can get upset if others do not appreciate the urgency of accurate information
- Can get upset if others do not follow the rules
- Can be too blunt and factual, ignoring the need for diplomacy and motivation
- Can be closed minded and stubborn
- Argues what is right without listening to others' opinions or input
- Can be so resistant to change that opportunities to improve are avoided
- May not be able to prioritize well
- Can be seen as aggressive, pushy, and arrogant
- Can bore people with too many irrelevant facts
- Can talk self into the wrong conclusion
- Verbally stubborn, argumentative, and self-righteous
- Humor can be sarcastic, with a negative connotation

ESTJ Case Study

Sherry worked in the QC department of a large company. She was well suited to keeping paperwork and defects under control. She had energy, an excellent memory, was organized, and was not afraid to confront people about defects or deviations. In fact, she loved her job, and the company loved how well she did it. But the other employees found her bossy, combative, blunt, and unyielding. Behind her back, they called her *The General* and did their best to avoid talking with her, even though they recognized that she was just doing her job. On one occasion, she lost her temper when production did not respond to her direction, but people knew that it was just part of her personality and the incident blew over. The defining moment came when the company was awarded the Supplier of the Year award from the top customer. The plant manager held a ceremony to thank both production and QC for their dedicated hard work. But everyone silently thanked Sherry for her leadership in setting and maintaining a high standard that everyone else had to strive to match.

Questions and Comments

List the evidence for the Thinker traits in Sherry's personality.

Thinker traits in a woman are sometimes difficult for people to accept, since women are traditionally thought to be accommodating and submissive. Had Sherry tried to be submissive, she would have been unhappy, and the company would have missed out on the award. The workers were irritated by her bossiness but, because they respected her, they made allowances for her blunt and demanding manner and occasional temper. This worked out well. But if Sherry had also made an effort to be a little more diplomatic, there would have been better teamwork and she would have felt more accepted. Most likely, there were workers who avoided her strong approach. With more diplomacy, they probably would have interacted with her more freely—to their benefit, Sherry's benefit, and the customer and company's benefit.

ISTP

Strengths

- Works independently, thinks deeply and in great detail
- Can remember and use large amounts of information effectively
- Can remember vast quantities of things and information with ease
- Verifies information to be sure that things are correct
- Can be a perfectionist
- Includes everyone and everything in the thought process
- Looks at many options—broad minded
- Can multi task well—has several projects going on at one time
- Can work alone for long periods of time

Weaknesses

- Can get bogged down in detail and forget the end result that is expected
- Can be out of touch with others and fail to communicate enough
- Can be seen as aloof, using perfectionism instead of communication
- Can get upset if others do not appreciate the urgency of accurate information
- Can get upset without some freedom to do things their way
- Can be too blunt and factual, ignoring the need for diplomacy and motivation
- Can be closed minded and stubborn, always ready to argue what is right
- Can be so resistant to change that opportunities to improve are avoided

- May not be able to prioritize well or keep track of time
- Can be eccentric, hoard too many things, get too messy, ignore relationships

Case Study: ISTP

Dewey worked in a machining department of a small company owned by Sarge, who had started the company in his garage after returning from Vietnam in the 70s. Sarge liked Dewey and thought of him as a son. He taught Dewey everything that he knew about machining, and Dewey responded by doing excellent work. His shortcoming was getting along with other workers. He was usually uncommunicative, except to say something critical about someone else's work. His blunt and sarcastic humor left people embarrassed and plotting revenge. Sarge often had to intervene in Dewey's defense, and had even once given him three days off without pay after one of Dewey's temper outbursts. Dewey spent the time fishing and thinking that, if he did not have a wife and two children, he probably wouldn't have a job at all. He would have preferred working in his garage and making parts for Sarge on a piece basis and wouldn't have to punch a time clock and work with others.

Eventually, Sarge wanted to retire and attempted to develop Dewey as the next manager of the company. This was a disaster. No one wanted to work for Dewey, and he admitted that he could not manage people. Left with no other choice, Sarge sold his company. Dewey remained at the company as a temperamental, but expert machinist—but one who set the standard for skill and precision.

Questions and Comments

You've already seen how the Sensor and Thinker traits appear in the prior case studies. Use this one to identify the Perceiver traits. List the evidence for Dewey's Perceiver.

Perceivers have trouble being comfortable in structured environments—like a job. They prefer freedom to do what they need to do when they need to do it. They can handle being responsible for a result, but schedules and deadlines are unnatural to them. Because most of our society is organized around Judger traits, they often carry the label of lazy, unmotivated, or rebellious. But if society were organized around Perceiver traits, the Judgers would be criticized for being too rigid and narrow minded. The bottom line for Perceivers is that they need a lot of freedom in their time off and often engage in creative projects or just having fun. If you are a Perceiver, please accept this about yourself, or you may become an organizational dropout. Do not criticize yourself or let other do so. If you stamp out your natural traits, you stop being you and can get confused and depressed. You are naturally a spontaneous, happy, and fun loving person—and that is a good thing.

ESTP

Strengths

- Works well in groups, speaks well in front of others, sociable
- Can remember and talk about large amounts of information effectively
- Can remember vast quantities of things and information with ease
- Verifies information to be sure that things are correct
- Can be a perfectionist
- Includes everyone and everything into the thought process
- Looks at many more options—broad minded
- Can multi task well—has several projects going on at one time
- Can be very persuasive, informative, and personable

Weaknesses

- Can get bogged down in detail and forget the end result that is expected
- Can talk so much that fails to listen enough
- Can be seen as overbearing, using perfectionism instead of communication
- Can get upset if others do not appreciate the urgency of accurate information
- Can get upset if forced to follow constricting rules
- Can be too blunt and factual, ignoring the need for diplomacy and motivation
- Can be closed mined and stubborn, always ready to argue what is right
- Can be so perfectionistic that no one can understand or please them
- May not be able to prioritize well or keep track of time
- Can become eccentric, hoard things, get messy, ignore relationships

Case Study: ESTP

Rachel worked for a publishing company in an office with many other women. She was sociable, outgoing, and humorous. She was willing to drop everything that was on her desk to answer a question, solve a problem, or to talk with someone. Her boss wondered how she accomplished so much with so many interruptions, but realized that socializing was part of keeping everybody trained, happy, and productive. Fortunately, Rachel worked closely with Wanda, who was an ISTJ with few friends. They were a good team because Rachel included Wanda in all of the fun social interaction, and Wanda took care of organizing and completing the work on time. Their boss was a wise woman who recognized the teamwork and took care to keep them on the same team—neither of them would be successful without the other.

Questions and Comments

1. Write a short explanation of how the E-I difference between Rachel and Wanda worked so well.

2. Explain how Rachel's Perceiver traits were a good match to the work situation.

3. Explain what would have happened if the two were not allowed to work together as a team.

INTJ

Strengths

- Independent thinker who has thoughtful things to say
- Takes ownership of ideas, departments, teams, and areas
- Can generate lots of ideas quickly—good problem solver
- Sees trends, issues, direction, and change, and drives to achieve the new goals
- Can organize, schedule, and plan for new and better change
- Has high standards, is objective, analytical, and is a good disciplinarian

- Has leadership traits that show confidence and control

Weaknesses

- Can be over controlling and uncommunicative—Do it because I said so
- Can drive self and others too hard until people leave the team
- Ignores the sensitivities and needs of people—relationships are a second priority
- Can fall in love with ideas and not see limitations and requirements
- So determined to succeed that the plan fails due to stress, discord, or lack of communication
- Not likely to include input from others

Case Study: INTJ

Sara worked at home making aprons for a specialty-clothing manufacturer. Her mind simmered with new ideas for designs and color combinations. She worked efficiently by herself while her children were at school. Her work was of high quality and she sent in complete orders on schedule each week. The company considered her one of their best home-based suppliers. Sara's coordinator felt that she needed little or no supervision, but called her weekly to discuss the new ideas and designs that she was generating. Some of Sara's ideas had been a great success, and Sara never took too much time on the phone. She felt lucky to be able to work this way and was able to keep a clean and organized home for her family. She valued her job and worked every day to improve.

Questions and Comments

Some might consider Sara a loner, but in truth, she loved working by herself for two reasons. One, she was an Introvert and liked not having much social interaction; and two, being a Thinker Judger, she could control her home environment without interruption from others. This worked well with her traits—the Intuitive was able to emerge in her creative designs. If the T-J traits had been frustrated, she might get angry and increase efforts to control—and the creativity might have been ignored.

1. Describe what you think her home was probably like.

2. If she had a Perceiver child, what would she have to be careful to avoid?

ENTJ

Strengths

- Persuasive, outgoing, sociable, and very engaging, with a purpose in mind
- Takes ownership of own ideas, departments, teams, and areas
- Can generate lots of ideas quickly—good problem solver
- Sees trends, issues, direction, and change, and drives to achieve the new goals
- Can organize, schedule, and plan for new and better change
- Has high standards, is objective, analytical, and is a good disciplinarian
- Has leadership traits that show confidence and control

Weaknesses

- Can be over controlling and unfocused—*Don't tell me you can't do it*
- Can drive self and others too hard until people leave the team
- Ignores the sensitivities and needs of people—relationships are a second priority
- Can fall in love with ideas and not see the limitations and requirements
- So determined to succeed, that the plan fails due to stress, discord, or lack of communication
- Communicates a lot, but does not necessarily accept input from others
- So committed to success that will do anything to succeed

Case Study: ENTJ

As a maintenance supervisor, Donnie was not a natural. He had started his career as a mechanic, moved to welding, and finally to electrical technician. It seemed that he could learn anything and loved to challenge himself. He was a good talker and convinced his bosses that he could do anything, despite the occasional complaint that he tended to bully coworkers. He was organized, disciplined, and outgoing, but his best skill was his ability to diagnose problems. He said that he could see the whole system in his mind. He was able to see where the problems might be, run diagnostic processes, and quickly find the problem. In addition, he was good at coming up with solutions when the correct part was not in stock or a secondary problem came to light.

But it was the task of supervising people that most interested Donnie. He was sure that everyone else could do as well as he did. As the new supervisor, he set out to train each mechanic. He quickly learned that few people thought the way he did, and his blunt and demanding words created more de-motivation than motivation. During his first year, he gradually became more aware of what he was doing wrong. He began to use his social skills to determine who was good at what and assign tasks accordingly. He never had trouble with discipline, as he was sure of the rules and enforced them impartially. As long as he didn't get too aggressive, things worked pretty well.

But his workers noticed that when he married Becky, he really started to mellow. She was a quiet, sweet person, and talked to him about how people might feel when spoken to so bluntly. In time, Donnie recognized that being more diplomatic would work for him, and he capitalized on it to increase the performance of his team. He and his crew liked being the best crew in the plant with the lowest maintenance downtime.

Questions and Comments

Donnie has natural leadership qualities from his Extraversion and Intuitive Traits. But what traits were causing him to be considered a bully?

Donnie and Becky are an example of opposites in some trait areas, but they were both Extroverts, and they talked about everything. This helped Becky give Donnie the Feeler perspective so he could see the benefit of being more diplomatic. So often, Feelers are so turned off or hurt by a strong Thinker that they clam up or avoid interaction. The Thinker goes through life never realizing that the Feeler world even exists. If Donnie practices this trait at home, Becky will feel comfortable too. And their Extraversion will continue to work well.

INTP

Strengths

- Independent thinker who has thoughtful things to say on many subjects
- Takes ownership of own ideas, departments, teams, and areas
- Can generate many ideas quickly—good problem solver

- Sees trends, issues, direction, and change, and drives to achieve the new goals
- Can organize and plan for new and better change—good at initiating plans
- Has high standards, is objective, analytical, and is a good strategist
- Has leadership traits that show confidence and control
- Will try to perfect a piece of work and get great joy from working on it
- Will include input from other people
- Is quick to adapt to change when confronted with a barrier or problem

Weaknesses

- Can be over controlling and uncommunicative—*Do it because I said so*
- Can drive self and others too hard until people leave the team
- Ignores the sensitivities and needs of people—relationships are a second priority
- Can fall in love with ideas and not see the limitations and requirements
- So determined to succeed, that the plan is changed over and over again
- Too much change can be confusing to people
- Can be so perfectionistic that loses sense of time and fails to complete project

Case Study: INTP

Steve worked as a drafting and design technician in an architectural firm's engineering department. Most of the work was speculative in nature, as clients tried to formulate their ideas of what they wanted within cost constraints. For most people this would be discouraging—almost all of Steve's prints were critiqued and changed, sometimes over and over for years. Few of them resulted in a completed project. But this did not bother Steve. He enjoyed doing the work more than seeing the project completed. He was thick skinned and saw criticism as an opportunity to create better designs. Although his multiple projects were sometimes in a big rush (and then left to wait for months), everyday he worked quietly at his computer screen contentedly thinking up better and better designs. The pay, vacations, and benefits were a plus, as was working with other engineers. Often the entire engineering department would get frustrated, irritable, and angry, but Steve would offer some sarcastic humor and they would all laugh and get back to work.

The only difficult part of Steve's life was finding a girlfriend. Most women found him difficult, sarcastic, and uncommunicative. Once a girlfriend asked him what was on TV for the evening. His answer—*dust*. The girlfriend dumped him shortly thereafter.

The department changed one day when they hired a female engineer. She was just as grumpy and difficult as the others. Steve admired and liked her, but wondered if that was how he came across to his coworkers and girlfriends. He took this to heart and tried to be more diplomatic with his words.

Questions and Comments

Many people assume that engineers are all Sensor-Thinkers, but Steve is an example of how the Intuitive traits come into play. Architects are another example of Intuitive traits used in a precise work environment. The Intuitive architects design the look and function of a structure, and the Sensor architects work out the fine detail. In Steve's case, he needed to be flexible (Perceiver) and not too focused on completion because so many projects were speculative in nature.

ENTP

Strengths

- Persuasive, outgoing, sociable, and very engaging—can sell anything to anybody.
- Takes ownership of own ideas, departments, teams, and areas
- Can generate lots of ideas quickly—good problem solver
- Sees trends, issues, direction, and change—drives to achieve the new goals
- Can organize, schedule, and plan for new and better change
- Has leadership traits that show confidence and control
- Appears logical and organized, at least at the beginning of a project
- Good change agent—can persuade a team to follow leadership

Weaknesses

- Can be over controlling and unfocused—*Don't tell me you can't do it*
- Can drive self and others too hard until people leave the team
- Ignores the sensitivities and needs of people—relationships are a second priority
- Can fall in love with ideas and not see the limitations and requirements
- So determined to succeed, that the plan fails due to stress, discord, or too much communication
- Communicates a lot, but does not necessarily accept input from others

- So committed to success that will do anything to succeed

- Can be unrealistic and fail to think things over completely before beginning

- Can be very poor at completing tasks on time or on budget

Case Study: ENTP

Tommy worked in a software company and was always talking, but rarely communicating. Thoughts poured out of his mouth rambling in confusing circles, littered with brilliance and strange humor. Despite these obvious verbal adventures, people liked Tommy immensely. He had the ability to think ahead to prevent problems. He could solve problems that baffled others. His intelligence and commitment to the job were legendary. For a short while, he was a supervisor. People found him to be a good disciplinarian, an excellent *go-to man*, and a ready source of humorous wisdom. He's no longer a supervisor because his technical problem-solving ability was so valuable that the company put him on the road to solve problems for irate customers. Tommy's humor and ability to think outside the box allowed him to see the customers' problems, his company's software constraints, and still come up with a solution. He made the customers laugh, which bought some time for a solution. He was the kind of person who could succeed at just about anything, anywhere—and he was always ready for the next adventure around the corner.

Questions and Comments

Tommy's personality seems to contain contrasting traits and unusual behaviors that seem to work so well in his job situation. The good thing is that he is comfortable with all of his traits and uses them to be productive. For that reason, he is valued in his job. This could be a good description of you when you fully understand and accept your many traits.

Considering his traits, explain where his humor comes from and how he uses it in his job.

INFJ

Strengths

- Good problem solver, especially when it comes to people issues

- Does not talk a lot, but when an idea is explained, it is a good one

- Avoids conflict through generating new ideas

- Good understanding of concepts of teamwork and how to apply them

- Can initiate and complete projects

- Comfortable with change—can be judicious about how much and what kind of change is appropriate

- Quiet and thoughtful, and can work independently with little direction
- Makes a personal commitment to work—can be an inspired leader

Weaknesses

- Can be unassertive and too retiring to lead
- Not a good disciplinarian
- Can get feelings hurt and retreat from a discussion
- Does not do well in meetings—does not promote self well
- Is not good at arguments, conflicts, or rationale
- Can be so attached to own ideas, that a lot of emotions are involved
- Needs a lot of praise, and suffers from stress
- Does not take criticism well

Case Study: INFJ

Rosy worked as a maid for a hotel in her town. It was not a good job, but it brought in needed cash and she had all daytime hours. She liked working by herself and took care to clean each room for new guests that would arrive that evening. The cleaning manager, Maria, was kind and helpful, but Rosy hated the repetition of cleaning room after room—over and over again. Each was just the same as the one before. She quickly lost interest and began to miss small details, such a replacing the tissue box and coffee cups. Maria sat down to talk to her occasionally and realized that Rosy needed more variety in her job. Hotel work had little to offer, but occasionally Maria would assign Rosy to set up and clean up for parties, weddings, and business meetings. This helped some. Rosy enjoyed doing the decorations and working with the customers to get the rooms set up to their best advantage. The work was more interesting, but she still found her job a chore—rather than a satisfaction. She decided to attend the local community college to upgrade her education and seek better employment. The college gave her a battery of tests to try to assess her ability and personality. She learned a lot from this experience and decided to take coursework to become a home health aide.

Questions and Comments

1. Explain why Rosy needed more variety in her work.

2. How could she better use her Feeler traits to find a new career?

Some institutions have testing resources to help people assess their abilities and chose a good career. But be cautious if the results do not seem to be a good fit for you. Some tests are not designed to test for personality traits, and some counselors have not been trained to coach people on traits. You are the final authority and judge on who you are and what is best for you. So be sure of who you are and be comfortable with your identity.

ENFJ

Strengths

- Good problem solver, especially when it comes to people issues
- Very outgoing, persuasive, and compelling speaker
- Avoids conflict through generating new ideas
- Good understanding of concepts of teamwork and how to apply them
- Can initiate and complete projects
- Comfortable with change—can be judicious about how much and what kind of change is appropriate
- Uses social skills to sell ideas, form teams, and motivate
- Makes a personal commitment to work—can be an inspired leader

Weaknesses

- Can be over talkative and unrealistic
- Not a good disciplinarian
- Understands people well, but may not listen enough to get cooperation
- Can get feelings hurt and become verbally aggressive or whine
- Does well in meetings—can over promote self and ideas
- Is not good at arguments, conflicts, or rationale
- Can be so attached to own ideas, that a lot of emotions are involved
- Needs a lot of praise, and suffers from stress
- Does not take criticism well

- If negative, can influence a lot of people to be negative as well

Case Study: ENFJ

Ken worked for a marketing agency as an assistant account representative. His boss was Howard, who made sales calls on customers. He then brought the customer to Ken to do the designs and manage the project through the production department. Ken's outgoing social skills and personal interest in the customers' needs were a real plus. He made the customer feel comfortable. In addition, Ken was good at planning and scheduling the work so that work was completed on time.

Howard was thinking about training Ken to be account representative. He recognized Ken's good social skills, high energy, creative abilities, and organization skills, but questioned his ability to tolerate the rejection inherent in outside sales. Only one out of ten companies that Howard called on would even give him an appointment. It took someone with tough skin to continue to make calls until that tenth company gave him a chance to sell his company's services. They talked at length about Ken going on a few sales calls. Ken decided that moving away from the job he loved would be a mistake. Howard did not want to lose the good performance that Ken lavished on the hard fought-customers that he brought to the company. They decided to keep the teamwork that they had and try to grow the company's business through exceptional service.

Questions and Comments

Explain why Ken decided that he would not be suited to the rejection inherent in sales.

Feelers often make excellent sales people because they sense what the customer needs and quickly build helpful relationships. They give the impression of a sincere desire to give good customer service. But the rejection part of sales is difficult. In many cases, the Intuitive sees this as a challenge and will make the effort to toughen up. In other cases, the Judger is so driven to set schedules and appointments and complete assignments, that sensitivity is not an issue.

INFP

Strengths

- Good problem solver, especially when it comes to people issues

- Does not talk a lot, but when an idea is explained, it is a good one
- Avoids conflict through generating new ideas
- Good understanding of concepts of teamwork and how to apply them
- Can initiate multiple projects at one time
- Comfortable with a lot of change
- Quiet and thoughtful, and can work independently with little direction
- Makes a personal commitment to work—can be an inspired leader
- Very creative innovator—capable of having genius experiences
- May be a leader through innovation, forms of expression, or vision

Weaknesses

- Can be unassertive and too retiring to lead
- Can *hole up* in own territory and disconnect from others
- Not a good disciplinarian—tries to do it all themselves
- Can get feelings hurt and retreat from a discussion
- Gets so lost in projects that loses track of time and resources
- Can be perfectionistic and has trouble completing work in a timely manner
- Does not do well in meetings—does not promote self well
- Is not good at arguments, conflicts, or rationale
- Can be so attached to own ideas, that a lot of emotions are involved
- Needs a lot of praise, and suffers from stress
- Does not take criticism well, can get feelings hurt
- Can be eccentric and care less about rules and conventional thought
- Difficult to control as this person can constantly change
- When confronted, will just go ahead and do own thing

Case Study: INFP

Tess worked for a catering company making cakes and pastries. She worked anywhere from 20 to 80 hours a week, mostly in the evenings. Her apartment was a hodgepodge of art and craft projects, most of them only half finished. Working alone in her apartment during the week, she sold her crafts on weekends at local art shows and flea markets. The catering company liked the fact that she was skilled and would come in at anytime, so they paid her well and made sure that she felt appreciated. Her former boyfriend, Theo, would attest that disorganization and lack of discipline were her worst faults. He had even bought some plastic boxes and a label maker to categorize and organize her huge pile of materials and projects. Initially, she liked the idea, but as it progressed, she grew anxious to see things boxed up rather than out where she could see everything and move freely from one project to another. Theo gave up the effort, and they eventually broke up. Then Tess met Salvatorie, an Italian glass blower. Moving in together into his cluttered loft, Tess was amazed to find that she was actually more organized than he was. Sharing their ideas, skills, and resources, they eventually opened their own art store and enjoyed local success with their coffee and cake art shows.

Questions and Comments

This case study ends with two similar types working together successfully. It is a strange feature of human nature, but a relationship seeks a balance. In this case, two creative and messy people could have buried themselves in clutter. But Tess asserted her mild organizational abilities to counter balance Salvatorie's stronger traits. Notice that Theo, who was organized (Judger), got the opposite reaction from Tess. This balancing is a positive dynamic that occurs when there are positive motives, acceptance, patience, and commitment.

This personality type is not just for artists, it shows up in many fields of work.

ENFP

Strengths

- Good problem solver, especially when it comes to people issues
- Excellent persuader and source of inspiration
- Avoids conflict through generating new ideas
- Good understanding of concepts of teamwork and how to apply them
- Can initiate multiple projects at one time
- Comfortable with a lot of change
- Uses social skills to sell ideas, form teams, and motivate
- Can discuss a wide variety of ideas that are spontaneously generated
- Makes a personal commitment to work—can be an inspired leader
- Very creative innovator—capable of having genius experiences

Weaknesses

- Can be unassertive and too retiring to lead

- Not a good disciplinarian—tries to do it all themselves
- Can get feelings hurt and retreat from a discussion
- Gets so lost in projects that loses track of time and resources
- Can be perfectionistic and has trouble completing work in a timely manner
- Can talk so fast and on so many topics that conversation is confusing
- Is not good at arguments, conflicts, or rationale
- Can be so attached to own ideas that a lot of emotions are involved
- Needs a lot of praise and suffers from stress
- Does not take criticism well
- Can be eccentric and care less about rules and conventional thought
- Difficult to control as this person can constantly change
- When confronted, they just go ahead and do their own thing
- Can be unrealistic and aggressive about ideas because they don't listen

Case Study: ENFP

Dale supervised thirty people in the production department of a mid-sized plastic injection molding company. He swam in a sea of people and equipment problems every day. But Dale thrived on constant interaction with people, solving problems, and responding to new situations. His boss, Albert, had told him repeatedly that he did a good job but was too accommodating to people. He needed to make people live within the rules. Seeing no improvement after several warnings, Albert decided to take a new approach. He recognized that Dale did a good job of handling most problems on the spot—only a few discipline problems went astray—so, he decided to be Dale's backup on discipline. They agreed that Dale would give the verbal warnings and counseling and, if a problem persisted, they would do the written warnings together. Albert was tougher on the rules, but Dale was supportive. The system worked well, even during a termination on a young man whose random drug test showed positive. Dale was anxious during the conference and said very little. He was glad that Albert was handling the situation. Through this teamwork, the department ran well, and employees felt that the treatment was supportive, objective, and fair.

Questions and Comments

1. Explain why Dale's supervisory environment of constant questions, problems, and interaction would not seem stressful to him.

2. Explain why Dale was so reluctant to discipline.

3. Explain why Dale's boss found helping Dale with discipline was a good tradeoff.

ISFJ

Strengths

- A very down to earth, friendly, reliable person who knows the facts
- Quiet and modest and takes care of family, friends, and teammates
- Interest in just about everything, and likes people
- Capable of remembering people and information from the past
- Takes care of everyday duties and takes responsibility
- Values family and friends and sometimes volunteers for school or charity
- Makes a personal commitment with any work attempted
- Manages schedules well—is always busy, but always on time
- Takes an interest in people and can manage small teams well
- Does not talk much, but is sincere

Weaknesses

- Can take things too personally, and is not a good disciplinarian
- Can get bogged down in detail and forget the goal
- Can attach emotional meaning to everything and lose self-confidence
- Does not delegate well and can take on too much responsibility
- Can fail to communicate well enough to get cooperation from others
- Does not take criticism well—might question the facts
- Can be too accommodating and not stand up to people

Case Study: ISFJ

Ross was a small man, but a great worker. He worked in the human resources department of a large department store with five other workers. He processed payroll and insurance claims, and published the company newsletter. This group of six people were surprisingly similar in nature and got along well most of the time. They all knew their jobs and worked quietly. They all knew the employees, the rules, and the schedules down to the last detail. It wasn't likely that any detail could escape their notice. But occasionally, the group had a meltdown that required the supervisor to step in.

Last week, Ross found a small mistake that Marilyn had made. He feared telling her about it because he knew she would be offended. Thinking about it too long, it soon loomed in his mind as a huge problem, and he blurted it out to a coworker. Marilyn found out and complained to Ross and the supervisor. The supervisor was amazed at the emotional nature of so small a matter, but responded by correcting the mistake and soothing the feelings of all involved. Peace was restored, at least until the next time. Despite these occasional incidents, they all liked their jobs and each other and had no ambitions to advance or work anywhere else.

Questions and Comments

Describe how the Sensor-Feeler traits play out in this story.

Remember that the Sensor point of view is a small, but intense area of interest. This ideally suits work that has to be exactly and constantly controlled. When a mistake comes to light, it is a major occurrence no matter how small. Think about what skills the department supervisor would need to keep this team functioning happily and productively.

ESFJ

Strengths

- Very down to earth, friendly, reliable—knows the facts
- Outspoken and sincere, talks about family, friends, and teammates
- Interested in just about everything, likes people
- Capable of remembering people and information from the past
- Takes care of everyday duties, takes responsibility

- Values family and friends, sometimes volunteers for school or charity
- Makes a personal commitment with any work attempted
- Manages schedules well—is always busy, but always on time
- Takes an interest in people, and can manage small teams well
- Draws people into conversations about the past, knows people and useful information
- Engaging and knowledgeable and well liked
- Good with research and stories

Weaknesses

- Can take things too personally, and is not a good disciplinarian
- Can get bogged down in detail and forget the goal
- Can attach emotional meaning to everything and lose self-confidence
- Does not delegate well, and can take on too much responsibility
- Can over communicate and bore people with too many stories
- Does not take criticism well—might question the facts
- Solves problems with research, not ideas for solutions

Case Study: ESFJ

Eugene loved being a schoolteacher. Teaching science to fifth graders at the local school, he wanted his students to have a good experience with school—just as he had. With his full schedule and large classes, many children needed attention and kind discipline. Eugene had the rare balance of being able to hold the students to the rules with a firm but kind word. He never seemed to tire of the constant flow of children through his classroom and was able to remember every child's name. Although the teaching material and endless classes were repetitious year after year, it did not bother him. Eugene's real interest was the children and their ability to learn. He had a stable job with good benefits and he enjoyed his work completely.

Questions and Comments

Do you think that the four traits in Eugene's personality are all equal in strength, or does one stand out as stronger than the rest? Explain your answer.

Certain careers attract many people of the same trait. For example, Sensors are attracted to accounting. Thinkers are attracted to engineering. Feelers are attracted to care giving. But, as soon as you make that assumption, you see people who are different happily working beside their opposite type. This is due to the blending of the strengths of the traits. If a trait is mild, it means that there is some strength in the opposite trait that can be utilized rather easily. The people who have a mixture of mild traits are versatile and hard to analyze—they seem to have all of the traits.

I hope that you enjoy knowing these people, because it is educational to see how they change to meet the needs of their situations and can find satisfaction almost anywhere.

ISFP

Strengths

- Very down to earth, friendly, reliable, and knows the facts
- Quiet and modest, takes care of family, friends, and teammates
- Interested in just about everything and likes people
- Capable of remembering people and information from the past
- Loves the feeling of getting lost in work—can be a perfectionist
- Takes care of everyday duties, takes responsibility
- Values family and friends and sometimes volunteers for school or charity
- Makes a personal commitment with any work attempted
- Is always busy, but rarely on time
- Takes an interest in people
- Does not talk much, but is sincere

Weaknesses

- Can take things too personally, and is not a good disciplinarian
- Can get bogged down in detail and forget the goal
- Gets involved in so many projects and topics that gets confused
- Can attach emotional meaning to everything and lose self-confidence
- Does not delegate well, and can take on too many tasks
- Can fail to communicate well enough to get cooperation from others
- Does not take criticism well—might question the facts

Case Study: ISFP

Laura worked for the records department of a hospital doing filing, typing, and billing. She worked in a little cubicle on a computer and surrounded her area with pictures of her dog, her family, and her friends. She really cared about the patients and their records and took great care to be accurate. Her supervisor liked this quality about her, but often talked to her about taking too much time to do a job and being too sensitive to office gossip. Laura recognized that she took every comment personally, but could not seem to overcome the emotional downside of comments and criticism. Fortunately, her supervisor had a great sense of humor and spent time each day joking and talking with each worker. Laura looked at her as a mother figure and loyally carried out her duties.

Through working at the hospital, Laura was able to support her family. Although she was not being considered for promotion, she did get good annual reviews, small raises, and outstanding benefits. The hospital was glad to have many workers like Laura because they were concerned about avoiding lawsuits for mistakes and incorrect records. People like Laura saw each file as a patient—not a piece of paper—and took the extra effort to get it right every time.

Questions and Comments

Not everyone is going to be promotable. Laura is an example of a person who makes a significant contribution by being herself and living within the constraints of her type and job. She would not do well with adding stress to her life and needs a particular type of supervisor to be successful. You could be that supervisor, helping Laura be her best and giving her the means to support herself and her family. And you will also be supplying the organization with the reliable accuracy that protects many companies and customers from major disasters.

If you were Laura's supervisor, what would you do to help her be a success?

ESFP

Strengths

- Very down to earth, friendly, reliable—knows the fact
- Outspoken and sincere—talks about family, friends, and teammates
- Interested in just about everything and likes people

- Capable of remembering people and information from the past
- Takes care of everyday duties, takes responsibility
- Values family and friends, and sometimes volunteers for school or charity
- Makes a personal commitment with any work attempted
- Is always busy and never on time
- Takes an interest in people and can manage small teams well
- Draws people into conversations about the past, knows people and useful information
- Engaging, knowledgeable person, and well liked
- Good with research and stories

Weaknesses

- Can take things too personally, and is not a good disciplinarian
- Can get bogged down in detail and forget the goal
- Can attach emotional meaning to everything and lose self-confidence
- Does not delegate well, and can take on too much responsibility
- Can over communicate and bore people with too many stories
- Does not take criticism well—might question the facts
- Solves problems with research, not ideas for solutions
- Gets lost in too many interests, and cannot focus or prioritize well
- If negative can influence a lot of people to be negative as well
- Can be a know-it-all, tell-it-all

Case Study: ESFP

Stanley was a part-time minister for a small church, as well as a truck route salesperson for a bread bakery. Everybody liked Stanley because he was quick to help anyone and always had a kind word or a funny story. When Stanley arrived at each store, he took time to talk. He remembered everyone's name and family situation. Some of his customers even started coming to his church because he was so friendly. All of his customers on his route looked forward to his delivery and would never consider changing bakeries although the product was not significantly better than others. His supervisor had no complaints about him taking so much time—orders were strong, and Stanley always accurately completed his paperwork. In fact, Stanley was a reliable person, except for an occasional day off, when he would call his friends and disappear for a full day of fishing and storytelling. Stanley was glad he didn't have to punch a time clock and have to work quietly at a boring, repetitive job. His family, his church, his friends, and job made up the web of a satisfying life for him.

Case Study: Another example of an ESFP

Candi was always an outgoing and sociable person, even though she had a hard childhood when her parents divorced. She graduated high school and went to work in the town's aluminum mill. After six months, she quit because of the harsh conditions, the rude treatment of employees, and the long hours. She felt like a failure, but her mother encouraged her to take a talent test for a modeling agency. She placed highly and was encouraged to compete for a local beauty pageant. Her sociable nature, interest in local people, and good humor made her an attractive candidate. But the other participants were competitive. They destroyed her self confidence with critical comments and discouraging predictions.

After that defeat, she was thoroughly confused about how she was going to make a living. By chance, a local restaurant owner offered her a hostess position. Her duties would be to greet guests, schedule reservations, and help the owner build his business by making conversation with regular local customers. She accepted just to have a job, but was pleasantly surprised when her knowledge of the local people and her ability to talk sincerely and sociably was the main part of her job. It wasn't long before the restaurant had a reputation for its friendly atmosphere, gracious treatment of guests, and concern for quality. Business people brought their customers, and the restaurant was soon the busy social center of the town. Candi was bewildered as to how she had been such a failure at factory work and the beauty contest, but such a success at being a hostess. And the restaurant conditions, hours, and pay were great. Perhaps, she had just found her place in life.

Questions and Comments

You now have two case studies of the same personality type in both genders. List the traits from the case studies that Stanley and Candi have in common.

As an exercise in developing a gender-free view of employees, imagine Stanley as a maitre d' and Candi as a bread delivery driver. Giving consideration to traits is a much better predictor of job performance than any other consideration that you could use. After that, experience, work ethic, and motivation are the next best predictors. If you see all of these positives in an employee, and there is a good fit to the job situation, there is a high likelihood for success.

Principles of Using Personality Types

Dangers of duplicating yourself

We all have the tendency to prefer people who are just like ourselves. We understand them best and do not find them difficult. Unknowingly, we might choose to work with only people who are like us and exclude others. If we do so, we would inevitably work in an environment with an oversupply of the same strengths and same weaknesses. We would have poor teamwork, not because people were not willing to work together, but because the mix of traits was strongly preferring one type and suppressing the opposite type. Research shows that a team with a mix of opposite traits usually outperforms a team that is limited to having all of the same traits.

This preference for the same traits can take place through hiring practices, promotions, or unconscious preferential treatment. If an organization creates such a teamwork situation, it has a tendency to self perpetuate, and the whole organization will reflect the performance of the preferred traits. For example if an organization has a preponderance of S-T traits, the whole organization will become slow to change or make decisions, but will be good with detailed and precise work. Another example would be an organization preferring the N-T traits and suppressing the S-T traits. It would have a tremendous amount of change and new ideas, but fail to be accurate in details. Such organizations would rapidly self destruct. It would be wiser to have a balanced team that can bring the best of all of the traits to address the goals.

Opposites attract

Your individual performance is determined by how well you can utilize and team up with the traits that are opposite yours. If you are good with detail, it would be to your advantage to also be good at direction and vision. The easiest way to achieve that is through teamwork with someone who is your opposite. In fact, the person who is opposite of you is the most important person in your life. That person has all of the traits that you lack, sees the world that you miss, and can solve the problems that you cannot. It is a joy to experience this kind of teamwork, as work gets a lot easier. You don't have to do the things that you are not good at. You have a teammate to rely on. You just have to put the effort into maintaining the teamwork.

This works in a personal relationship too. Often, we so admire and respect people who can do what we cannot that we are attracted to them. They seem to complement and support us. You now see that this is just human nature. But the requirements for maintaining such teamwork are: respect for traits that we only barely understand, patience with traits that seem to be annoying, and wisdom to know when to assert your traits and when to let others assert theirs.

Let's take as an example two parents, one a Feeler and the other a Thinker, with a difficult child. The Feeler will be patient, kind, and understanding –something the Thinker finds difficult to do. But when it comes to misbehavior, the Thinker will provide organization, limits, and appropriate discipline—something the Feeler finds difficult to do. The net result is a child who gets the best of both, a kind and loving family with good discipline and organization. This assumes, of course, that the Thinker and Feeler have learned to get along. They no longer criticize each other's traits. They no longer try to change the other into a copy of themselves. They respect and support each other for who they are. Sounds like a good marriage, doesn't it?

Balanced teams perform best

Can you imagine how wonderful it would be to have the perfect team? This team would be good at: talking and listening, setting appropriate goals, implementing, quality as well as quantity, good with numbers as well as people, good at solving problems, good with perfecting processes, good with creativity, and good with meeting schedules. This team would have to consist of people who represent all ends of all of the ranges. Understanding, accepting, and utilizing these differences is the glue that would keep this perfect team together.

You are now prepared to do just that. Look at the people with whom you work, and you will find parts of this perfect team. It is up to you to identify all of the traits and to put them together in an appropriate way so that they can function.

Remember, you are the helpful coach. After coaching individuals, the next task is to put the individuals together into a team. You now have the basic tools to do just that. Have fun and be proud as your team begins to function better and better.

Self guidance is essential to this perfect teamwork

Once you have assembled the different combinations of personality type and abilities, you then have to teach the team members to guide themselves. They need to learn how to adjust their traits so that they use their strengths and avoid their weaknesses. They need to know when it is appropriate for them to assert their abilities and when it is time to wait while others asserts theirs. They need to do this without jealousy or arrogance, content that each set of traits is just as important as the others, knowing which trait is needed for each part of the project. Here is an example of how this concept might work:

- Research data to analyze a problem: Sensor
- Visualize the eventual goal achievement: Intuitive
- Develop a solution to a problem: Intuitive
- Critique the solution for feasibility: Sensor

- Use relationships to form a team: Feeler
- Set and enforce standards of performance: Thinker
- Listen to input from others: Introvert
- Communicate the project needs to others: Extrovert
- Drive the team to successful conclusion: Thinker and Judger
- Think outside the box to achieve excellence: Perceiver

In the first two items, the Sensor would have to know when to do the research and when to stop and turn it over to the Intuitive. The Intuitive would have to know to wait until the Sensor had completed the research and then turn it back over to the Sensor for critique. This is much like a relay team or a baseball team—the players wait until the ball is passed to them. As you learn your own strengths, and when to use them and when to moderate or accelerate them, you can begin to teach others to do the same.

What does it take to learn to self guide?

The first step is to identify your own traits, as you have done in these classes. The second step is to determine which of your traits are strongest and which are used inappropriately and look like weaknesses. An example would be an Extrovert who is so talkative that no one else can get in a word. If the Extrovert begins to reduce the amount of talking, others can begin making a contribution—and the teamwork improves. Moderating just one of your traits even a little bit has a huge effect on how well others can work with you. Another example is the Thinker who is so blunt and rude that no one wants to get into a conversation. If the Thinker begins to be just a little more diplomatic and considerate, others begin to participate. You only have to move an inch or so to get some outstanding results. What are your strongest or most inappropriate traits that you are willing to moderate? Make a note to yourself of at least one that you intend to work on after this class. Shortly, I will provide you with a Self Guidance Work Sheet.

The personal benefits of self-guidance

People who have seriously undertaken this self guidance find that others (who can best support them) start working with them more effectively. Instead of being in conflict with them, they see a good reason to seek them out and work with them cooperatively. They now have someone who loves to do what they hate to do—and someone who is good at what they struggle to accomplish. Both parties greatly benefit. Working together, these two can effectively handle many more situations without great stress or effort. In fact, failures and hassles begin to disappear because they are not trying to do something in their weak area.

When the two are successful, more people are attracted to work with them, and teamwork becomes the primary method of getting work done.

Self Guidance and Coaching

You are probably aware that there are several people in your life who have coached you about your strengths and weaknesses. These might include teachers, parents, spouses, friends, bosses, supervisors, or co-workers. This feedback might have come in the form of evaluations, advice, corrections, praise, complaints, or observations. If you look back, you might be able to see a common theme. Others can see the same traits exhibited in your life repeatedly, and they would like to see you succeed by mastering them. In fact, if you find that what you have been coached on are the same traits you identified through this program, you can be sure that you have found a good opportunity to improve your life. The great advantage of the self-guidance approach is that you take the initiative to make the change yourself because you understand how much you have to gain. Once you start to make these changes, you will see the benefits and will never again be willing to go back to what you were doing before. The interesting thing that will happen next is that these trusted coaches in your life will start giving you feedback on how good the change has been and how happy they are to see you doing so well.

Case Study of Self Guidance

Billy is a big and strong man with a tough attitude. He is the supervisor of a large department where the work is hard, hot, dirty, and dangerous. Only the strongest and toughest workers stay, and Billy is the strongest and toughest of them all, having worked his way up through the ranks.

When he was promoted to supervisor, Billy wanted to show everyone that he was tough and would not take any backtalk from anyone. He came across as hot-tempered, demanding, narrow minded, aggressive, rude, and insensitive. Management received many complaints about him, and turnover was high. People voted with their feet as to what they thought about working for Billy. He was written up for his unprofessional manner and passed over for a promotion. Those who saw his good work ethic, knowledge of the department, and desire to be promoted tried to help.

After several years of setbacks, he finally decided to try to improve his manner—no matter how distasteful it was to him. After much coaching, he knew exactly what his faults were, and he started to work on listening to his lead men better. They started to notice that he did not bite their heads off when they came to talk to him. As a result, they began to tell him more about what the workers were saying. Billy tried to fix the problems that the workers were complaining about and, as they saw that he was listening to them, they started to talk to him even more. Billy understood that they were really trying to do a better job, so he didn't get so angry when they failed. He began to look for the real causes of failures and tried to resolve them. As workers began to trust him, he got more cooperation from them. Many of the problems that had made him so angry before just seemed to vanish.

His lead men began telling him that the workers respected him and that made their job easier. The department performance improved dramatically, turnover declined, and the managers started telling Billy that he was doing a much better job. Billy was surprised at how much good came from just trying to listen a little better. His job became so much easier, and he went home each night with less stress. Having gained his confidence, he requested an evaluation from his boss, asking him what he needed to do to be considered for the next promotion. His boss was pleased. They outlined three things that he would have to achieve before they could recommend him. Billy set about achieving the three improvements and felt much better about applying for the promotion. It was an unforgettable experience for both Billy and his workers.

Case Study in Self Guidance

Judy supervised a cleaning crew of six women. She had been a cleaner herself and was selected to be the supervisor—mainly because everyone else quit under the former supervisor. She started her supervisory career ill prepared and nervous about managing her crew. Judy was a nice person and a dedicated worker, but she was not so sure about disciplining people and getting people to work as hard as she did.

Trouble started the first week. The workers sized her up as a pushover. They came in late and slacked off their work. Unless Judy wanted to do all of the work herself, she had to do something. She remembered some advice that a former boss had given her—*Get comfortable with telling people no.* Judy acknowledged that telling people *no* was her weakness, so she decided to try to improve. When Colleen asked to leave early, Judy said, *No. Two more hallways and then you can go.* Colleen was mad because Judy had not said no before. Why did she say no to Colleen? But since Judy looked comfortable with the statement, she stayed and completed her work. When Alice asked to come in late the next day, Judy said, *No. Fridays are our busiest days, we all have to come in and work together to get all of this work done. When it is done, we can all go home.* Alice was mad, but did not want to let the others down, so she came in on time. After a few weeks of this, the crew decided that, since Judy was nice but firm with them, it was a pretty good job after all. They even figured out better ways to work together, so they could all go home when the work was finished. Eventually, Judy's crew was known as the hardest working and happiest crew in the company. Few people quit and others wanted to transfer in. Judy was surprised to see such a wonderful result from just one change. She wished that she had done it sooner. Actually, it was easy and made her job so much better. She thought that if she ever had an opportunity to develop someone else for supervision, she would pass on the same advice.

SELF GUIDANCE WORKSHEET

NAME _____   DATE_____

Instructions: By this time, you probably have a good idea of your strengths and weaknesses. If you want more input and confirmation, review your past evaluations, talk to your bosses, your spouse, or your co-workers. Write a brief description of your strengths and weaknesses and note how each might help or hinder you. After you have completed the list, circle the most dominant weaknesses, and work out an action plan at the bottom of this page. Work on your weakness for several weeks, and then ask for feedback. Make notes on the results that you see developing. Later, you can refer back to this page and identify another weakness to address. Lastly, you can also get a good result by looking at your strengths and finding ways to utilize them better. You might consider those coworkers that you can team up with—those who would find your strengths to be a complement to their weaknesses.

INTROVERT-EXTROVERT

My strengths   My weaknesses

SENSOR-INTUITIVE

My strengths   My weaknesses

THINKER-FEELER

My strengths   My Weaknesses

PERCEIVER-JUDGER

My strengths   My Weaknesses

My Goal to Work on a Weakness:

My Goal to Work on a Strength:

GRADUATION EXERCISE

We have traveled a long journey together in these classes. Now you are ready to graduate to a fulfilling and effective career as a supervisor. In order to review and answer some final questions that you might have, recall what you said in the first class about what makes a good supervisor and what makes a bad supervisor. We can now comment on these features of supervision in terms of what we have learned. I hope that you will find it interesting and helpful to evaluate what type of a supervisor you wish to become.

Characteristics of the worst supervisors:

> Bad supervisors ridicule people and destroy their self-respect. This leads to high turnover. Employees leave and try to find a better supervisor as soon possible.

Comment: This shows a lack of understanding of the importance of motivation to effective performance. If people experience an unpleasant consequence when trying to perform, they become de-motivated to work and motivated to leave. I know that you would never do this because you want to develop workers who are motivated to work for you.

> Bad supervisors can be out of control, have drinking problems, or other personal issues that seriously interfere with their work and hurt their employees.

Comment: Supervisors need to meet the basic criteria for becoming a supervisor by having their own life under reasonable control. They need to lead by example and to counsel their workers to control themselves to be effective workers.

> Supervisors who communicate poorly leave employees in the dark, forcing them to decide what to do. These employees are often criticized for doing something wrong, even though they were given no instruction.

Comment: This might be an Introvert who has to work a little harder at communicating. Supervisors might think that they have communicated, but workers need much more—especially Extroverts who do not listen well and Sensors who need more detail and lots of repetition.

> Taking credit for others' work causes people to look for ways to sabotage their supervisor.

Comment: This shows a lack of understanding motivation. Every time you give a person credit for their work, they are motivated to do more work and thereby make you, the supervisor, look good. Employees can get so angry over this behavior that they even think about sabotage—and that could jeopardize their job. A helpful coach would always want to avoid this. The goal is to help people succeed at work.

> A poor supervisor does not admit when he or she made a mistake and may blame it on others. It actually improves credibility to admit to mistakes and then correct them, just as an employee has to do.

Comment: This might be a Sensor-Thinker, needing to always be right and hating to admit mistakes. This stubborn mindset indicates that the supervisor is not listening to workers—the ones who know what is really going on. This supervisor is in great danger of being wrong and alienating his people. Eventually the workers will let the supervisor fail and say nothing.

> Confusion seems to follow bad supervisors. They may assume that someone knows something and not follow up or train the employee thoroughly. This sets the worker up for failure.

Comment: This could be an Introverted supervisor who is not communicating enough or an Extroverted supervisor who is not listening enough to be sure that people understand the training. The more motivated the worker is, the more he will try, but still could possibly fail due to poor communication. This would then cause de-motivation. You can see how this is a way to quickly turn a good worker into a bad worker.

> Second-guessing a person detracts from trust, whereas checking work and pointing out strengths and weaknesses increases trust.

Comment: I'll assume that second guessing in this example means criticizing work after the fact, without sufficient input. When a supervisor criticizes a worker, there is a separation that occurs—the supervisor who is correct separates from the worker who is obviously in error. There goes teamwork and the helpful coach role. Every good supervisor wants to take responsibility along with the worker for any errors or mistakes, so they both feel free to get it right—right now.

> Being inflexible and unrealistic makes people anxious. Workers know that no situation is black or white. When a supervisor does not listen to what the team members are saying, it communicates that responding to the actual situation is not a priority. This is the *do it my way or else* approach.

Comment: This sounds stubborn and controlling. It might be a Thinker-Judger insisting that the T-J is the only ones who could possibly know what is right—and everyone should perform without question or comment. The final de-motivator, of course, is the threat of someone's job. This only serves to raise anxiety and de-motivation. The helpful coach wants to establish an honest and realistic conversation with the worker, who joins in a sincere effort to determine the best way to reach the department's goals.

> Being a liar is a very bad trait, even if bad news is presented as good. People need to hear the truth delivered in a personable way so they can improve.

Comment: This might be a Feeler, afraid to deliver bad news because of the conflict that would result. It might also be an Extroverted Intuitive who is trying to put a *spin* on the truth. The helpful coach must always be respectful and personable, but also honest. Workers need know what they have to do to be a success.

> If supervisors are unavailable to their employees, it heads to confusion—and a feeling of lack of support. The most frequent cause of being unavailable is a supervisor who has not trained a worker well and is essentially doing their job for them. This leaves both the worker and the supervisor ineffective.

Comment: You might find this situation with rookie level supervisors who have not mastered the skills needed to get the workers to do the job—and are thus trying to do too much themselves. They are probably stressed and might be abrasive when asked a question. At any rate, they are not able to be helpful coaches, not able to train, counsel, discipline or solve problems. This is a difficult situation, as the problems are sure to multiply. The supervisor is destined to be overwhelmed with too many problems and too little time, while others are standing around doing nothing. I wouldn't wish this on anybody, certainly not you.

> Not being organized communicates a lack of support because people have to redo work or wait around while things are organized.

Comment: Thanks to all of you Thinker-Judgers who are so good at organizing, this does not need to happen. This is an example of how quickly things can go wrong without the basic skills of organizing, scheduling, training, information management, and communication.

Comment: I've met supervisors who are so poorly supervised by their bosses that they feel that they need every opportunity to sell their worth and value. They steal thunder from their workers efforts. In trying to upgrade their image, they suffer the loss of worker motivation—an important ingredient that would make their department perform well.

> A lack of consistent and fair policies leads to jealousy and resentment—a situation that is difficult to resolve.

Comment: This might be a Feeler who is playing favorites and unable to be objective enough to separate feelings from fair treatment. It might also be a case where the communication with upper management is so poor that the supervisor does not know what the policies are—and is often reversed on decisions. In either case, the employees take personal offense and question their good job future. If two Feelers get into a jealousy situation, they might build a *clique* of people who agree on the perceived unfairness and create as much discord as possible. This can be disruptive to work. This mess can be avoided, of course, by being fair to everyone and by helping everyone to be a success at work.

Characteristics of the best supervisors:

> Good supervisors always look for ways to help their people and to make them a success. Their training and discipline comes across as helpful.

Comment: This helpful role is comfortable for anyone to use, even if you have to address difficult issues, such as discipline. You will generally get good motivation from this approach.

> Successful managers know and organize detail so that the job goes smoothly.

Comment: A supervisor who is knowledgeable about the job has his foot in the right place. If that is followed up with good organization and communication, you will see a department that runs smoothly without disorganization, confusion, and unnecessary mistakes.

> They follow up on tasks assigned to others and their own responsibilities. Getting things done well is a priority.

Comment: This implies that the pocket notebook has been used consistently. As people learn that they are held accountable for their work, they start to take it more seriously and begin to improve. When they know that their supervisors hold themselves accountable, they start to trust them and perform even better.

> Good supervisors are knowledgeable of the equipment, product, customers, and policies. They can answer questions with credibility. Most of this knowledge comes from actual experience of having done this job themselves.

Comment: Job know how is a rich resource for credibility and training opportunities, but it also implies that, having reached the moderate level supervision, the supervisor has the time to attend management meetings, ask questions, and get timely and accurate information to communicate to the workers.

> Effective supervisors have a positive attitude toward problems, avoid blame, and seek to solve problems. Even if an employee has made mistakes, a good supervisor looks at it as a retraining opportunity. They rarely lose their temper when mistakes are made.

Comment: This supervisor is comfortable with *peeling the layers* and uncovering problems. This supervisor also appreciates that an employee's motivation is at risk after a mistake and needs reinforcement in order to get a good result from retraining or correction.

> Some supervisors have charisma, a useful characteristic of leadership. They inspire people to work hard to achieve goals. As a result, their employees feel loyal and satisfied.

Comment: Charisma emerges as supervisors gain years of experience and confidence in their ability to organize, communicate, motivate, and train. The foundations for this are in positive expectations and effective motivation. Employees are drawn to this supervisor—and will even put up with a lot of difficulty and inconvenience to maintain the relationship.

> All good supervisors lead by example and observe all policies. They can demonstrate the job processes themselves and model good attitudes.

Comment: The transition into supervision forces the decision to be part of management and to live by the rules and policies in order to achieve the goals of the organization. A secondary benefit is that people can see what behaviors and attitudes are preferred and are motivated to adopt them. If the unprofessional supervisor is still acting like an hourly worker, can you imagine how difficult it is to motivate people to perform better?

> The best leaders are open to all and do not hold grudges or exclude people. Communication is consistent, open, and friendly to everyone without exception.

Comment: Do you sense the comfort level with the helpful coach in this statement? It allows you to feel good about yourself, what you do, and the people you work with. People can feel this and want to be a part of your team.

> Personable managers are approachable. Bad news delivered in a personable way is easier to bear.

Comment: *Personable* does not mean that you have to be a politician. Think of it as respect for people, listening to them, and being helpful. Avoid being too sympathetic, too rude, too blunt, too critical, sarcastic, argumentative, or pushy.

> Professional supervisors delegate tasks so that they are not doing the jobs of their people for them. This conveys a lack of confidence. Good supervisors attend to many duties, but always have time to attend to their workers' needs whenever they arise.

Comment: This is the moderate level supervisor, who has achieved the valuable status of having motivated workers. Our deepest respect and admiration go to you.

> Good leaders are good communicators, meaning they listen well and give clear instructions.

Comment: Basic communication skills will carry you far. They can be simple, but have a far-reaching benefit. Of all of the communication tools that I have ever studied, I rate listening as the most important. It allows you timely access to the real problem and the opportunity to solve it. Solving employees' problems is a huge motivational opportunity, as many of you have already experienced. Follow that up with clear instructions, and you have the whole package.

> Some supervisors are hard driving and push their people to work hard, but in a reasonable way with positive and negative feedback. There is consideration given to each person's abilities, but everyone is challenged to improve.

Comment: This supervisor has high goals and a resilient team to count on. When the pressure is on, this supervisor can push for excellence and get it. The good supervisor can achieve this by knowing each person's capabilities and motivation.

> Good supervisors are organized and avoid wasting time and rework, which is frustrating for workers. They effectively schedule the day and have all necessary materials and resources available. These supervisors address problems promptly.

Comment: Good organization makes work easier with fewer de-motivating mistakes and setbacks. Problems that are promptly addressed remove de-motivators and install motivators. The better you do this, the better your department performs.

> Successful managers have the trust and credibility of their workers. This is a difficult trait to define. But commitment to telling the truth, effectively solving problems, and working for the benefit of the company earns trust and credibility.

Comment: This is the crowning glory—trust. Notice how much of our study has gone into the many skills that create trust. Trust is a fragile commodity and can easily be destroyed. But, if it is in place, it can be the energizer for excellence.

This completes the Supervisory Development Course. Thanks for participating. I hope that you take much from this program that will improve your life both at work and at home.

APPENDIX

Supervisory Development Feedback

You will find a copy of this feedback form on our website. Please fill it out. We'd love to hear from you.

Name_____ Company_____ Date_____

Position_____ City and State_____

Email address_____

1. List three important things that you learned in this class.

2. Describe how this class has helped you improve as a supervisor.

3. What aspects of the class did you like the best?

4. What suggestions for improvement would you suggest for the class?

5. What would you recommend to further improve your supervisory skills?

6. What improvements in your organization would you like to see as a result of what you have learned in this class?

7. Share a supervisory story that we can use in future programs and books. Use the back of this form or another sheet. Thanks.

Please complete this form on our website so we can continually improve our program. You comments may be included in future publications.

www.PositiveOpt.com

Survey of Your Personality Traits

Name:_____ Date:_____

Directions: Read each item and place a number **0-2** in the Score column. **Zero** indicates those statements that you think almost never apply to you. **Number 1** applies to you some of the time. **Number 2** applies to you most of the time. Add your totals for each group.

0. Almost never applies to me.
1. Applies to me some of the time.
2. Applies to me most of the time.

		Score 0-2
1.	Prefer to work independently by myself	
2.	Do not like interruptions. I have to concentrate	
3.	Don't like people coming into my space unless expected	
	Total for I	
4.	Want to interact with people to get my work done	
5.	Want to express what's on my mind right now	
6.	Like to share my space and things with others	
	Total for E	
7.	Prefer to focus on facts and details	
8.	Like things that I know are true because they already happened	
9.	Accuracy and precision are more important to me than good ideas	
	Total for S	

10.	Good at solving problems quickly	
11.	Love to imagine possibilities and work them out in my mind	
12.	Find decision making easy and don't mind a few risks	
	Total for N	
13.	Find myself focusing on how I feel about people and events	
14.	Need to have harmonious relationships—and avoid conflict	
15.	Prefer cooperation and likes to help people	
	Total for F	
16.	Like setting clear goals and strategies to achieve success	
17.	Like to debate and test people's commitment—don't mind arguing	
18.	Insist on objectivity and consider myself tough and strong	
	Total for T	
19.	Prefer to have a lot of options from which to chose	
20.	Like having several projects going at one time—don't like schedules	
21.	Enjoy creative and innovative work and dislike repetition	
	Total for P	
22.	Prefer structure, rules and discipline as a way to get things done	
23.	Like to organize and to get a lot of work done in a given time frame	
24.	Like to follow tried and true rules rather than change things	
	Total for J	

Personality Type Handouts

Introvert	Extrovert
6------------------------------------0---6	

Introvert	Extrovert
Thinks in terms of territories	Sociable, no boundaries
Concentrates on task at hand	Interacts with people
Lives in an internal world	Lives in the external world
Goes into depth on something	Goes for broad surface information
Is intensive	Is extensive
Has few relationships	Has many relationships
Loses energy with people	Gains energy with people
Gains energy alone	Loses energy alone
Is self-reflective	Is external, little self-reflection
Prefers to listen, then talk	Prefers to talk, then think
Slow to make decisions	Quick to decide
Thinks independently	Uses group thinking
Hates being interrupted	Likes interruptions
Good in one-on-one situations	Good with group situations
Keeps secrets	Tells all
When disagrees, gets quiet	When disagrees, talks more
Seems distant, takes time to respond	Seems friendly, outgoing and responsive
Serious	Engaging, often humorous
Talks conclusions, not thoughts	Talks thoughts, not conclusions
Very time efficient	Takes more time
Avoids attention, freezes up	Likes attention
Tends to be passive	Tends to be aggressive
Good listener, poor talker	Poor listener, good talker
Needs quiet to work	Likes noise and activity to work
Often misunderstood by others	Often overrated by others

Best Case

Thoughtful, efficient worker who can make independent decisions.	Likable worker who builds teamwork.

Worst Case

Uncommunicative, stubborn, slow, and suspicious.	Disruptive, superficial, aggressive.

Weaknesses

Doesn't communicate well enough	Disrupts and can seem aggressive
Others think the Introvert doesn't like them	Tells things that shouldn't be told
Avoids others and group situations	Makes impulsive decisions on poor info

Personality Type Ranges

Sensor

Intuitive

6---0---6

Sensor	Intuitive
Practical minded	Idealistic person
Likes concrete things	Likes ideas and concepts
Realistic	Imaginative
Focused on today only	Focused on tomorrow
Prefers facts	Prefers possibilities
Must verify data	Makes possibilities come true
Steady, methodical worker	Likes beginnings, then bored
Likes detail	Bored with detail—not accurate
Dislikes change	Requires constant change
Accurate and precise	Insightful, sees big picture
Likes step-by-step routine	Visionary, likes big ideas
Dislikes unclear situations	Bored when everything is known
Poor at long range planning	Good at long range planning
Slow to make decisions	Makes decisions too fast
Likes things	Likes relationships
Good at data gathering	Good at problem solving
Good at evaluating	Good at brainstorming
Avoids conclusions	Rushes to confusions
Compares facts to past facts	Thinks of similar situations, trends
Prefers the tried and true	Willing to try new ideas
Avoids taking risks	Likes to takes risks
Knows the lessons of the past	Can forecast the future

Best Case

Reliable, dependable, and accurate	Flexible, responsive problem solver
Controls, administers	Leader, designer, visionary.

Worst Case

Suspicious, critical, resists change	Inaccurate and over confident

Weaknesses

Can become obsolete and avoid changes	Can be unrealistic and underestimate
Head in the sand, doesn't see future	Can make fast decisions, ignores facts.
Gets stuck with problems, makes do	Sees many solutions, but can't decide.

Personality Type Ranges

Thinker   Feeler

6------------------------------------0-------------------------------------6

Thinker	Feeler
Uses logic to make decisions	Uses relationship issues to decide
Avoids emotional issues	Likes emotional issues
Likes conflict, it generates performance	Avoids conflict, wants harmony
Competitive, wants to win	Values relationships over winning
Sacrifices feelings to get performance	Builds loyalty through feelings
Goal directed	Relationship directed
Wants to excel	Wants to serve
Seeks to control	Seeks to cooperate
Sets standards and gives discipline	Is flexible and accommodating
Reacts objectively	Reacts subjectively
Very persistent, never gives up	Can be a crusader for causes
Highly organized and uses charts	Influences people through relationships
Hash marks everybody	Green stamps everybody
Respects strength	Understands feelings, has compassion
Performance oriented	People oriented
Driver, sees no need to persuade	Uncritical, very accepting
High tolerance for stress	Suffers from stress, pleasing everybody
Critical thinker	Takes criticism personally

Best Case

Thinker	Feeler
Good manager, gets performance	Good teambuilder, gets loyalty
Sets goals and achieves them	Good friend, sensitive and giving
Good controller, rule enforcer	Good at customer service, helps people

Worst Case

Thinker	Feeler
Cold, insensitive, negative bully	Weak, easily manipulated, cries
Highly critical, discourages people	Holds grudges, cultivates cliques

Weaknesses

Thinker	Feeler
Can destroy teamwork with over control	Fails to discipline and loses authority
Too critical, gives no positive feedback	Too subjective and performance falls
Builds resistance and people rebel	Suffers from too much stress
Overlooks people issues and fails	Keeps everybody happy, but loses control

Personality Type Range

Perceiver	Judger
6---------------------------------------0---------------------------------------6	
Takes time to gain perfection	Wraps things up ASAP
Quality thinking	Production thinking
Avoids decisions	Pre-empts decisions, avoids input
Flexible, adaptable, experiments	Inflexible, gives orders, controls
Open for changes	Limits change and flexibility
Bends rules	Enforces rules
Thinks the unconventional thought	Conventional thinker
Has time for everything	Prioritizes and ignores secondary
Often doesn't finish projects in process	Makes lists and gets things done
Has multiple projects	Likes one project at a time
Wants to lighten things up	Wants to tie things down
Does not manage time well	Manages time very well
Asks important but unpopular questions	Makes good time on wrong road
Very patient person	Very impatient person
Is scarce in manufacturing	Dominates manufacturing
Likes to challenge with alternatives	Hates alternatives, wants to control
Values disorder and chaos	Values order and structure
Is capable of being brilliant at something	Prefers to conform to standard
Is interested in having fun	Workaholic
Seems irresponsible and uncontrollable	Overly responsible and controlling
Works well without structure	Always creates structure
Frequently tardy, but works overtime	Fiercely punctual
Resists schedules	Makes and enforces schedules
Does not manage money well	Manages money through budgets
Free spirit, likable	Hard worker, reliable, humorless
Doesn't like to be boxed in, needs options	Likes to box people in and limit options

Best Case

Perceiver	Judger
Takes on difficult, time consuming jobs	Good scheduler and production mgr
Argues for better quality	Gets goods out the door

Worst Case

Perceiver	Judger
Sloppy, unorganized, unproductive	Humorless, controlling taskmaster

Weaknesses

Perceiver	Judger
Can destroy teamwork with perfectionism	Fails to get enough input, teams suffer
Takes too much time, money, unrealistic	Doesn't allow enough time for quality
So late and disorganized that can't function	Works too long and hard; dies in boots
So rebellious, disruptive—people avoid	Over controls until people rebel

Resources

Organizations:

Positive Options, Inc.
www.PositiveOpt.com
937-288-2790

This is our consulting and training company. We can answer questions, get you some copies of the book, and arrange for some in-house training and consulting on the topics presented in this book.

***

Association for Psychological Type (APT)
9140 Ward Parkway
Kansas City, MO. 64114
816-444-3500

This is the foundation organization for learning more about Personality Type. This organization offers a wide variety of training programs and tests, as well as a journal and printed information.

***

Center for Applications of Psychological Type, Inc. (CAPT)
2815 N.W. 13th Street Suite 401
Gainesville, FL 32609
800-777-CAPT
352-375-0160

This is the organization founded by Isabella Myers-Briggs and her family to compile and publish findings from Myers-Briggs™ test scores, information, research, books, and journals. They have a library there that is interesting.

Additional Books about Types

Brownsword, Alan. *It Takes All Types*. Herndon, VA: Baytree Publication Company, 1987.

Kroeger, Otto, and Thuesen, Janet M. *Type Talk*. NY: Delacorts Press, 1988.

Myers, Isabel Briggs, with Myers, Peter. *Gifts Differing*. Palo Alto, CA: Consulting Psychologists Press, 1980.

Myers, Isabel B., with revisions by Myers, K. and Kirby, L. *Introduction to Type*. Palo Alto, CA: Consulting Psychologists Press, 1993.

Tieger, Paul D., and Barron-Tieger, Barbars. *Do What You Are: Discover the Perfect Career for You Through the Secrets of Personality Type*, Rev. ed., Boston, MA: Little, Brown, 1995.

Books about Type in the Work Setting

Barr, Lee, and Barr, Norma. *Leadership Equation: Leadership, Management and the MBIT*. Austin, TX: Eakin Press, 1989.

Berens, Linda, and Isachsen, Olaf. *Working Together-A Personality Centered Approach to Management*. Coronodo, CA: New World Management Press, 1988.

Benfari, Robert. *Understanding Your Management Style*. Lexington, MA: Lexington Books, 1991.

Brock, Susan. *Using Type in Selling*. Palo Alto, CA: Consulting Psychologists Press, 1994.

Kroeger, Otto, and Thuesen, Janet M. *Type Talk at Work: How the 16 Personality Types Determine Your Success on the Job*. NY: Bell Publishing, 1993.

Disclaimer Statement

The characters, situations, and conversations in this book are a compilation of many experiences by the author. All are fictitious, but reflect actual experiences and comments. The lessons are guidelines for instructional purposes only and are not recommendations for specific situations. In addition, all recommended words and actions are subject to the management and policies of your company. The author recommends that supervisors check with their managers before taking action.

Acknowledgements

I would like to thank the many supervisors, managers, and business owners who gave me a chance to make a difference in their workplaces. By sharing your lives, goals, and problems with me, you have taught me what good supervision should be. Most of all, I am so impressed with the honesty and effort that all of you put into improving yourselves and your work performance, as a result of the classes and *walkarounds* that we shared. I am humbled and awed by you. I also wish to thank the consultants who worked with me over the years, adding their insights and encouraging me to continue.

I wish to thank my husband, Charles, for his consistent support and his own supervisory stories, and my daughters, Erica and Jill, for encouraging me, offering feedback, and being so giving of their time. Thanks to my sister, Kathy Kilgallon, who helped me with marketing. You have all been a supporting cast that could not be duplicated. The bad news is that I have plans to do other books, so you will be again called in for reinforcement. I also wish to thank my wise and patient publishing partners at Cincinnati Book Publishers and my first office assistant, Lorna Smythe, who got me started and explained so many of the mysteries of word processing. Thanks so much. I appreciate each one of you.

Joyce Karnes
Cincinnati, Ohio
2008

For Additional Copies of

Supervisor's Training Guide

The "How-To" guide for being a supervisor success story

Copy the form below or go to **www.PostiveOpt.com** and click on *Ordering Copies*

Reply to: *Positive Options for Productivity*
P.O. Box 127
Fayetteville, OH 45118

Price: $28.95   x   _____ quantity $ _____

Shipping:
$6 first book; $2 each additional book to the same address $ _____
(Call or email for shipping rates outside of the USA and Canada.)

Tax: Ohio residents *only* add 6.5% ($1.88 ea.) $ _____

Total number of books   _____   Total amount $ _____

◯ Check or money order enclosed (make payable to Positive Options).

For discounts and shipping options on 10 or more copies, go to www.PositiveOpt.com and click
on *Contact us*, or telephone us at 937-288-2790.

If you are ordering for your company, provide us with a purchase order number. _____
Give us the following information:

Name _____

Company Name _____

Address _____

City _____ State _____ Zip _____

Phone _____ Email _____